FORBIDDEN STRAWBERRIES

By Cipora Hurwitz

MULTI

M

EDUCATOR

NEW ROCHELLE, NY

Publishers since 1994
244 North Avenue
New Rochelle, NY 10805
www.multieducator.net

Originally published in Israel in 2009
under the title "Tutim Asoorim"
by Moreshet Publishing House
and the Mordecai Anielevich Memorial and Research Center

Forbidden Strawberries, translated by Geremy Forman–
1st American ed.
ISBN 978-1-885881-38-0

Table Of Contents

3

PREFACE TO THE ENGLISH EDITION

The book, Forbidden Strawberries, was written originally in Hebrew and was intended, mainly, for an Israeli audience. Its publication was made possible thanks to Moreshet, The Mordechai Anielevich Memorial, Holocaust and Research Center. In Israel, the book was well received and the reviews commended it both for its content and for its style.

The translation of the book into English was made possible thanks to a generous donation from Mr. Ira Drukier, and I am deeply grateful to him. I also want to express my gratitude to the Koppelman Family Fund for its contribution and help in having the book published.

The Holocaust, as described in the book, is that of my own personal experience as a "lucky" child, who managed to survive from among the one and a half million Jewish children whose lives were cut short by the German nation in the period of the Nazi regime.

Cipora Hurwitz
Kibbutz Gal On, Israel
July, 2010

ACKNOWLEDGEMENTS

I would like to thank my husband Ariel for the great help and support with which he provided me as I wrote my life story. I would also like to thank Moreshet Publishing House for deciding to publish the book. Finally, I wish to express my deepest gratitude to the Committee of Jews of Hrubieszow for their contribution toward the publication of this book.

4

THE VOW

Avraham Shlonsky

By these eyes that have seen the woe and the grief

Their outcries heaving to my hearts' embrace,

By this compassion which taught me:

Forgive till the time did come too awful for grace

I have taken this oath: as I breathe and live,

To forget not a thing

Of that which took place

Till the tenth generation forget not,

Till each of my insults be completely assuaged,

Till the last of my lashes has chastened their lot

Cry heaven, if in vain passed that night of rage

Cry heaven, if by morning I resume my trod,

Not learning the lesson taught me by this age.

(Translated from the Hebrew: Ada Holtzman)

PREFACE

I remember that which I cannot forget.
(Aba Kovner, Seventy Years)

I do not recall the exact moment I felt compelled to sit down and tell the story of my broken childhood in a book -- a book to be composed of letters that combine to form words, which together depict the terror of Hitlerism, the most horrific embodiment of terror humanity has ever known. How was I able to survive such terror? Perhaps I survived as a result of a young girl's will to live. Then again, one-and one- half million other Jewish children also had the will to live. Perhaps I survived by chance, perhaps by luck. I am unable to explain the miracle of my survival based on pure logic alone. I was a girl who grew up before her time.

This book focuses primarily on the physical events that I experienced and their impact on me, my loved ones, and my surroundings. It is impossible to convey a true understanding of the general atmosphere of the period of the Holocaust and the way we felt at the time. What the Jews of Europe experienced under Germany's Nazi rule simply cannot be expressed in normal language, and not even in lofty language. As human beings, we are almost incapable of translating into words the sense of fear that penetrated our souls and which became an important aspect of the nature of the Jewish people. The death sentence that was issued against the Jews was absolute and final.

The Jews throughout history have known many tragedies, but until the Holocaust it was always possible to find a way out, whether through conversion to Christianity, flight to another country, or a pledge of allegiance to the ruling regime. The period of the Holocaust was unique in that its death sentence against the Jews enveloped them completely and with decisive finality. In the pages that follow, I recount the miracle of my survival.

I give testimony in schools, before units of the Israel Defense Forces, and on kibbutzim. I travel to Poland with teenagers and give testimony there as well. I refuse to call Germans "Nazis" just to be politically correct toward the Germans of today. If we continue to call the Germans who

6

murdered Jews during the Holocaust "Nazis", the day will soon come when future generations of Germans will not know who among their people were really the murderers. After all, there is no such thing as a Nazi people. Those who killed were born German, fought for Germany, and, in the name of Germany, and strived to kill anyone and everyone in Europe who was born Jewish.

Although Germany is a democratic country today, I still regard it as the country that murdered everything that was dear to me. Democratic Germany never took serious measures against the soldiers who participated in the killing and never rooted out the evil. Today, the murderers' progeny continue to live in Germany in comfort, and do all they can to disassociate themselves from the evils perpetrated by their ancestors, as if nothing significant had taken place. Even today, the members of Josef Mengele family live normal lives, even though they knew where he was hiding all along. His name was not forgotten in the city where he had lived. It was as if Mengele had been just another soldier.

People who experienced the Holocaust as children will always be different, even though they may function normally in the world of the free. Children who experienced such deep hatred and humiliation at the hands of other human beings will never be able to escape the frightening image of those who coolly and indifferently murdered and butchered those around them, as if they were no more than shadows. Those who were born in cities teeming with Jewish life and were suddenly uprooted without taking leave of the landscape, their friends, and of their closest family members will always live in longing.

1. A Visit with a Strange Jew, Years After the War

It was late in the evening and my husband Ariel had already returned home from work when the phone rang in our New York apartment. When I picked up the receiver, I heard a man's voice who identified himself as Ariel's childhood friend whom Ariel had neither seen nor heard from in years. I did not know him, but when I told Ariel who was calling, I could see a joyful sparkle in his eye. He quickly took the phone from my hand, and I heard him give his friend an enthusiastic, affirmative response to an obvious proposal being made at the other end. I returned to my own affairs.

As I had no idea who this friend was, I did not listen to the rest of the conversation. Still, the pleased expression on my husband's face made me curious. When he hung up the phone I asked Ariel about the friend. His name was Abe and Ariel explained how he knew Abe. Then, he told me that he had made a date with him for Sunday evening at the home of his friend's elderly mother in Manhattan. The reason Abe had come to New York, Ariel told me, was to take his mother back home with him to Chicago.

Abe's family left Germany in the late 1930s, along with many other Jews fleeing persecution, the revocation of their rights as citizens, and imprisonment in concentration camps. The majority of these Jews settled on the West Side of Manhattan, not far from the George Washington Bridge. Most lived in red-brick buildings with large apartments. The former U.S. Secretary of State, Henry Kissinger and his family were among them. As the years passed, the German Jews of New York managed to acclimatize to the city and its culture, make a living, and ultimately disperse throughout the United States. Time inevitably marched on for those who stayed in New York. Some moved to old-age homes, and others died. People from many backgrounds and cultures moved into the neighborhood, changing the character and appearance of the area. By the time Abe returned to bring his mother back to Chicago with him, she was the only long-time Jewish tenant left in her building.

After telling me all about Abe, Ariel noted the upcoming meeting in his date book. Like Ariel, Abe had also been a member of the socialist Zionist youth movement Hashomer Hatzair. Unlike Ariel, however, Abe had not moved to Israel. Over the years, he had become a well known engineer. He was an intelligent man, and people liked to be in his company.

That's all well and good, I said to Ariel, but you made plans for a problematic time.

What do you mean by problematic? he asked.

Have you forgotten that Iris invited us for dinner on Sunday?

"Listen," said Ariel. "Iris does not live far from Abe's mother's apartment. Why don't we just apologize and explain that we can't stay after dinner. I'm sure she'll understand. We can catch a bus from Iris' house and still make it there on time."

I was not completely convinced, but the plans had already been made and I could not change them.

We arrived at Iris' house as scheduled, but I became extremely tense when I noticed that her husband, Jack, was still working in the kitchen and that they were in no hurry to sit down. The table was immaculately set and ready for guests. At each place were a beautiful wine glass, a water glass, two forks, a soup spoon, and two plates. Clearly, all this signified that we were in for a lavish meal. "Wow!" I gasped in astonishment, "a five-star restaurant!"

"Yes," said Iris, "we were so happy to have you over that Jack worked especially hard to prepare his best meal." Jack had lost his job, and he was now putting all his effort into learning how to cook. This time, he'd made Italian food.

Soon after our warm reception, Jack finished his work in the kitchen and we all sat down: Iris, Jack, their daughter Sigal, Ariel, and I. We made a toast and started talking about this and that. But inwardly, I remained completely tense, watching the hands on the clock and realizing that we would probably need to leave even before the main course was served.

9

"Ariel, you look a little tense," Iris remarked suddenly, apparently noticing the same anxiety in him. "Why so restless?"

"I'm sorry," he began to explain, "but I promised a friend who's only in town from Chicago until Monday that I would meet him at his mother's house at 7 o'clock. It's important for me to be there on time," Ariel continued, "because for as long as I can remember, he's been not only a yekke [German Jew] by origin but by nature as well." When Iris heard this, she began rushing Jack to serve the food more quickly and to forego wasting time on mere conversation.

All I can say is that I felt terrible. I was so embarrassed! They had gone to so much trouble to prepare for our visit, and look how we were acting. Although he was not a certified chef, Jack had put all his energy into his minestrone soup! To make matters worse, both Ariel and I had arrived to their house famished.

When Jack served the salad, he told us the evening's menu: a choice roast beef, mashed potatoes, broccoli in white wine sauce, salad, and, of course, minestrone soup. We managed to eat the salad, which was delicious, and to just barely taste the soup. Actually, I was prevented from truly tasting the soup by the anger building up inside me. Why was it so important for Ariel to see a friend whom he had neither seen nor heard from in more than twenty years, I thought to myself? He was clearly anxious and making signs that it was time to leave, but I kept my feelings to myself. When Ariel looked at his watch and got up to go, it was already 6:30 PM. By the time we'd be able to get to the bus stop, catch the bus and get to his friend's mother's house, it would already be 7 PM. To my great embarrassment, most of the food was still on the table when we got up to leave. Moreover, Ariel and I were still quite hungry!

I hoped that our friends, who had hosted us so graciously, would be able to understand how important this visit was to Ariel, and that they would be able to forgive us for our unmannerly behavior. We apologized again and said goodbye, taking the elevator down to the lobby and stepping out into the evening air. We walked along silently, saying nothing about the unpleasantness we had caused our hosts.

The streets on the West Side of Manhattan are particularly long. Every few blocks, the appearance of the buildings changes, a landscape that breathes life into the streets. We saw the shops ranging from stores specializing in gourmet food, clothing, and electronic appliances to less extravagant emporia selling less expensive merchandise.

We got off the bus and searched for the address. When we found it, we walked up to the second floor and knocked on a truly ancient-looking door. It opened and Abe welcomed us inside. He led us into the large living room with walls that had not been painted for many years. High windows were concealed by heavy drapes that darkened the room. It was almost completely devoid of furniture. All that remained were three old wooden chairs on which we sat in a small circle. Because I did not know Abe, I began to look around the large room, which seemed like it had seen better days.

When Ariel and Abe started talking, Abe apologized that the apartment was virtually empty. Because his elderly mother was about to move to Chicago, he explained, they had decided to donate its contents to the Salvation Army. I was surprised that he had decided to donate the things to this, of all organizations, particularly when he added that the donated furniture was extremely old and valuable. Then, he took us into a dark side room containing an antique beautiful chest of drawers that held a large number of decorative handbags, which Abe indicated was going to be given to a woman of their acquaintance. The piece of furniture was obviously worth a great deal of money. The chest of drawers, which I suspected may have been brought over with them from Germany, left quite an impression on me. It was clearly decades ago, at a time when furniture was handcrafted by talented woodworkers.

When we returned to the living room, Abe called for his mother to come out of the kitchen, and after brief introductions and a bit of small talk, she left the room. Then, Abe began to tell us about his recent visit to the town in Germany where he had been born. Awestruck and with extraordinary enthusiasm, he described the good-heartedness of the people of the city, and added in amazement, "Not only did they invite us – the Jews who had been born in the city – to be their guests there, but they even paid our airfare out of their own pockets." He recounted the warm welcome they had been shown and the great efforts that had been made to assure their comfort. It was unlike anything he had ever experienced, he told us, again stressing that it was all done at the Germans' expense. Finally, he told us how pleasant it had been to spend time with these people. Abe's enthusiasm startled me out of my thoughts and the depressing feeling brought on by the empty, run-down apartment.

"They didn't pay anything out of their own pockets," I interrupted suddenly. "They paid with the money, gold, valuables, and jewelry that they stole from my parents and the millions of other Jews victims, in addition to the millions of gold teeth they pulled from their mouths! " Abe appeared visibly shocked.

"So, you're one of those people who believe all the lies about the Germans and help spread them?" he asked.

At his response, it was my turn to be shocked. Was this is a normal Jew? He had appeared so as I sat across from him. Now, I gasped.

"Is that a serious question?! Are you a Holocaust denier?!"

But Abe was so focused on his defense of the German people that he continued asking questions without, apparently, noting my emotional response. Had I heard of an Austrian Jew named Peter Sichrovsky, a journalist and author who wrote a book entitled Strangers in Their Own Land? One of the stories, Abe explained, was about a Jewish girl of German origin who lived in New York and whose parents had fled Germany in the 1930s. For many years, she had had no interest in even hearing about Germany. One day, she received an invitation from Germany. It stated that she was eligible to receive compensation for the property lost by her parents. When she made the trip to Germany, she was enamored by the country such that she no longer understood why everyone was giving the Germans such a hard time. Ultimately, she fell in love with Germany and its people and decided to stay. At that moment, Abe appeared to have forgotten about the reasons that had initially caused the girl's parents to flee their homeland.

As someone who was miraculously spared the certain death that the German people had planned for me, my entire past flashed before my eyes at that shameful moment. I was completely flustered and I felt like shouting out, With whom am I arguing, anyway?! I was unable to decide if I was sitting across from someone mentally unbalanced or merely a Jew from Germany who simply could not come to terms with the fact that his country had spit him out, a Jew who still wanted with all his heart to return and to be accepted there, like an excluded child doing everything possible just to be liked by the cool kids at school.

Abe's mother, who had been sitting in the kitchen the whole time, heard the conversation, entered the room, and asked us if we would like some tea. They finally offered us something, I thought to myself. No, thank you, we answered in unison. Until that point, Abe had not even offered us a glass of water! She then turned to leave, hesitated for a moment in the doorway, turned back to us, and said, "Don't pay any attention to the things he is saying. He's an idiot." And with that, she disappeared back into the kitchen.

The large, empty apartment had been depressing enough, even without the conversation. I was still angry that we had to leave a delicious meal served by good friends just to experience this. But now, I was sitting across from a Jew raised in a Zionist youth movement and I was unable to accept what had been said. It was one thing to decide not to move to Israel, but to deny the fact that the Germans had butchered six million Jews?! How could a Jewish man from such a background defend Germany? The inhabitants of his city of birth invited the city's few surviving Jews back and had succeeded in distorting the facts so cleverly that Abe's opinions had been thoroughly changed. All that mattered to him now was his unreserved appreciation of their generosity.

His words implied that all I had gone through as a young girl was a figment of my imagination, including the murder of my city's Jewish population and my parents. My parents have no grave; there is no evidence for their very existence. Their names would have been forgotten had my brother and I not survived, each in a different place and each under different circumstances.

I managed to overcome my emotional distress and respond to Abe. I told him that the Germans had burned my mothers body, with the help of the Ukrainians at the Trawniki concentration camp and that, as far as I knew, my father was murdered (to the sound of loud music composed by civilized Germans), along with another 19,000 Jews from different locations who had also been sent to Majdanek. I told him that my brother and twenty other 16- year-old boys had been ordered to dig a giant ditch in the cemetery of my home town, and that when the ditch was deep enough they were all shot to death while standing in it. "Yes," I told Abe, "one of the men who shot my brother may have even been someone from your city who you now think is a very nice person! How would you know? After all, they do not talk about their past! Did one of those generous Germans reveal to you, in his old age, that he had been involved? I have never heard any one admit it. Have you?"

I was shaken to my very core, and I lost my temper. "And do you know what?" I continued, raising my voice louder now, "I did read Sichrovsky's book! It also talks about the Jews who returned to Germany, usually in order to receive compensation payments, and who nonetheless still feel like strangers in their country, even today. How could you distort the book's contents in order to justify their 'generosity'?!" I screamed from the depths of my soul. "Are you even a Jew?!"

As far as I was concerned, the conversation was over. Although Ariel had hardly said a word to his friend whom he had not seen in twenty years, I told him that I wanted to leave immediately. I stood up to leave. My husband clearly understood that on this matter there was no room for discussion. During the conversation, in response to Abe's disdainful question, 'what do you know about it anyway,' Ariel had tried to explain to him that he was arguing with someone who had experienced the German atrocities first-hand. But Abe completely ignored my husband and continued to hold his ground.

When we were about to leave, Abe stopped talking and offered to walk us to the bus stop. I was more than ready to forego the pleasure of his company, but Ariel, not wanting to make an embarrassing situation any worse, did not dare to decline. After saying goodbye to his mother, we walked down the dark stairs, out the door of the building and soon arrived at the bus stop. There was no one else at the stop, and the neighborhood was quite frightening. The three of us stood silently awaiting the bus that was supposed to arrive any minute. I suddenly turned to Abe and said, "I have met some strange Jews in my life, but a Jew like you who defends the German nation, which killed six million of your own people in ways the human imagination is incapable of comprehending – a Jew like you I have never met! For me, meeting you was a painful experience, which I hope I won't have the opportunity to repeat!"

14

With that, I turned my back to him in order to not hear his response. I looked around, but I do not think I saw anything. At the time, my mind was racing, the bus was late, and I had no patience to wait for it with Abe's presence so close. "Let's take the subway," I said to Ariel, who agreed immediately. He felt bad for me not only because we had abandoned Iris' wonderful dinner (and were still famished), but also, and especially because he had not expected such a disturbing experience with Abe.

We said goodbye, and as we walked away he called out after us, le'hit'ra'ot (Hebrew, for 'see you again'). "Never again, " I said to Ariel. He had not expected such a meeting. First, he was certain that, since we were invited for 7:00 p.m., dinner would be included. Second, he thought they would talk about the past, about the kibbutz, and about mutual friends. Who could have guessed that the visit would turn out as bizarrely as it had?

We walked a considerable distance before we reached the nearest subway station. Ariel looked for a restaurant of some kind on the way to the station, as we were both hungry and as he wanted to offer me some recompense for the unpleasant experience. It had been difficult for both of us, and to top it off, we could not find a restaurant. Hungry and dispirited, we descended into the subway station, when suddenly my emotions took over.

"Abe is crazy," I said to Ariel. "He even dared to say le'hit'ra'ot! Has he no shame? If, and when he visits us as he said he would, I will not let that man set a foot in my house." Ariel remained silent. He felt terrible. "Look what had happened," I continued. "Not only did we leave our friends with a great deal of food and miss out on their company, but we were also embarrassed at leaving them in such an impolite way."

"I can't understand it at all," Ariel said in a sad voice. "What happened to him? I guess I didn't know him as well as I thought I did."

"Ariel, look at the time!" I said, realizing how late it was. And despite all our plans for this evening, we were still starving.

"You're right," said Ariel. "What do we have in the house to eat?"

"Nothing," I answered. As we were talking, the train arrived.

From the moment we got off that train until we reached our apartment, we said not a word to one another, and the silence was deafening. The whole time, Abe's words reverberated in my head like the pounding of a hammer: So, you're one of those people who believe that the Germans were like that? What do you know about it anyway? I wondered how a living, breathing Jewish person could say such a thing. When had his memory been erased? When had he forgotten why his parents fled Germany? When had he forgotten the millions of Jewish men, women, and children who the Germans tortured and slaughtered in ways that decent people still struggle to understand?

The next morning, I went to work as usual, although the almost-surreal events of the night before weighed heavily on my heart. As soon as I found a seat on the train into Manhattan, I decided that the most important task on my day's agenda would be to call Iris to apologize, and also to tell her about the upsetting visit with Ariel's friend. Unfortunately, I would not be able to call her from the office because Iris taught at the university during working hours and was therefore unreachable during the day. When I arrived at work, I found it difficult to concentrate. My thoughts remained focused on the previous evening, which in turn provoked vivid memories of the horrors of the war.

I worked in the New York office of the Institute of Contemporary Judaism of the Hebrew University of Jerusalem. It was an independent office in a building occupied by different organizational supporters of the University. Each day, I fielded dozens of phone calls from Holocaust researchers in Jerusalem and throughout the United States. I conducted countless phone conversations about the publication of books relating to the Holocaust. The office shelves sagged with the heavy weight of innumerable historical tomes on the Holocaust written in different languages by top scholars. The books seemed to whisper to me, saying, Cipora, you don't have to give testimony in order to prove history to a misinformed Jew. The German people murdered six million Jews and erased them from the face of the earth. The history is already recorded in the books on the shelves in your office.

In an effort to lift my somber spirits, I went to the coffee area we shared with the other offices on the floor. There I met Evelyn, who worked in the office next to mine. Because the weather was fine, we walked to the park for lunch. After that, I went back to my office, walked down one floor to send a few faxes to the Institute in Jerusalem, and then returned to my office to try to work on the bills. Still, I was unable to concentrate no matter how hard I tried. The day crawled by, and I was extremely relieved when 5 o'clock rolled around and I could go home.

The subway ride home took close to an hour. At 5 o'clock, the trains routinely fill with masses of people, like me, on their way home from work. Like herds of sheep, thousands of people squeeze into train cars, trying to get in before the doors close. The cars are so crowded that there is no need to lean on anything or to hold the grab-bar above your head for support. At that hour, commuters only desire a comfortable place to stand with their feet on the floor and not on someone else's feet. And, if someone vacates a seat nearby and you manage to sit down before someone else does, it is your lucky day. It is not an easy trip.

When I got home I was tired and worn out, as usual. After completing a few unavoidable chores, I went to the phone and called Iris. No one answered, and I realized that the family must not have arrived home yet. I hung up and decided to call again tomorrow to apologize, but, more importantly, to tell her about the unsettling meeting with Ariel's friend. But the next day, I was also unable to reach Iris at home. Later that week, on Thursday, I received a call from Gertel, my adopted father who lived in New York and owned a few buildings on the West Side of Manhattan. In Poland his name had been Shmuel Gertel, but in the United States he was known as Samuel Gertel. He invited me to visit him in his office. I wrote down his address and promised to stop by some time next week.

Finally, I managed to speak with Iris the following Saturday. After first apologizing, I told her what had happened during our visit with Abe.

"Cipora," she said, interrupting me, "you are always telling me bits and pieces of your past that make me curious about you. Why don't we meet again at my house and you can tell me your entire life story, once and for all?"

"It would be my pleasure to meet with you again," I told her, "but I doubt you have the days necessary to hear my life story."

"Days?" she asked in disbelief.

"Yes," I said. "Actually, just a few days will not be enough for me to tell you all my experiences as a child. In any case, I'll be happy to come, and to tell you as much as your emotions can handle and your ears can bear to hear."

"Okay," said Iris. "Come on over." But this time would be without the five-star restaurant accoutrements.

Neither one of us could have guessed the outcome of our meeting this time.

Because I kept Iris's address in my address book under "S" and Gertel's address under "G", I had never realized before that their addresses were one and the same. I had not memorized the address of my adopted father. I had always assumed that his office was located in a commercial building of some kind. Imagine my surprise when I entered the lobby of Iris' building and heard the voice of an older man speaking in a loud but familiar voice to a security guard. I looked up to see him on a mezzanine located half-a-story above the lobby. All of a sudden, it hit me that I was looking at my adopted father, and I made a quick escape into the elevator to avoid being recognized. I wanted to see Iris first.

With great anticipation, up to Iris's apartment I went. We greeted each other with a hug and a kiss. Unable to wait any longer, I asked her, "Tell me, who is your landlord? What's his name?"

"He's an older Jewish man," she answered without missing a beat. "His name is Sam Gertel. He's a Jew from Poland." She went on to tell me that her daughter had been ill, but was now feeling a bit better. The doctor had prescribed a new medicine, which she had not yet purchased because she couldn't go down to the pharmacy and leave her young daughter alone.

"Iris," I told her with as much calmness as I could muster. "Go down and buy the medicine now. I'll watch Sigal. And do me a favor. Before you go to the pharmacy, go into Mr. Gertel's office and tell him that Faygeleh [the name my parents used to call me] is in your apartment."

"What? What do you mean? Who's Faygeleh? Have you lost your mind? Do you know him? Why in the world should I go into his office and start telling him about someone named Faygeleh?! He'll think I'm nuts, that I've gone crazy!" she replied.

"Iris," I said to her, "do I seem confused to you?"

"But why in the world Faygeleh?" she asked again. However, after seeing how serious I was, she agreed to do as I had asked.

"Okay," she told me. "I'll go see him, but only after I come back from the pharmacy."

"Not after the pharmacy," I insisted, "on the way to the pharmacy. Believe me, I know what I'm talking about, and I am quite serious. That man you referred to as a Jew from Poland was my adopted father after the war."

Iris looked at me wide-eyes in disbelief and asked no more questions. She went downstairs, and I stayed with Sigal, all the time imagining how Gertel would take the news that I was just upstairs, in the apartment of one of his tenants. No more than five minutes had passed when I heard a knock at the door. When I opened it, I was met by Gertel, who had tears in his eyes and was shaking with excitement. He hugged me and asked in Yiddish, "Faygeleh, di bist du?" (You're here?) He then turned to Iris, who in the meantime had returned from the pharmacy and said, "You know, she's like a daughter to me, she was almost my daughter." Then he stopped suddenly and burst into tears. I was standing next to him, and I tried to comfort him by hugging him again warmly and stroking his troubled face. "Enough, Gertel," I said. I had always called him by his last name. It was my pet name for him.

"Sit down Mr. Gertel," said Iris, watching the amazing reunion taking place in her apartment. "I'll bring you a glass of water."

"You know," he said to Iris, who was still holding the glass of water, "I said goodbye to her when she was still a young skinny girl, but I really didn't want to leave her. I wanted to officially adopt her as my daughter. She was the same age as my only son Chaimke. Had she stayed with me, she might have been able to fill the hole, the empty space that remained in my heart after she told me how my son died. She was the only one who could tell me. At the beginning of the war, I managed to sneak across the border to Russia. I was hoping to get things set up there and then somehow to have my young family join me." He abruptly stopped speaking as tears streamed down his face, and then continued, the emotion apparent in his voice. "What can I say? The plans of Hitler and the German people succeeded more than my plans." He fell silent and drank some of the water that Iris gave him. He looked at me again, gazing at me with a loving fatherly look and stroking my cheek affectionately. Then, he arose and apologized that he had to get back to his office. He invited me to visit him at his home.

After Gertel left, Iris gave her daughter the medicine and the little one went to her room. Iris sat down next to me, surprised and curious. It was hard for her to digest the fact that her landlord whom she had known for many years – was my adopted father. It was difficult for her to make sense of it all. She had suddenly learned, in a rather unbelievable fashion, that her friend – whom she believed to be Israeli in every way – was a Holocaust survivor, one of 'those' people with horrible stories. After learning about my relationship with her landlord, her curiosity began to get the best of her, and she asked me to tell the story of exactly what had happened to me.

"Everything?" I asked. "How many days do you have?"

"Is your story that long?" asked Iris. "Why don't you just start and we'll see how it goes. My family is from Iraq, so all I know about the Holocaust is what I learned in high school. Until now, I have never had a close enough relationship with a Holocaust survivor to learn first-hand what happened over there. Most of my conversations with you have been about academics and your children, and I never thought of you as someone who came from there. Your relationship with Gertel has been the surprise of my life!"

"Perhaps because I arrived in pre-Israel Palestine as a girl," I explained, "I was able to adjust to my new environment relatively easily such that the signs of my suffering were not apparent on my then-young face. Also, you know that when I arrived in Palestine in the late 1940s, just a few years after the end of the war, it was immediately clear to me that I needed to conceal the fact that I had gone through the Holocaust. It seemed to me that the veteran Jewish inhabitants of the country saw Holocaust survivors as people who were not completely sane. Those 'vatikim' were extremely arrogant toward the diaspora Jews who came to the country after the war. They accused the survivors of thinking they were entitled to everything. Some even criticized us for not having immigrated to the country as pioneers as they had. As they saw things, they had suffered, sacrificed, and received nothing in return. I encountered such people personally. Iris, I did everything I could to become like the sabras as quickly as possible. I even asked my Israeli cousin how to pronounce the letters resh and lamed, and I practiced pronouncing those letters regularly to make my Hebrew sound more Israeli."

"How did you get to Israel anyway?" asked Iris. "You were only a little girl."

"I came to Israel with my uncle who, like your landlord Gertel, returned from Russia with the repatriation. We met in the city of Lodz, when I was already in a kibbutz of Hashomer Hatzair. After the war, most survivors gathered in Lodz, where they reestablished all the Zionist youth movements. The Jews who survived the war were homeless and had no families. Many young people children and adolescents joined together in what were then referred to as kibbutzim. Each youth movement tried, in different ways, to attract as many people as possible to join their kibbutz. Most work of this kind was carried out at the train station of Lodz. At that time, Polish Jews were returning from Russia as part of the repatriation, and they had no one else to turn to. Believe it or not, there was a real competition among the Zionist youth movements to see which could attract more people."

"Is that how you joined Hashomer Hatzair?" Iris asked.

"Of course not," I answered. "After all, I didn't return from Russia, and my experience was completely different. In any event, the answer to your question is a long one. It's late, and there's not enough time to answer it. It will take me more than an hour-and-a-half to get home to Queens, and I still have to make dinner. Let's plan to meet again, perhaps this time at my house?"

"Great," said Iris. "I'll be looking forward to your call."

When I got up to leave, she added, "You know, I am still astounded by your connection to my landlord, Gertel. I can hardly believe it. I also just realized that with all the excitement since you've been here, I didn't even offer you anything, not even a cup of coffee."

She then went into her small, narrow kitchen and brought out some cake and a cup of coffee, and we continued to chat about different things, but mostly about little Sigal. Instead of waiting until I got home, I opened my pocket calendar then and there and we made another date, this time at my house. After I finished my coffee and said goodbye, I kissed little Sigal and left.

By this time, it had already started to get dark, so I picked up my pace, the walk to the subway station taking about five minutes. I had bought my subway token ahead of time, and I walked down to the platform amid all the other weary commuters on their way home from work. I waited for the train. When it arrived, I squeezed into one of the cars with the rest of the crowd, and I even found a place to sit!

I was still full of emotion after my reunion with Gertel, whom I loved dearly. From the moment we met after the war, he took care of me with love, compassion, and understanding. There I sat on a New York City subway and no one in the crowd of people could have ever guessed how far away I was in my thoughts.

I imagined my parent's house, located on the main street of my home town. In those days, our house was considered large and spacious. It had a roomy kitchen with a brick oven and an iron stove with six burners. A baking oven was mounted on the wall above the stove, which had different size iron knobs to control the intensity of the flames. Today, more than seven decades later, stoves like that are only seen in old movies. On the windowsill facing the alley stood a collection of glass jars of all sizes and colors in which my mother stored chicken and goose fat, apple vinegar, and different kinds of jams. I never tasted them, but I was mesmerized by their appearance. The entrance to the house was located on a side street. The front door opened into a long hall, across from which there was another door leading down into a dark cellar, where I never dared to go alone. It was a very dark room that held barrels of pickled cabbage, pickled cucumbers, jams, and fish that my mother had prepared for the Sabbath. I liked going down into the cellar with mother to bring up the gefilte fish. Exiting the cellar meant climbing a number of wooden steps that brought you back into the hall of the house.

Off the hall, one door led to the kitchen, another door led to the bath room, and a third door led to a balcony that opened into a common yard shared by neighbors. In the yard beneath the balcony was the outhouse, which was made of wood and which had no running water. I almost never used that toilet, as I was scared to go into the yard by myself.

A heavy table with closed sides covered with a curtain stood in the kitchen. This was the table on which my mother prepared all the Jewish culinary specialties that I, as a young spoiled girl, never ate willingly. I always had to be cajoled to at least taste a bit. Those delicacies disappeared along with the Jews of Europe. My mother never passed on her delicious recipes to me. What remains of those savory and succulent recipes must also be viewed as Jewish survivors of the Holocaust; they are only remnants like partially charred pieces of wood that are pulled out of the inferno.

This house, with all its rich contents, was connected to neither running water nor a sewage line, and for this reason water was kept in a large tin barrel at the entrance to the house between the worktable and the door. We still received the services of a personal water carrier, an old man who had spent his entire life delivering water. He filled our barrel every day, and twice on Fridays, because on Fridays we took baths. I have no recollection of how bath water was heated and drained.

When the train pulled into the station, I was still deep in thought of memories of my parent's house. Once I got off the train along with the throngs of other people, I had to walk up to another platform to catch the train to Queens. The train to Queens was much more pleasant, with newer cars and comfortable seats. My regular subway station was a fifteen minute walk from our house. On the way home, I passed a supermarket where I always stopped to buy ingredients for dinner. After a long day at work and a tiring train ride home, I was usually worn out by the time I reached my stop. However, today I was not only physically fatigued when I got home, but emotionally drained as well.

My reunion with Gertel had evoked memories that brought me back to my childhood, when Rafael found me in Lublin, in a long line of other Jewish survivors, standing outside the offices of the newly-established Jewish Committees, waiting to receive precious allotments of sugar and soap.

23

Lublin, which had only recently been liberated by the Red Army, was still, at that time, a battle-scarred city. Burned cars and out-of-commission tanks littered the streets and the previously Jewish-owned stores were closed and gone. Jews who were still alive in the camps and in hideaways, or with the partisans, or with falsified Aryan identity papers, who had been in Eastern Poland at the time, were the first to be liberated from the terrors of the Germans. With no place to go, they all began to gather in Lublin. Nonetheless, much time passed before I found another Jew, and until that point I naively thought that I was the last remaining Jew in the world. At the time, I was living in a Catholic orphanage run by a nearby convent. The nuns cooked lunch for the orphans, and every day two children carrying buckets were sent from the orphanage to the convent to bring back soup for lunch. The soup was supposed to be enough for all the children, even though new orphans arrived almost every day. I was the only Jewish girl at the orphanage, which was located on the main street of Lublin and which occupied one full floor of a multi-story building. To reach the entrance of the building, one first had to pass through an enormous wooden gate that was painted dark brown.

Still immersed in thoughts about my past, it was as if I had never stopped telling my story to Iris. I heard Ariel open the door. As he always did, he came straight into the kitchen, gave me a kiss, and asked me how my day had been.

"It wasn't a typical day," I answered.

"What happened?" he asked, and then added, "Actually, as soon as I came in, I could see in your face that something unusual had happened."

"You were right," I answered.

"Well, what happened?" Ariel persisted.

"Don't ask," I said only half in jest.

"Come on!" he said. "Now you're getting me curious. Was it something at the office?"

"No, it wasn't at the office," I replied. "Actually, it was at Iris'."

24

"You also managed to go to Iris' house today?" he asked in some surprise.

"You don't remember? I had plans to go see her today," I reminded him.

"So, what happened when you were there?" he asked curiously.

"Do you know who Iris's landlord is?"

"No, I don't. Come on, tell me already! Who is it?"

"Gertel," I said

"No way!" said Ariel in astonishment, "Did you see him?"

"Of course," I answered.

"Iris was completely blown away by the fact that her Polish Jewish landlord is my adopted father. At first she completely refused to believe it, because it wasn't consistent with how she saw me. But after she personally witnessed our emotional reunion, she was convinced."

While we talked, I heated up the soup, put the chicken in the microwave and Ariel set the table. We were about to sit down for dinner when the telephone rang, and I answered it. It was Shlomo, from the Hashomer Hatzair leadership in Israel.

"What can we do for you?" I asked.

"Listen," he said, "an international group of Hashomer Hatzair members is leaving for Poland in a month. The group consists of young members from Mexico, the United States, and Hashomer Hatzair chapters in Israel, which will supply most of the participants. We would like you to be responsible for the members from the United States, and most importantly to give testimony before the movement members regarding your life during the war. What do you say?"

"Shlomo, this is a very surprising offer," I answered, "and I am having trouble digesting it. Actually, I am shocked," I continued. "I never, ever thought I would return to Poland. I fled Poland with a terrible feeling, as if my time in the country was a part of my life that had been erased forever, buried deep within my soul where I would never look again. I cannot give you an answer immediately. Give me a few days to think about it. I also need to talk it over with Ariel. Okay?"

"Of course," he said. "I'll call you again in a few days."

"All right," I said, and hung up the phone. We sat down to dinner, talking about this unexpected turn of events, which had also served to spark conflicting emotions within me.

Ariel immediately said that I had to make a decision regarding Shlomo's offer within a few days because I had no visa for Poland, and getting one during that period, the 1980s, would definitely take some time. He also pointed out that I would have to inform the rest of the delegation of Israeli emissaries in New York and ask for their agreement. In short, I had very little time to make an extremely complicated decision. On the one hand, I was quite frightened about facing my past. On the other hand, something was also pushing me to go back there. Was this almost a sort of masochism? I did not know and could not explain it.

A few days later when Iris phoned to discuss our planned meeting, I told her about the trip to Poland and about my difficulties in making a decision.

"Go," she said. "It's very important to tell the younger generations about the terrible things a supposedly cultured people did to another people. In that sense, you almost have no choice."

"Thanks for the advice," I said, "but if this trip actually takes place, who knows how long it will be before we get another chance to sit down and talk?"

"Never mind that," she answered. "Go! We'll be patient and we'll surely find another opportunity to meet again at some point."

That night, I couldn't fall asleep. I was having a hard time with the decision, and I only fell into a restless sleep towards morning. I awoke in a panic, because I'd dreamed that the Germans had found my hideaway and that I had to flee. I decided to join the trip to Poland.

A few days passed, and all the members of the Israeli delegation in New York at the time were summoned to the Hashomer Hatzair office. The issue under discussion was my invitation to join the trip to Poland as the group-leader for the members of the American movement, and as a witness for the entire group in Poland. Who is paying for the trip? asked one emissary, with clear distaste for the whole affair.

Another member remarked that I was a logical choice, "because she is the only emissary who was there as a child and survived. She is the best suited to make the trip with the movement members."

The discussion lasted for some time, and for most of it I remained silent and listened to the debate. Who apart from myself could offer testimony to the youth about what happened there? I thought to myself. Ultimately, the delegation approved my participation in the trip. Now, I had to deal with my visa to Communist Poland, which was still not easily accepting of visiting tourists from the West.

When I entered the Polish consulate in New York City, it was if I had entered a different, threatening and frightening world. Everyone there was stern and ill-tempered, red flags were waving at every turn, and guards stood by every door. When I finally reached the right window and explained my request, I was immediately turned down.

"Were you born in Poland?" the clerk asked me.

"Yes," I answered.

"But you're an Israeli citizen."

"Yes," I said again.

"Why are you requesting a visa in New York and not in Israel?" asked the clerk, with a suspicious look in his eyes.

"I am in New York temporarily," I explained. "I left Poland in 1945, right after the war."

"I cannot approve anything now," he said. "First I have to contact Poland."

"I'm sorry," I said, "but I need a visa urgently."

"If that's the case," he said, "you can send a fax. It will cost you ten dollars."

"A ten-dollar fax?!" I asked in disbelief.

The clerks face grew angry. "If you don't want to pay," he said sternly, "we can not help you."

After taking ten dollars out of my purse and paying the man, he told me that the answer would arrive in one week.

"What?!" I responded incredulously. "If we are sending a fax, why can't I get an answer today?!"

The clerk looked at me, stunned and angry, and disappeared. I left the consulate disappointed and in disbelief at what had happened inside. Nonetheless, I called the consulate every day to check if an answer had arrived. After all, we had sent a fax in order to get a quick answer. It was impossible to understand what was really going on behind the scenes.

With every day that passed with no answer, I grew more and more frustrated. To be on the safe side, I told my superiors at work that I might be absent for a week. Although that is what I thought, that was not how things eventually worked out.

During the week leading up to the trip, I received calls from the parents of many New York area movement members who were registered to participate in the trip. For the most part, their questions had to do with issues such as clothing, money, and security. They also wanted to know exactly when I would know for sure whether I would be joining the trip. They were only willing to send their children if there was an adult chaperone present, which seemed completely justified to me. But, I had no idea what was going on. I did not even know if I should start packing. The day of the trip arrived and I still had no visa. That morning, it was decided to try to convince the parents to send their children without me by assuring them that adult movement leaders from Israel would be awaiting them in the airport in Warsaw. By the time the members of the delegation accompanied the movement members to the airport, not only had the parents been convinced to allow their children to make the trip (most of the youngsters were almost 18 years old) but all the registered participants – except one – showed up. Because I had not received a visa, as had the movement members, I went to work that morning like every other day. It is better that it turned out this way, I thought to myself. The Poles had made my decision for me.

But my anxieties about confronting the past dissipated prematurely, as late in the evening two days later, after we had finished dinner, I received another call from Shlomo. This time, he was calling from Poland. He told me that because I had not arrived with the American movement members, he had gone to the Israeli representatives in Warsaw (this was before there was an Israeli embassy in Poland) and told them my story. They had arranged my visa from Poland and sent it by fax to the Polish consulate in New York.

"You have to pack right away," he said. "We will be waiting for you at the airport in Warsaw."

When I hung up the phone, I was completely shaken and confused. Ariel prodded me to start packing, repeatedly reminding me that there was no time to spare. The next morning, I picked up my visa from the Polish consulate and even made it to my flight on time. During the flight, I had time to dig down deep within myself and think about what I would tell the young members of the movement. I could not imagine what awaited me there. For the past forty years, Poland was merely a country in Europe. I had hardly thought about it.

2. In Poland

After landing at the Warsaw airport, I took my first look around. To me, the airport looked like a small, grey industrial zone. I walked to the border control area, which was located in a small hall with walls that had obviously not been painted for many years. I stepped up to the control window. There sat an older, stern and frightening-looking man dressed in an official's uniform. He reached his hand through the small window to take my passport and looked it over a few times, periodically throwing an angry glance in my direction as if to reassure himself that the picture in the passport was, in fact, the person standing in front of him. He looked at me with menacing eyes which reminded me of a black-clad Ukrainian from the days of the war and finally stamped my passport. The entire procedure was conducted with an air of extreme seriousness. He asked me in broken English if I had any dollars. After I declared the amount of money I was carrying with me, he warned me that I was prohibited from changing dollars on the street. He also told me that I could only make purchases in dollars in places that provided receipts, because when I left Poland I would be expected to show receipts indicating where I spent my money and where I had exchanged dollars. He spoke with a heavy Polish accent. When the implied warnings came to an end, I was extremely relieved.

Because my plane was the only one that had landed at that hour, my suitcase arrived immediately. So I had only a few minutes to examine my surroundings. The place looked more like an old, abandoned garage than an airport in the 20th century! In the arrivals hall, I was met not only by Shlomo, but by Chaim Auron, who was then serving as the secretary of the Kibbutz Artzi Movement. After greeting each other and shaking hands, Shlomo suggested that I ask one of the taxi drivers in the parking lot how much it would cost to go to our hotel.

"Shlomo," I said, "I really don't remember how to speak Polish. You can ask just as well as I can."

We walked over to the first car in line, told the driver the name of the hotel where the members of the group were staying, got into the small taxi and were on our way. As soon as we left the airport, my eyes began to

30

scour the familiar yet foreign and distant Polish landscape with curiosity tempered by restrained pain. All in all, I was terribly confused. Could it be that I had once belonged here, I thought to myself?

During the drive, we passed a few road signs and I tried to read them.

"Shlomo!" I suddenly blurted out, "I remember how to say, how much does that cost in Polish!"

I then posed this question to the driver and found myself remembering word- after-word the language I had spoken until I was twelve. The fact that I knew how to read the street signs, which for some reason seemed familiar to me, had me feeling confused about my own identity. Once, I had been a local, but now I was a foreigner.

I understood what was written, but it had nothing to do with me. Was I a nostalgic tourist? Shlomo was a bit surprised by my confusion, but pointed out reasonably that now I would be able to translate for the group from Hebrew to Polish and vice-versa. This is how I started to remember my Polish, which immediately swept me back to my childhood.

When the war broke out, I was not even six years old and had only been in school for two weeks. (Nonetheless, after I was liberated from Majdanek in July 1944, the heads of the Christian orphanage enrolled me directly in the third grade.)

At the beginning of the war, my parents hired a private teacher to tutor me at home. After the Polish children taunted me with cries of 'Jew, go to Palestine,' they were afraid to send me to school. The tutor was Chedva Russak, a Hashomer Hatzair leader who knew Hebrew. She not only taught me Polish, math, and Hebrew, but made an indelible impression on me that lasted my entire life. Together with a friend (who was later killed during the first aktion – an operation designed to assemble and deport Jews for extermination) I studied with Chedva. The basic knowledge that she taught me remained in my memory during the years that followed, even in the concentration camps, when I was starving, in constant fear, and treated with such merciless cruelty.

So when I was tested on reading and writing skills after being placed in the Polish orphanage, the teachers complimented me on my abilities and enrolled me in the third grade. This is how it came to pass that I neither attended nor completed 1st or 2nd grade. I never finished 3rd grade either, and the sense of inadequacy that resulted followed me later in life, so that when I met kids my own age, I usually felt different and inferior to them.

When we arrived to the hotel, another surprise awaited me, courtesy of Shlomo.

"Listen, Cipora," he said suddenly. "In addition to the extremely large group of participants, we brought a film crew with a professional director with us from Israel.

They've been waiting for you since we got here. They want to interview you before we leave for the extermination sites in Poland."

"But I just arrived," I told him. "I really need some time to get things in order. I don't even have a key to my room, yet."

"We'll get you your room key while they interview you," Shlomo said reassuringly as he led me to the members of the film crew, who were sitting with some of the young group members. After initial introductions, we got down to business. As I had just arrived I asked at least to be allowed to comb my hair, and I was given the time to do so.

"Cipora," said Carlos, the director. "Tell me about yourself and about your experience during the war. Are you ready?"

"You went to such great lengths to bring me here," I said, "I suppose I really can't refuse."

Though still clad in the same clothes in which I'd flown to Warsaw, the crew sat me down in a chair and I started telling my story as the camera rolled.

3. Hrubieszow Under German Occupation

I was born in a town called Hrubieszow, located in Eastern Poland in a region known as Lubelszczyzna. Before the war, the town had a Jewish population of approximately 14,000, which included the Jewish residents of a number of nearby villages and towns. Traditional religious Jews accounted for the majority of the local population, and this had a decisive influence on the character of the town. Jewish influence was prominent in the economic, cultural, and religious life of the city, but every ethnic group maintained its own separate existence.

My father was born in Radom. During the early years of their marriage, my parents lived in Radom. However, due to economic problems, they decided to move to Hrubieszow, my mother's hometown, where she had a large family. My mother's parents probably helped them financially as they started out in Hrubieszow.

We were three children. I was the youngest and the only daughter in the family, and I had two older brothers. My eldest brother Nathan was born when my parents still lived in Radom, but my brother Shalom and I were

Brother Nathan
Poland 1946

Brother Shalom Killed in
Hrubieszow 1943

Cipora, Age 5,
Hrubieszow 1938

both born in Hrubieszow. When I was very young, I vaguely remember living in a home with a large courtyard. After that, I remember living in a different multi-story house. But more than any of the other places where we lived I remember the large house my parents built in the center of the city, after they established themselves financially. This was the house in which I lived until the war and in which my childhood was shaped. There, I met the Orensteins, our neighbors, whose children had already attended university in Warsaw. At that point I only knew Chanka, their daughter. At the time the war broke out, Chanka was sixteen years old the same age as Nathan, my eldest brother. Chanka still lived with her parents. I only met the other children during the war.

Plac Wolnoscy was not a long street. It was lined with Jewish-owned stores on street level, which had apartments above them. The one exception was the store that sold non-kosher meat, which was not owned by Jews. Two stores on the street were exceptionally large: "Radomsky" was my parents' shoe store (named for the town of Radom), and the Orenstein family's clothing store, which was slightly smaller. Our shoe store was well-known throughout the area. It had two floors displaying shoes of every type: from inexpensive felt boots for the peasants of the area to high work boots (whose 'descendants' are sold today as fashionable shoes in the chic stores of Tel Aviv's Shenkin Street) to the elegant footwear that women used to wear to synagogue or on Saturday walks along Panska Street.

I remember my life before the war as a happy childhood. Though I did not have many toys, any boredom I experienced was easily overcome because the world outside was full of activity and magic. Outside the house, I would meet my Jewish friends. Together, we discovered smooth

(From Right-Left: Mother Rivka, Aunt Chayaleh, and Father Mendel. Cipora in the front. Hurbieszow 1938.

34

sidewalks for playing hopscotch, walls for playing ball, and flowers from which we could make bouquets, all according to the season of the year. In the summer, we would play tag or hide-and-seek on the grass near the river, but the most fun came in the winter. Because new shoes were never a problem for me, the beginning of winter was always an opportunity for me to show off my white felt, brown-leather covered boots to my friends. I loved sledding down the hill next to our house, and the feel of the cold wind brushing against my cheeks was a pleasure. We used to build snowmen, and on especially cold days we would go for rides in horse-drawn sleds accompanied by the sound of the jingling of bells hanging from the sides of the horse's head. I played only with Jewish girls, all of whom were dead by the end of the war. Most were gassed to death in Sobibor or one of the other death camps located near Hrubieszow.

Because I was the only girl in the house, my mother treated me like a little princess. She was very particular about the clothes I wore. I had a private seamstress and was usually the fashion leader among my friends. I was enveloped in love from everyone around me, and I was a happy child. But all that came to an end on September 1, 1939. After that day I grew up overnight. Happiness, my childhood, and my family would all be lost to me forever.

Even before the Germans occupied our city, I remember standing on our balcony and noticing an extremely loud airplane flying overhead. It was the first time in my life I had seen an airplane. "Father," I asked, "is that a metal bird? Why does it make so much noise?"

"It's an airplane bearing bad news, my daughter," was his response. But even my father, with his sense of foreboding regarding the future, could never in his worst nightmares have imagined what would actually come to pass.

From the moment the Germans entered the city via the main street, we could see the violence they brought with them from our window. They jumped out of vehicles and broke display windows, screaming the whole time. No one was outside in the street except the occupying German army. Immediately upon their arrival, they became the rulers of the street.

On the second day of the German occupation, there was a loud knock at our door and two German soldiers entered the house and barked at my father to collect all the Holy Scriptures in the house and place them in a pile in the kitchen. In our house, all such books were kept on a shelf in the far room. My father's native language was Yiddish, so he understood the German that the soldiers spoke. One of the soldiers accompanied my father to the last room to make sure he was telling the truth. When my father opened the door of the cabinet and the German saw the collection of books, he began pushing them and quickly removing all the books from the cabinet. All the books were placed in a pile in the kitchen, and the other soldier ordered my father to spit on them. I do not remember whether my father actually spit on them, but after a short time with no further explanation and with faces full of ridicule they left the house as suddenly as they had arrived. When they left, we still trembled with fear, but we were also relieved.

The war broke out on September 1st, 1939, and the Germans occupied Hrubieszow on September 14th, which was Rosh Hashana, and quite symbolic. However, in accordance with the Molotov-Ribbentrop Pact, the Germans left the city on September 23rd, just after Yom Kippur, and were replaced by the Red Army.

"Cut!" said Carlos, the director, to Motti the cameraman. Then, he turned to me and said, "Cipora, I see that it is starting to get a bit difficult for you. Why don't you drink some water, and then we'll continue?"

"Thanks," I said. "I really do need a few minutes. Don't forget, I just landed in Poland, where almost everyone I knew as a child is buried with no sign and no grave my mother, my father, my brother Shalom, my uncles and aunts, and my friends. My reunion with Poland is really shaking me up and bringing back memories, some of which are nice, but others of which are too difficult to bear."

After drinking a glass of water, I managed to compose myself.

"Cipora," Carlos asked, "can we continue?"

"All right," I said, sitting up in my chair. "Where did I leave off?"

"The Russians had just entered the city," Carlos reminded me.

36

"Ah, yes," I said, and I continued telling my story.

A large number of Jews were serving in the Red Army, many in high ranking positions, and these soldiers sought ties with the local Jewish population. As for the local Jews, not only were they relieved to see Russian soldiers, but the mere fact that there were many Jews among them made them feel a bit better. As a result, every Jewish family with the means to do so would invite Jewish soldiers to eat Sabbath dinner with them on Friday nights. This was considered a great honor. I remember that we hosted two Jewish officers, and the picture I remember most vividly from that evening is one of the entire family sitting around the table with the Jewish officers talking about the war in Yiddish. Although I was only six years old at the time, I already understood the importance of these matters. The possibility of fleeing to Russia was always on the agenda. Sitting next to the soldiers, who were not just any soldiers but Jewish soldiers, made a permanent impression on me. Even today, so many years later, I still remember their uniforms and the medals-of-honor they wore. In my eyes, as a young girl, they were magical, heroic figures. Every word they spoke lodged deep in my heart.

That evening, the soldier sitting across from my father suggested that we pack up all our belongings and flee to Russia while it was still possible to do so. They warned my parents that, in their opinion, it was not at all certain that the Russians would remain in Hrubieszow. For this reason, they explained, they would be willing to help us escape by placing a military truck at our disposal and transporting us and our belongings to Russia. They promised to provide us with the addresses of their families, who would be able to help us upon our arrival in Russia. When my mother heard this suggestion, she immediately agreed, and began trying to convince my father. She was even willing to contribute all our embroidered pillowcases in order to pack up the shoes remaining in the store. We already experienced treatment at the hands of the Germans, she argued, let's go. Of course, as a child, I was expected to remain quiet, which I did. But I must admit that I found the idea exciting – a journey, an adventure! For the first time in my life, I would ride in a military truck and see new places! I was in complete agreement with mother.

In response to the points made by my mother, my father argued that he could not just abandon all he had worked for his entire life in a single moment of weakness. It was not just an issue of the shoes. What would he do with the store? Of course, he was the one to decide the issue. Even when the soldiers came back and told my parents that if the Germans were to return, we would find ourselves in a bad situation, no one, in their wildest, most pessimistic dreams, ever imagined the new horrifying realities that would result. Although he had already had some experience with the Germans, Father simply did not believe what the soldiers were telling him.

With this, we lost our golden (and final) opportunity to escape the approaching inferno. This memory will remain with me for the rest of my life. I even remember where each person sat around the table. The two Jewish soldiers sat on the left, next to my mother, I, the youngest, sat to her right, and my brothers sat across from us.

The short period of Russian occupation was no more than a slight break enabling us to catch our breath momentarily. It was not long enough us to prepare ourselves for what lay in store for the Jews.

Hitler's army returned to our region in early October, and occupied Hrubieszow once more. Even after the Germans returned, Father continued to go down to the store every once in a while. Our shoe store was on the street level, and the rest of the house was located above it. The balcony overlooked the main street. It was from this balcony that I had first seen the metal bird that had made so much noise. October in Poland is cold, and by this time in most years snow would have already covered the few roads in the proximity of the city. That year, snow had already covered the train tracks. In order to prevent disruption to the German war machine, the Germans began abducting Jews on the street in order to clear the tracks. They also put them to work in order to help the German war effort. My father and my eldest brother tried to minimize their time outside the house out of fear of being snatched by the Germans. Nevertheless, one day Father went out and did not return until very late.

When he got home, he told us that he had been abducted and forced first to clear snow off the tracks and then to dig some sort of ditch, two jobs that were too strenuous for him. That night, he was more than just tired; his spirit had been broken.

38

The store remained partially open for only a short time, even though it was no longer frequented by paying customers. The villagers who once came in droves to Hrubieszow for market day, and who would use the opportunity to do their shopping as well, disappeared. Not only did Jews stop buying things now, nobody bought anything. The only people who entered the store were German soldiers, and they simply took as many pairs of whatever type of shoes they wanted. The store stayed open until one morning when only my father and my eldest brother were in the store. That morning, a German officer walked into the store and demanded that they provide him with a pair of shoes in a specific size which had already sold out.

Trembling with fear, my father explained to him that he could take any shoes he wanted, but that he did not have those particular shoes in stock. In response, the officer removed his pistol from his holster, aimed it at my father and my brother, and ordered them down into the cellar at gunpoint. There, he made them stand against the wall and threatened to kill them if they did not supply the shoes he wanted, which was of course impossible because we were out of them. Only after they had pleaded for their lives did he agree to release them.

Moments after the German officer left the store, my father and brother returned home, pale and still shaking. My brother Shalom and I were at home, and we listened as they described what had happened to them. That was the day my father brought the rest of his merchandise home and closed the store for good. Having no other choice, he decided to give the store to a Polish friend, assuming that they would settle up after the war. During that period, all I heard my parents talking about was giving up the store. I remember having the merchandise from the store in our house. Later, after moving into a different apartment in the ghetto, I watched as my father hid some fifty pairs of shoes inside a niche in the kitchen that was meant for firewood. When I went back to Hrubieszow after the war, I insisted that my adopted father look for the shoes, and, although he could not believe that someone my age could remember such things, I actually found them. I will tell you later under what circumstances we found the shoes.

In the meantime, we continued living upstairs, even though the Polish family to whom my father entrusted the store quickly converted the lower level into a restaurant for the German army. Because I could no longer play outside freely, I used to go downstairs to the restaurant to see what was going on. This is how I got to know Mr. and Mrs. Gotlewski, the new owners of the restaurant, and their four daughters.

The German army's reoccupation of Hrubieszow on October 4th, 1939 brought back all the fear and uncertainty about the future. The difficult living conditions called for unusual solutions, and many Jews in the city now began actively looking for ways to escape. My father had many friends in town, most of whom were merchants with stores that sold fabrics, bicycles, sewing notions, and other goods. Before the German army's reoccupation of the city, most of the merchants would meet in the synagogue of the General Zionists on Friday evenings and holidays. During the prayers, the children would play in the courtyard of the synagogue. It was a large yard, but particularly well-kept. The ground was of hard earth. The game I remember most was one we would play on Simchas Torah, when we all came to the synagogue with flags bearing words that we could not yet read because they were in loshen koydesh (the holy language, Hebrew). What turned the flags into a game was the red apple stuck on the top of the flag. There was always a serious competition to see whose apple was the reddest. After a democratic process of judging, with the majority of kids voting in favor of the reddest apple, the winner was awarded a piece of candy, which in those days was a highly prized commodity among children.

When the Germans returned, we stopped going to synagogue. Now, the Jews preferred to meet in private homes. One day, a close friend of my father convinced him that it was a good idea to try to sneak across the border into the Soviet Union. First, the men would try without their families. If they managed to cross the Bug River, which was only five kilometers from Hrubieszow, they would first get things organized on the Russian side of the border and then bring their families over.

Crossing the Bug required bribing a Pole or a Ukrainian who owned a boat. Not only was the bribe expensive, but many Jews tried and were unsuccessful. This time, after his first-hand experience with the Germans had destroyed any illusions that he would be able to protect his property if he stayed in Hrubieszow, my father was persuaded to steal across the Bug into the Soviet Union with three other friends. One morning, they left the house carrying money and a small bag, with the goal of crossing the border.

All I remember from that day is my father returning home soaking wet and dejected, and telling us that the non-Jew they had hired to help them cross the river had cheated him. Not only had they not made it to the other side, but they lost all they had brought with them in the process. My father recounted how the owner of the boat had made the boat capsize, how everyone had fallen into the water but had managed to get back in the boat, and how the Russian border guards had apprehended them and returned them to the Polish bank of the river. Despite the short distance between our house and the river, reaching the boat owner with a heavy suitcase was no less complicated and dangerous an endeavor than actually crossing the river. On the way to the Bug, my father and his friends had to pass villages whose residents would feel no shame about robbing passing Jews with suitcases and reporting them to the German authorities. Thus, those embarking on such crossing operations needed to be cautious, calculating, and in possession of finely-tuned senses in order to cope with the dangers that awaited them. When my father's friend Gertel, who had convinced him to try the first time, showed up again and said, Mendel, don't give up hope, I've found another boat owner who will take us to the other side, my father appeared to have already lost all hope. Go on your own this time, he said, I don't trust those boat owners anymore.

But maybe we'll make it this time, Gertel insisted, trying to convince my father to join him.

I'm done running, my father said. Whatever the future holds for the rest of the Jews here, it holds for us as well.

But Gertel did not give up, and he eventually managed to convince my father to try to cross the river a second time. Again, they went to the river, and again they were unsuccessful and returned home. I do not know the details of the second failed attempt to cross the border, but one day some time later Gertel showed up at our house, not to try to convince my father for a third time but rather to inform him that he was going to attempt to cross over on his own. I have one request, he said. During the time it will take me to cross over to the Russian side and get things organized there, take care of my wife Bella and my son Chaimke.

I will treat your family like my family, my father assured him. We will do all we can for them. It is difficult in such times to know what the future holds in store, when we are hit with new troubles every day. Have a safe journey. I hope that that this time you succeed.

Gertel said goodbye to my father, and the next day we learned that he had disappeared. One day later, he sent a message to his wife via a messenger that this time he had made it across the border and that he was already on the Russian side. My father was sorry that he had not taken part in the third attempt, because by that time things in Hrubieszow were getting progressively worse, day- by-day. All we could do was to be thankful that, for the meantime, we were all still alive. From that point on, my parents were also responsible for Bella and Chaimke, although the situation could not have been more deceiving. At that point, my father could have never dreamed that it would be Gertel who would end up caring for his little daughter.

"Cut," Carlos said to the cameraman, and then turned to me. "Cipora, why don't you have something to drink and rest for a bit? he said. It might also be better to leave out some of the details, as we still need to eat dinner and go on a walking tour of Warsaw."

"Carlos," I said, "even if I cut out all the extraneous details, it will still take me more than a day to tell the story of what happened to me."

"If that's the case," he said, "just go on as you see fit, and we'll work it out."

I went on with my story.

I was born in December. That much I know. I have no birth certificate, and I have no one left to either confirm or deny the actual date. From the beginning of the war to the end of the war, I thought I knew my own age. However, I paid no attention to the date. We definitely did not celebrate my birthday. December birthdays are inconvenient when registering for 1st grade, because you are either too young or too old. I remember going to a Hebrew kindergarten called Tel Chai. One day, my parents took me to the local school to begin the first grade, despite the fact that I was so young. My parents enrolled me in the first grade before I even turned six, two weeks after the beginning of the school year. I don't remember having any special problems learning to read. I can remember my first school book. It was a kind of notebook, with large letters and a picture of a dog.

I loved walking to school. Our house was located in the center of town. A grass boulevard with bushes and flowers divided the two sides of the street, and I needed to cross it to get to the other side of the street, where there were many stores.

Sometimes, on days that I left the house early, I would peek into the store windows, which were not glamorous but which nonetheless interested me a great deal. Every morning, I entered the Polish-owned bakery to buy a fresh roll, which I would use to make a sandwich with the kosher salami my mother packed for me every morning before school. Just the fact that I was already old enough to buy things with money was a feeling I enjoyed a great deal. However, this pleasant experience, which I still remember well, lasted only two weeks. Yet I actually still remember a Polish song that I learned during those two weeks.

One day when I got to school, a few girls came up to me and started shouting: Jew, go to Palestine. The shouting frightened me, and I ran home crying. My father was quite concerned, and, as I said, things by this point were getting worse each day. From then on, my father did not let me go back to school. Although this marked the end of my formal education for many years to come, my parents nonetheless insisted that I continue my education. This led them to an alternative solution.

I have no idea how my parents found Chedva Russak as a home tutor for me. Chedva had been a member of the Wloclawek chapter of Hashomer Hatzair and was sent by the movement leadership to Hrubieszow to run the Hashomer Hatzair chapter there. She of course knew Polish, but as a member of Hashomer Hatzair and an enthusiastic Zionist, she also knew Hebrew, including a number of Hebrew songs. My father hired her to tutor me at home so that I would not need to walk around the city unnecessarily. I was joined by my friend Freida, whom I liked a great deal.

Chedva would come to our house everyday to tutor us. I cannot remember how many hours per day she worked with us, but I have vivid memories of her stories about Hashomer Hatzair. Also, because as a child I was somewhat musical and had a good voice, she taught us Hebrew songs which I loved to sing. Although Chedva's job was supposed to be limited to tutoring us because we were no longer able to attend school, her infectious personality made her a much more compelling influence, one which actually determined the future direction of my life. My brothers, who also ceased going to school and were unable to continue life as usual, helped my parents in the store as much as they could.

The events I have recounted so far took place between Wednesday October 4, 1939, when the Germans reoccupied Hrubieszow, and Friday December 1, 1939. This was the day the Germans announced by means of the Jewish community leaders, the beadles of the synagogues, and signs posted on the walls of homes that all male Jewish 'parasites' (as they referred to us) between the ages of sixteen and sixty were to assemble near the train station on Saturday morning. There, it was announced, they would help the Jews cross the border into Russia. From the moment they set foot on Polish soil, the Germans referred to Jews as parasites and pigs. They justified their supposed desire to help the Jews cross the border into Russia by asserting that the Jews in Hrubieszow did not work and were parasites.

I remember that fear was already in the air as many of Father's friends visited our home that Friday night. The topic of conversation was, of course, what the Germans meant when they said they would allow us to cross the border. Did they really mean it, or was this simply a German trick?

There was a real desire to move to Russia, and the hopes for a more secure life had already motivated many Jews to flee the city. For this reason, people wanted to believe the Germans. After all, the Germans wanted to get rid of the Jews, and this was a good way to do so. Nonetheless, deep in their hearts, people remained frightened about the Germans true intentions. At this point, the Jews of Hrubieszow knew nothing about what had happened to the Jews of Chelm two days earlier. Throughout the entire war, the Germans shamelessly lied to the Jews, misleading them and concealing information from them for the sole purpose of killing as many Jews as possible without allowing them to disrupt the smooth operation of their killing machine.

44

Hrubieszow and the nearby city of Chelm were two cases in point. Two days earlier, approximately 2,000 Jews were removed from Chelm under false pretenses and taken on a death march through deep mud, during which more than 1,500 were murdered. Every time the Germans planned to murder Jews, they first took their money and their valuables, even removing gold rings from the fingers of young children. The German greed for material wealth was unparalleled, and to them, the Jews of Chelm and Hrubieszow were to be no exception. The first thing the Germans did after their arrival was to order the Jews to hand over their valuables.

The surviving Jews of Chelm reached the suburbs of Hrubieszow early Saturday morning, at 4 a.m., and were immediately forced into a Jewish-owned barn located in close proximity to the train station. They were placed under guard, and no one left the site. The Germans kept the presence of the Jews from Chelm a closely guarded secret in order to prevent the Jews of Hrubieszow from discovering what was happening. And so despite the small distance between the two cities and because of the lack of any means of communication the Jews of Hrubieszow knew nothing of the fate of the people of Chelm. The Germans issued their instructions to the Jews of Hrubieszow on Friday, and the next morning many members of the Jewish community assembled in the designated location in a relatively calm atmosphere, based on the belief that they would be walking toward the Russian border, which after all was not far away.

My father, who was then in his 40s, and my eldest brother Nathan, who was then 16 years old, also planned to meet at the designated time and place that Saturday morning. As teenagers sometimes do, my brother left early. My father, however, first wanted to pray and to eat his usual Sabbath morning breakfast of gefilte fish, for which my mother was deservedly famous. As a result, he was in no hurry to leave on time. I also think he was waiting for a friend with whom he planned to walk to the meeting place. In any event, my father left relatively late, and when he started walking toward the train station, he found himself completely alone, as if he were in a ghost town. Even Poles were not on the street. Growing increasingly concerned about what was happening, and after he had already walked almost half way to the station, he suddenly saw a Jewish man running toward him, screaming from a distance, Mendel, don't go! Run! As most of the houses on the street where he was walking belonged to Jews, he immediately took shelter in the nearest house the moment he heard the man's cries.

In the meantime, we were at home, completely unaware of what was taking place. I vaguely remember my mother being nervous and worried by the fact that there were not even any Poles in the street, only German soldiers. The atmosphere in the house was extremely tense. What was really going on, we wondered? Later, we learned that as soon as approximately 2,000 Jews had gathered at the designated location, (which was more than the Germans themselves expected would show up) they were surrounded by S.S. soldiers, German gendarmes, and Polish and Ukrainian policemen with machine guns.

When they saw the situation they were now in, the men of Hrubieszow began to fear that something terrible was about to happen. Still, hours passed and they were told nothing about what to expect. Someone tried to escape and was shot dead. As noon approached, a Volksdeutsche (a Pole of German extraction) S.S. officer appeared before the Jewish men and ordered them to organize themselves into two lines and to leave room between the rows. Into this space, the Germans sent the remaining Jews of Chelm, who were suddenly brought out of the barn where they had been held. The shocking appearance of the Jews from Chelm made the Jews of Hrubieszow understand that they were apparently destined to suffer the same fate. Once they realized the intentions of the Germans, some tried to escape. However, escape at this point was impossible, because the Germans now started shooting at anyone who started to run. In one instance, a young girl who had accompanied her father that morning screamed Tata! and, after being separated from him, was shot dead as well.

There was no mercy on the part of the Germans. The word had been erased from their vocabulary and now had no significance to them. Before the Jews of Hrubieszow started their march, they were ordered to hand over all the money and valuables in their possession and were warned that anyone who did not do so would be killed. They allowed every Jewish man to keep a maximum of 10 zlotys.

At home, we waited amidst great tension, with no information about what was happening to the men. Today, in the era of high speed communications, it is hard to imagine such a situation. No one was outside in the street, and we had no other source of information. My father and my eldest brother had left the house in the morning, and since then we heard nothing from them. It was only toward evening, after it had started to get dark, and it gets dark early in December, that my father suddenly arrived home, looking forlorn and knowing nothing of what had happened to those who had reported to the train station in the morning. Among them were my brother and my cousin, who were the same age and who were both named Nathan. We were almost certain that something terrible had happened. My mother was in hysterics. Where was her son?!

My mother was born in Hrubieszow, and she had a very large family of five brothers and four sisters in the city. They were all married and they all had three or four children, which meant that I had many cousins. I was the youngest of all the cousins, seven of whom were named Nathan, apparently after a beloved or respected grandfather or great-grandfather. Of all of my mother's many brothers and sisters, only the wife of my mother's brother, Uncle Yitzchak, remained alive after the war. I spent the war with her and her daughter until my uncle from my father's side of the family returned from Russia. During the days that followed the war, we did not spend much time remembering the dead or thinking about what we had been through and how we survived. We were too busy with the day-to-day struggle of existence, our new temporary lives, and the question of where to settle down. Today, everyone knows that the people who survived the hell of the Holocaust needed a long period of time to rise above the pain and to deal with the memory. It is extremely unfortunate that as time has passed, the names of the dead have been forgotten. Our memory of the cruelty of the Germans has also faded and in a very real sense has been forgiven, based on the assertion that not all Germans took part in the murders and that the Germans of today are somehow different from the Germans of the past. For this reason, many people refer to the Germans from the period of the Holocaust as Nazis, in order to distinguish them from the Germans of today. Nonetheless, the people who committed the murders back then were Germans!

"Cut! Cipora," said Carlos. "This is a good place to stop for a while. You seem to be getting a bit upset, and it is also time for dinner. We can't be late. In the meantime, they also found you a room in the hotel."

Upon hearing Carlos's words, the cameraman packed up his filming equipment and we walked out of the room together. Although the hotel was located in the center of Warsaw, its external appearance was grey, like most of the houses on the street. Warsaw itself was grey. It had almost no stores, and most of the people walking outside, especially the men, were drunk. At first glance, Warsaw seemed to be a sad, poor, and extremely colorless city, but it did not make me particularly sad. As for the Jews of Warsaw, most had been burnt at Treblinka and their absence from the city could be felt. In those days, the only place for travelers in Warsaw to eat was the hotel restaurant. There was also a store at the hotel entrance, which was a delicatessen of sorts that carried things that the average Polish citizen did not even know existed. The store accepted only dollars, and for this reason there were money changers at every turn, asking us if we wanted to exchange dollars.

The hotel room I was given was about the size of the bed itself. However, as I had not come to Warsaw as a tourist, and because it was my first visit to the city, I made do. At the end of the corridor on my floor was a large samovar with boiling water for tea. Next to the samovar sat a woman whose purpose was ostensibly to serve the guests but who was actually there to provide the authorities with information about the guests in the hotel. She followed every step of every guest on her floor, and she knew exactly who entered each room. The day after my arrival, it became clear that she was also there to collect a few zlotys to add to her meager salary, as after nightfall she would direct prostitutes to rooms which she thought would be profitable for them.

Dinner was good, and despite the years that had passed since I left Poland, the Polish roll I ate reminded me of the rolls I used to buy in the bakery in Hrubieszow on the way to school, during my two weeks in the first grade. The American teenagers in our group were exceptionally well-behaved, and because English was still not popular in Poland, I became the group's only translator from Hebrew into my broken Polish, and from English into Hebrew and Polish. During all my years in Israel, I had never had the opportunity to speak Polish and I was certain that I had forgotten the language. However, my Polish had actually been stored in my memory, and it improved with each day I was in Poland. In fact, it got to the point that I became the only person who could tell our five

Polish drivers where we would be going the next day. The only other person who could help with translation was our Polish guide who also spoke excellent English.

Many of the teens on the trip were vegetarians. Back then, Polish waiters did not understand the phenomenon of vegetarianism and found it extremely difficult to accept the fact that some people simply do not eat meat. They were not prepared for the vegetarianism of our kids, and all they had to serve them instead of meat was more cabbage salad or another egg. In 1980s Israel, it was already known that buying food in Poland was difficult; the organizers of the trip had brought along plenty of candy and cakes from Israel with which the vegetarians in our group proceeded to fill their stomachs.

After dinner, we took a tour of the area where the Warsaw ghetto once stood. Our tour guide, who was also an historian, explained every detail, including the fact that Jews from the entire region had been brought to Warsaw. He described how people lived in the ghetto, how people were killed in the ghetto, and how they fell ill and died in the ghetto. He also told us about the place where Jews were concentrated before being sent to Treblinka, and the circumstances in which this took place. At the end of the explanation, he spoke about the uprising. When I saw the expressions on the kid's faces after hearing the detailed account, it seemed to me that they had not truly understood and internalized what they had just heard. Perhaps such things can never be understood.

The place was now completely different, and the new landscape appeared quite restrained. Gray multi-story buildings stood where the ghetto had once been, and it was almost impossible to imagine how the ghetto looked like back then, with its streets and all its residents; to visualize entire families being brought there as a first step on the road to certain death. All that remained of the ghetto were giant heaps of ashes that ran the entire length of the rebuilt houses, because even by that point, they had still not managed to get rid of them.

I, who did not need to use my imagination, rummaged through the heaps and without much difficulty found a piece of burnt sweater, which illustrated perhaps better than anything else how the entire ghetto had gone up in flames. I keep the piece of sweater in my album of pictures from the trip. The kids listened attentively, but how could they truly understand anything of what they had heard?

We returned to the hotel, and the organizers met to discuss the plans for the following day, which was supposed to begin at the Majdanek concentration camp. Carlos said that because I was supposed to give testimony about Majdanek the next day, we should continue filming into night, at least until I reached the point of my story when I entered the camp. I agreed with Carlos' suggestion although I was weary from the flight, and coping with the overwhelming emotion that had gripped me during this first visit to Poland since I fled the country decades ago. This would be my only opportunity to finish telling the kids everything I had experienced before I entered Majdanek. We went back to the filming room, and Carlos again instructed me how to sit and where to look. And, again, I asked him to remind me where I had left off.

"You stopped when the Jews of Chelm met the Jews of Hrubieszow, before they began their death march," Carlos said.

That evening, after my father returned home, my parents realized that my cousin, also named Nathan, had reported to the train station as well. (The second Nathan was the son of my Uncle Srumeir.) By evening, the news of the round-up had circulated through the city. It seemed to me that on that night, my parents understood that something terrifying was about to happen. And all the while, my mother kept screaming: My son! My son!

Later that evening, my mother disappeared and returned home late at night. Early the next morning, she dressed herself in clothing typical of the local peasants, her head was covered with a large colorful wool kerchief, and she wore a long black dress and carried a basket filled with food. My mother was a tall, thin woman with brownish-blondish hair and green eyes. She did not look Jewish to begin with, and, dressed in the clothes of local peasants, it was hard to tell that she was Jewish at all. From the window of the house, I could see a horse-drawn wagon carrying a coachman and my uncle Srumeir waiting in the street. My mother left the house and got into the wagon, which, moving slowly, gradually disappeared from view.

50

My mother did not return home that evening. She and my uncle had met a peasant from one of the villages close to town. They had paid the peasant a large sum of money to help them follow the trail of the Jews that had been taken in the round-up. That evening, they found a Volksdeutsche to whom they also paid a sum of money to forge papers stating that the two boys, Nathan Rozensztajn [my brother] and Nathan Sher [my cousin], were professional tailors employed by a German military garment factory and that they must be released for the sake of the war effort. The Volksdeutsche had joined the passengers in the wagon in mid-journey.

The road to the villages to where the marching Jews had been led was unpaved. Polish soil is heavy and black, and someone who gets his foot stuck in the mud on a rainy day will always have an extremely difficult time getting it out. Feet simply sink into the deep Polish mud. For this reason, the Jews who had set out on Saturday had travelled only twelve kilometers by Sunday. At nightfall, the procession reached a wet, marshy area.

But despite the rain, the deep puddles, and the mud, the marchers were forced to keep walking. On Saturday alone, more than forty Jews drowned to death. Only at nightfall were they ordered to stop and to lie down just as they were, wet to the bone, and whoever lifted up his head was beaten mercilessly. Late Saturday night, some 200 people, including many highly respected figures, were persuaded to enter a nearby shed under the pretext that they would be provided with an explanation of why the Jews were responsible for starting the war. The 200 men who entered the shed never returned to the group, and the rest of the marchers did not know what had happened to them. The next morning, they discovered puddles of blood nearby.

Only a relatively small number of people were killed during the march on Saturday, and these included primarily those who had been walking at the end of the line and those who had been taken into the shed. On Sunday morning, however, the Germans began murdering people on the spot, in front of all the other marchers, usually when they took notice of someone who did not meet their standards. When this happened, they forced the person in question to lie face down and then shot him. The German guards competed with each other to see who could kill the most

Jews. Things changed somewhat when the guards themselves started to find it difficult to walk through the deep mud. It was only on Sunday afternoon, after hours of walking, that the group reached the village of Dolwicow, where they were all forced to lie down with their faces to the ground.

That is when the wagon carrying my mother, my uncle, and the Volksdeutsche caught up with the procession. They parked by the home of a peasant whom my mother knew, and she went inside and asked if she and my uncle could stay with them for a bit. The coachman waited outside, and the Volksdeutsche walked until he found the group, with all the Jews lying face down and the German guards speaking with the commander of the march. He walked up to the commander and handed him the forged letter, which he said had arrived from the high command. After reading the letter and concluding that it was authentic, he called out: Nathan Sher and Nathan Rozensztajn, report to me!! No one answered. He called their names a second time, and again no one answered. After the third time, the two Nathans decided that since they faced certain death no matter what they did, they would be better off reporting to the commander. Perhaps something good would even come of it. Hungry, thirsty, and covered with mud, they approached the commander, who then turned to the Volksdeutsche and informed him that the two Jews were now at his disposal.

When my brother and cousin entered the peasant's house and my mother saw the shape they were in, barely recognizing her own son, she fainted on the spot.

Everyone present was gripped by emotion, even the peasants, who wept with my mother, as she told us later after everyone had returned home. I am not certain of all the details, perhaps because I did not usually pay attention to what was discussed by my parents during serious conversations. What I do recall, however, is that my father apparently did not trust the Volksdeutsche. Father suspected that the Volksdeutsche would eventually tell the Germans that the letter he had delivered to the march-commander had been falsified. That very night, my parents decided to smuggle both Nathans across the border. I do not know the fine points of the transaction, but I remember hearing that my parents quickly found a non-Jew with a boat to whom they paid a large sum of money for his services, but not the entire sum. This was because it was known in town that many non-Jews had promised to help Jews cross the border into Russia for financial gain, but had actually killed them on the way. This is why my parents paid the man only half the agreed upon sum, and promised that if he succeeded in smuggling the two boys across the border and could tell them the code-word that the boys were instructed to reveal to him only after they crossed the border, he would be paid in full.

The whole family stood in the living room as my parents packed Nathan a few razor blades. They knew that this was an expensive commodity on the other side of the border, and he would be able to sell the razor blades and use the money to buy food. They also packed him photographs of all the members of the family, and one outfit of clothing. He had a small suitcase that would not burden him as he tried to cross the river.

It sometimes seems strange to me the details I remember and those I find difficult to recall. I remember what the small suitcase looked like, but I do not at all remember saying goodbye to my brother. When the man who helped them cross the border returned with the password, my parents paid him the rest of the money. From that night until we moved into the ghetto, we heard nothing from my brother. Ironically, it was only in the ghetto, when we had already moved out of our house, that we received our first postcard from Nathan, telling us that he was in Siberia. Although the Germans had succeeded in demonstrating their power over the Jews before we moved into the ghetto, the postcard from my brother caused my mother to begin weeping hysterically, pitying her son, her sensitive boy, and worrying about how he would survive the cold and hunger of Siberia. My brother Shalom sent him a postcard in return, and wrote that despite the difficult conditions, the situation was not terrible; he still got new boots and was still able to see his friends. This made my mother very angry: How can you dare to tell him that you have new boots, she asked incredulously, when I don't even know if he has bread to eat? she cried, incensed. Her heart was broken by the fact that her son was in Siberia and because she had no way of knowing what the future held in store for us.

My father appears to have been wise to suspect the Volksdeutsche, who after completing his task, walked to a pub in town to the jingling sound of new coins in his pocket and got completely drunk. From there, he went straight to the Gestapo and told them about the forged document he had used to have the two Jewish boys released from the march. That night, my brother was smuggled across the border, and by approximately ten o'clock the next morning two gendarmes or Gestapo men were already searching our house for him and my cousin. When they could not find them in their homes, the soldiers took my father and Uncle Srumeir instead, locking them up in the local jail located not far from our house. I think my mother hid from us what my father had been forced to endure while being interrogated about the boys' whereabouts. She sent me every day to bring my father food in jail. Upon reaching the jail gates, I was able to get a glimpse of my father through a crack in the wooden walls. He got thinner and thinner.

As I already mentioned, my parents were quite wealthy in the late 1930s. But during those frenzied first days of the war, they used their money primarily to rescue members of the family. When my mother saw that they were not releasing my father and her brother, she tried unsuccessfully to bribe those supervising his incarceration. One day, after the two men had been imprisoned in the local jail for quite some time, my mother returned home in tears. They had been transferred to a jail in Lublin and placed in cells designated for prisoners who had been sentenced to death.

Remember, my father had closed his store and entrusted it to a Pole by the name of Gotlewski who used the location to open a restaurant for German soldiers. We lived above the store, and during the early days of the Gotlewskis' restaurant, when I was still a very little girl, I used to visit the kitchen, which had previously served as a shoe storeroom. The kitchen was a happy place. My mother always warned me not to taste anything there, because nothing was kosher.

Nonetheless, Mrs. Gotlewski would periodically invite me to taste some of the food. To be honest, the variety of food in my house was no longer what it used to be, as it was already extremely difficult for Jews to acquire food. Jewish stores closed one after the other, and most of the peasants stopped coming to market day in Hrubieszow because the Jews had no choice but to stop buying from them. It was also a cold winter. One day, Mrs. Gotlewski convinced me to eat a bowl of cabbage soup containing a big bone with meat on it. Don't be afraid to eat it, she said with a smile on her face. You don't have this kind of soup at your house. Eat.

I sat by the piping hot soup, which smelled wonderful. Unable to resist the temptation, I started to eat hungrily. Here I was, the spoiled girl whose parents often threatened to make her stand in the corner if she did not eat everything on her plate, sitting on a tall chair in Mrs. Gotlewskis kitchen eating non-kosher soup! The moment I swallowed the first mouthful, I was gripped by a very real and terrible fear that the sky was about to fall on me. Conscious of my transgression and certain that I would receive a horrible punishment on the spot from the heavens above, I abruptly stopped eating and never finished the soup. When Mrs. Gotlewski noticed, she guessed the reason. Leaving her large pots on the stove, she walked over to me and asked in amazement: How do the Jews instill a sense of what is allowed and what is not allowed in such young children? You can keep eating, she continued in a convincing tone. Nothing will happen to you, and you do not have to tell your mother that you ate here. Doesn't the soup taste good?

Mrs. Gotlewski was a short, slightly plump woman with sparkling green eyes and short blond-brown hair, and she ran her kitchen with great skill. Aside from Mrs. Gotlewski, there were others who helped her prepare the food. Of course, all of them were Polish. What attracted me most about the kitchen was all the activity that went on there.

When I got home, I was afraid to tell my parents that I had eaten in the Gotlewski's kitchen. I also think that my realization that the sky had not fallen when I ate non-kosher soup was my first break with religion. Still, despite the fact that I was drawn to this place that was teeming with life, I never ate in the Gotlewski's kitchen again. At the same time, I suffered the anxieties stemming from my secret, and I never told my parents about it.

The Gotlewski family had four daughters who already looked like quite grown-up to my eyes. As I remember it, they were also pretty, and after the restaurant opened they quickly found themselves boyfriends among the German soldiers who ate there. Although their youngest daughter was four or five years older than me, she befriended me. At that point, my parents had already stopped allowing me to walk around town by myself to visit friends, and I had no toys at home. All I had left now to pass the time each day was my friendship with the Gotlewski's youngest daughter, Zoya. She was not as pretty as her sisters, and I noticed that for some reason she was somewhat of an outcast in her family. She did not have any friends, at least none that I could see, and despite my young age, she too grew to rely on her friendship with me.

One day, Zoya suggested that we go walking in the forest to look for berries. Because she was older than I was and she assured me that she knew the way, she succeeded in convincing me, and the next morning we set out for the woods. We walked a long distance before we reached the part of the woods we sought. When we left home, we told no one about our plan. Zoya said that there was no reason to tell anyone, because we would be back early and, in any case, no one would look for us. I did not dare challenge her. However, when we got home, it turned out that people had been looking for us after all. Initially, it was Mrs. Gotlewski, who had been looking for her daughter for one reason or another and, when she was nowhere to be found, began searching for her in earnest. This is how my mother realized that I was also gone. There was a great commotion in the house upon our return, and Zoya was punished with a beating and by being grounded for a few days. My mother seriously reprimanded me and warned me never to repeat the offense, especially, she said, because of the precarious situation of the Jews. This is my last memory of any interaction with the Gotlewski family during the war. As time passed, however, we would soon get to know who they really were.

When my father was transferred to the prison in the ancient fortress in Lublin, my mother decided to follow him in order to try to save him, even if this meant bribing the guards. When she left, I remained home with my brother Shalom, who was then fifteen years old. One of our aunts brought us food, and my cousin Freida, who was living in Lodz at the time, came to look after us. When Freida arrived, I was sick in bed with dysentery, apparently due to some fresh milk I drank straight from a cow while visiting a farm not far from town with my brother. Freida was like a substitute mother, providing for all our needs with the help of our aunts and uncles, and we grew rather attached to her. Because she had no work waiting for her in Lodz and could no longer attend classes, she continued to live with us even after my mother, who was also eventually arrested, was released from jail. Still, because my mother spent a great deal of time in Lublin in her desperate effort to get my father released from prison, she was not at home most of the week. When the whole family was finally reunited, Freida had already become one of us. I loved her very much.

I do not remember the exact date it happened, but one day we learned that the Germans were recruiting young Jews to work in the nearby military base and that the working conditions there were good. Freida volunteered for the job. I do not recall the type of work they did, but I do remember that Freida would come home from work with a sense of satisfaction. As time passed, she found a boyfriend among the other young Jewish workers on the base and even brought him home to meet us. The young man belonged to one of the many Zionist youth movements operating in the city and made a good impression on my parents. However, their freedom to come home every day was short-lived, and the Germans soon began to force them to sleep on the base at night. After that, I never saw Freida again. I missed her, but every once in a while she managed to send us a note through circuitous channels informing us that she was fine. Later, when the aktions began, the Germans declared the area Judenrein (cleared of Jews) and my family hid in the Jewish cemetery for a few days. We then learned that all the young Jews who had been working at the military base had been murdered and buried in a mass grave there. When I heard this, I started to cry out loud, but my mother silenced me immediately, and told me that we now had to think only about how to avoid getting caught. But despite the fear, the hunger, and the overall situation, I kept on talking about my cousin Freida, and about how she was no longer with us. I continued to miss her and eventually, my memories of her were all I had left, like those of my other loved ones who were to be murdered by the Germans.

Every week, my mother would return home from Lublin as the Sabbath approached. I do not remember if she told us where she slept at night, but I do remember her saying that she spent most of her days near the prison trying to find ways to sneak some food in to my father and to bribe the guards to get him released. One weekend when my mother got home, she was immediately arrested by two Gestapo agents, who took her directly to jail. We learned of my mother's arrest from one of our uncles. With this, my days as a little girl bringing food to a parent in jail returned only this time it was for my mother, not my father.

A few days after my mother was arrested, it became clear who was responsible. When the Gotlewski family learned why my mother was not at home, they went to the Gestapo and told them that my mother was trying to bribe the guards in Lublin to get my father released. They informed on my mother in the hope that, since they already had turned my father's store into a restaurant, and since their older daughters were entertaining the German troops, perhaps they could get our house as well. If they were to inform the Germans that my mother was trying to bribe the guards, the accusation would come from the Germans. This would be a good reason to arrest her, and with only two children left in the house, it would be easier for them to get a two-hour eviction order issued. The Gotlewski family, who were supposedly friends of my father, decided to take advantage of this opportunity in order to take possession of our house. Freida was in hysterics. How could we vacate such a large house in only two hours? She alerted all my mother's brothers, and together, we emptied the house. We took all the movable furniture to a storage shed that belonged to one of my uncles, and we left all the things that could not be moved in the house.

Initially, we lived with my Uncle Srumeir. I liked his house, because it was located far from the center of town and had a large yard with animals and a lot of chickens. I even saw a chicken laying an egg, which truly amazed me. Two weeks later, my mother was released from jail. After she got home, she learned that it had been Mrs. Gotlewski, always so friendly, who had informed on her to the Gestapo because she wanted the whole house.

"Cut!" said Carlos. "I apologize. We need to switch cassettes, and I also hear a strange noise coming from outside."

We went out into the lobby to investigate the source of the noise, and there we saw Yossi, one of our own adult escorts from Israel, standing by the door of the hotel, white as a sheet. "What happened?" asked Carlos.

"They stole all the dollars I took from the kids to exchange for zlotys," Yossi told us. Still upset and trembling, he informed us that he had taken ten dollars from each participant to exchange for zlotys and had left the hotel. After quickly finding a Pole who asked him if he wanted to change money, which was a very popular question on the streets of Warsaw at the time, Yossi answered affirmatively, but first asked to see that the man was carrying enough Zlotys to make the transaction. The Pole pulled out a stack of bills topped by a 100 zloty bill and started to count out the rest. He made it appear as if the amount he was going to give Yossi was correct. But after he left which he did extremely quickly Yossi counted the money and realized that instead of a stack of 100 zloty bills the man had given him a stack of one zloty bills.

"I have no idea how I will ever make it up to the kids," he said, extremely embarrassed. After calming him down a bit, we went back into the hotel, talking about how we would be able to return the money to the kids.

Carlos, Motti, and I returned to the filming room.

"Cipora, let's continue," Carlos said. "I'll tell you where you left off." I thanked him, and we got back to work.

After about two weeks in jail, my mother was released just as suddenly as she had been arrested. In the meantime, we had already moved in with my uncle.

The Zubermans, who were close friends of my parents, lived in a large apartment with two entrances. Before the war, one entrance had been the home of the Stein family, a young couple with one child. The Steins fled to Russia with the Red Army, and we moved into the apartment in their stead. The apartment had a kitchenette with a door leading into a spacious living room. Another door led from the living room into the bedroom of the Zuberman family. For most of the day, the door between the two apartments remained closed. However, I the little one was allowed to enter the Zuberman's apartment whenever I wished. The apartment was located on Szefska Street, the street later designated by the Germans as the Jewish ghetto of Hrubieszow. Szefska (Shoemakers) Street was populated by the poorest Jews of the city. It had no sidewalks and was not paved, and most of the houses were mere huts without proper flooring. For this reason, the Germans decided to move the thousands of Hrubieszow Jews onto that street. However, the Zuberman's house was different. It was located at the beginning of the street, and there were only two or three other houses like it. After the Germans packed all the city's Jews onto Szefska Street, a serious food shortage ensued.

Approximately half a year passed between the day my father was arrested and the day we moved into the Zuberman's apartment. Although for the most part I do not remember exact dates, I do remember the particular half-year in question because we talked about it a great deal at home. I do not know how it came to be that my father was released, but he came home when we were still living at the house on Szefska Street. Shortly thereafter, he came down with typhus. I was very attached to my father, and when he vanished from the house I missed him terribly. When first I saw his physical state, I started to cry inconsolably. As my father was extremely sick with a contagious illness, I was immediately removed from the house and not allowed to return. This, they told me, was why my brother and I were sent to live with the Zubermans, where we slept in one big bed together with their children Chana and Itsche. We had fun telling each other riddles and playing other such games each night before falling asleep. Nonetheless, I missed the touch of my father's hand, and after he came home from prison I spent most of the day standing by his bedroom window just to see him. My mother wandered around him with eyes red from crying. They told us that he was very ill, that there was no medicine, and that it was not possible to call a doctor. But despite the lack of medical care, my father eventually recovered from the typhus. One day, my mother told us that my father was starting to get better and that my brother and I could return to the house.

Although no day during that period was similar to the next, life nonetheless returned to some semblance of routine. On Szefska Street, I gradually found new friends. They taught me how to play Palki, which means "sticks" in Polish. My mother said that the game was not appropriate for me because it was for boys. Palki was played by using a thick, strong wooden branch to keep a small piece of wood spinning in the air over a hole in the ground. I was great at the game. With other friends, I also learned how to knit. Because we had no knitting needles and we were no longer able to buy any, we made them out of pieces of wood and used wool that we found. But it was most exciting in the winter, when it would snow. Szefska Street was a long street lined on one side by a tall hill that descended into a long valley. We used to ski down the hill. I have no idea how my parents got me a pair of skis, but I, too, used to descend the hill on skis that fit over my shoes with the help of a special key. On the Jewish street, where Jewish children were permitted to live, we would play these and other challenging games, until someone would shout out, they're coming! They, in this case, referred to the Germans, who would enter the ghetto without warning only to suddenly disappear again, as if the ground had swallowed them up.

While I played outside, my parents scurried around town trying to buy food at any cost. My father somehow managed to hide pairs of shoes in different places, the locations of which were unknown to me. In return for a piece of leather or a pair of shoes he had stored away in a special hiding place, local peasants would meet him at the border of the ghetto with food. One day, after we had not eaten meat for quite a while, my father managed to acquire a piece of non-kosher meat. Over my dead body, my mother said, when my father brought the meat home and my mother realized it was not kosher. We are not going to use this. We simply won't eat meat. I won't cook non-kosher food! she said.

After the Jews of Hrubieszow and the surrounding villages, and the Jews who had fled from Warsaw, were crowded into the houses lining the long, poor street, the Germans found a new way to continue humiliating the Jews and robbing them of their remaining possessions. Periodically, they would use the Judenrat to issue instructions. For example, Today, all Jews must hand over all furs in their possession. Then, a wooden horse-drawn cart would stop in front of each house and the occupants were required to hand over all their fur. I, too, had a fur coat. It was almost brand new, and I was very proud of it. I remember how difficult it was when my parents forced me to place it on the pile of furs on the cart. My hands trembled and tears streamed down my face. A few days later, we were ordered to hand over all the gold and jewelry in our possession. After these demands were met, Gestapo officers continued to make surprise visits to the ghetto to conduct searches (Revizia) in randomly-selected houses. If they found a piece of gold jewelry, they would kill the owners of the house on the spot as punishment for not handing over their property as instructed.

When a German officer entered the ghetto and a Jewish person walked toward him, the Jew was afforded no more than a moment to salute the officer, otherwise he would be shot on the spot. That is how my Uncle Yosef Leib was killed. Uncle Yosef was a tall man with a huge potbelly who apparently failed to satisfy the expectations of a German who suddenly appeared in front of him on the street. Therefore, when Jews saw a German enter the ghetto, the rumor spread like wildfire among all its residents, and everyone would immediately go inside and lock their doors until they were certain that the German had left the ghetto. But even under these conditions, my parents were still not willing to give up on my education.

I was too young to understand that the Germans had not succeeded in breaking the human spirit of the Jews, despite the persecution, the humiliation, and all the other malicious actions taken against us. In spite of it all, the Jews of the ghetto still made a concerted effort to remain active. The Zionist youth movements continued to operate, and Chedva Russak, my tutor whom I mentioned earlier, continued teaching Hebrew, Polish, and math to Frieda and me. What I remember most, however, were the Hebrew songs Chedva taught us, such as Melafafon Tzamakh b'Gan (A Cucumber Grew in the Garden) and Avatiakh, Avatiakh (Watermelon, Watermelon). I admired Chedva to no end, to the extent that when she was sick and I went to visit her in her apartment, I simply could not believe that she went to the bathroom like everyone else! My admiration for Chedva made me want to join Hashomer Hatzair, but the people in the movement told me that I was still too young and that I could only join when I got older. I was completely crushed when I was not accepted into Hashomer Hatzair, and I was jealous of the older kids I met who were members of the movement.

I felt that, despite the hunger, the suffering, and the lack of certainty regarding what could happen at any moment, my life at the time provided me with many great experiences, perhaps because I still had a brother and a family, and a warm, loving, and supportive home-life. Overall, however, it was a life of fear, sprinkled with relatively ordinary positive experiences, such as making tasty pumpkin jam and trading dry bread (to be fed to the pigs owned by non-Jews who lived at the edge of the ghetto) in exchange for dill and parsley straight from the non-Jews' gardens. This life continued until 1942. Whenever the Germans issued an order of some kind, they would always add a humiliating epithet to the word Jew, like 'Jewish pig', 'cursed Jew', 'Jewish parasite', and others. I still remember how these names sounded in German. On June 1st,

1942 the Germans announced that all unemployed Jewish parasites (and by that point, Jews were not permitted to work) should report to the train station the following morning for resettlement in a better place with employment opportunities. Masses of Jews who had lost their livelihood left their homes willingly, without the Germans even having to issue threats to persuade them to do so.

I remember watching from our kitchen window as a family left their house with a large number of children. The first to leave was a tall bearded man wearing a coachman's hat and carrying a large fabric-covered bundle on his shoulder. He was followed by a few young women and men, and then the children (Whenever I tell teenagers about the Holocaust, it is the image of this family walking out of their house that always comes to mind). They still believed the German announcements and that the Germans stated intentions could be taken at face-value. When they arrived at the train station they found themselves being prodded onto freight cars that were so densely packed that it was almost impossible to sit down. They were forced onto the train with machine guns trained on them in order to prevent them from escaping.

From there, they were transported to Sobibor, a death camp, which in 1942 could perhaps still be more accurately described as a primitive death factory. Before they were killed, and again based on false promises, they were forced to write postcards saying that they had arrived in Minsk, that they were working, and that they were pleased. During this aktion, 3400 Jews from Hrubieszow were murdered. This time, the Germans did not go house-to-house looking for Jews, and for that reason I was able to stand by the window and see what was happening. The quota of Jews was filled even without the Germans having to bring them to the train station by force. During one of the periods between the aktions, I remember walking outside and hearing two Jews arguing passionately with one another. Because I was ever the curious child, their argument caught my interest. The disagreement was over whether the postcards that had arrived from Minsk were real, or whether they were merely another instance of German propaganda. One of the Jews shouted that it was a lie, that he was worried about the fate of those who left, and that there was no way to know what happened to them. But there are postcards! the other one shouted. By using such deceptive psychological measures, the Germans succeeded in killing as many Jews as possible without a Jewish uprising or rebellion. Media outlets, such as radio and newspapers, were inaccessible to Jews.

I do not know exactly when the Zuberman family managed to build a hideaway beneath their house. The front of the house was on the ground floor, at the edge of a hill. However, its back walls faced the valley and therefore stood on pillars. During most of the year, the space between the floor of the house and the ground below held firewood, which at that time was the only means of cooking and heating. After the adults stopped believing the German pronouncements, they decided to build a hideaway in the space, to be used in the event that the need arose.

First, they closed the space off by building sealed walls between the pillars. Then, they moved the large cabinet in the Zuberman's bedroom and made a hole in the floor large enough for a person to enter the hideaway, with a wooden cover that matched the floor. When the cover was closed, the hole in the floor was impossible to see. They then returned the cabinet to its original position. In order to enter the hideaway you had to first open the cabinet and pull out a large drawer. Only then was it possible to remove the cover of the hideaway. A wooden ladder was positioned in order to descend from the inner entrance of the hideaway into the cellar itself.

On June 7, less than one week after the first aktion, the Germans again ordered the Jews of Hrubieszow to report to the train station. By this time, the lies were not believed. Whoever had made preparations in time, would not go to the train station willingly. Instead, they would go into hiding. When the Germans realized that few of the city's Jews had reported as ordered, a German company entered the ghetto and went house-to-house searching for Jews. Many people were caught because they had been unable to prepare hideaways, and those who were caught were removed by force and made to walk to the train station at gunpoint. The abruptness with which the removal had taken place became clearly apparent when the process of clearing out the now-vacant houses began after the aktion. Food found burnt on the stove after having been left unattended, remnants of breakfast still on the table, and beds that had not been made. Everything had been left as if the residents of the house, having been momentarily distracted, were soon to return. These people, about 2000 Jews, were removed from their homes and brought to the

64

train station by force. Their lives were to be snuffed out at Sobibor. This aktion lasted from June 7 to June 9 and was extremely brutal, as the Jews would no longer report freely. After the aktion, 400 local Jews who were found in hiding were taken directly to the Hrubieszow cemetery and shot to death. After the first aktion, the Jews in the city had learned that another was scheduled to take place. It was then that the Zubermans and my family along with Bella and Chaimke (Gertel's wife and son), together with a next-door family that had an eight-month-old baby, entered the hideaway. All in all, some forty individuals took refuge in that small space.

From the moment we had moved in with the Zubermans, I began playing with the neighbor's baby and grew extremely attached to it. The baby's family included not only her two parents but her mother's mother. The entire family lived in only one room. Aside from this family, I remember neither the names nor faces of the other Jews who hid with us. All I remember is that there were forty of us. Our hideaway was full of bunk beds built from wood, padded with straw and covered with blankets so that the straw would not itch. Two buckets of water were supposed to quench the thirst of forty people and a baby. I remember that despite the constant shortage of food, we did have food to eat. The worry and the tension caused us to lose our appetites, and we all made do with dry bread, which had most likely been prepared ahead of time. From the very beginning of our time in the hideaway, everyone found a place to sit on one of the beds near their family and did not move from it. It was too crowded for unnecessary movement. Except for going to the bathroom in a bucket that stood on the other side of a divider made of blankets, everyone sat quietly, and in great tension, both to prevent being discovered and to hear if someone was entering the house. The baby slept most of the time, and before she woke up her mother would shove a bottle into her mouth just to make sure she did not make a sound. Her grandmother also helped care for the baby. On the night between June 7 and 8, my father left the hideaway to get a sense of what was going on outside. I assume that he knew people who would give him information.

Fortunately for us, the Germans did not enter homes to search for Jews in hiding. On the night of June 9, my father knocked on the cabinet above the hideaway using an agreed-upon signal indicating that we should let him back in. Inside the hideaway, an oil lamp burned. When my father entered, we saw that his face was sad and that his hair had gone grey in some places almost overnight. He told us that the Germans had already filled their quota of Jews for the aktion and that we could therefore leave the hideaway toward morning. I do not know for certain where my father had been when he was outside the hideaway. After all, there were no Jews in their homes during the aktion, and those who were found in their homes were either taken to the train station or shot on sight.

I seem to remember that my father told the people in the hideaway, including those closest to him, that he had a few friends in the Judenrat building who let him inside. This was important, because the Germans did not forcibly remove people from the Judenrat building at gunpoint. It appears that the Germans did not want to kill the members of the Judenrat until the city was completely Judenrein, as their help in the process was crucial. From their part, based on their naïveté and their belief in the human spirit, the Judenrat members hoped that satisfying the Germans with Jewish-owned property, silver, gold, and other valuables would serve to soften the impact of the German demands. Their intentions were not only sincere, but seemed reasonable under the circumstances.

During the two days that we lived in the hideaway beneath the floor of the house, we were completely cut off from what was going on above us and outside. Our only connection was a tiny window in the wall facing the main street through which we could see out but which could not be seen from the outside. In this way, we were completely detached from the hostile, threatening outside world in which death was waiting at our doorstep. We felt like mice that were being pursued not only by hungry cats, but by all the world's ravenous creatures.

We were still in the hideaway when the Germans assembled the Jews for another death transport. This time, however, it was not just the Jews of Hrubieszow who were involved. During the period between the first and second aktions in Hrubieszow, the Germans had brought Jews from the entire region to the city.

Everyone was assembled for transport at the Hrubieszow train station. All the apartments from which Jews were removed remained open with doors broken in, beds unmade, and meager breakfasts still on the table.

Under the circumstances, the Poles were eager to loot the remaining property and to take everything they could. At the same time, they were scared to death to enter Jewish homes after a few Poles who dared to sneak into the empty houses during the night were shot and killed on the spot. The Germans had apparently issued an order strictly prohibiting the looting of what had been Jewish property.

When the aktion was completed, we left our hideaway and all returned to their homes. The Germans deviously tried to reassure the Jews who remained in the city by leading them to believe that their futures were secure. To this end, they informed the local Jewish leadership that the Jews would henceforth be expected to organize their own lives, as those who remained faced no danger of deportation. The establishment of a cultural center was ordered and a house in the ghetto was appropriated for the purpose. It was painted in bright pastel colors. The Germans also ordered that a choir be established, and I seem to remember the publication of a newsletter, which was a sort of local newspaper. For their part, some of the Jews started to believe that the Germans might actually leave them alone after all. I still remember the adults debating the significance of the events that took place between the aktions.

For my friends and me, it meant that we suddenly had somewhere to go. Even though I was very young – only eight years old at this point – I nonetheless enjoyed the activities at the Center. Fear and uncertainty reigned, however, tinged with the merest glimmer of hope. How can this be? many asked. Why are the Germans taking care of us? Why are they establishing cultural institutions? The Jews had no confidence whatsoever in the seeming transformation of the German policy toward the Jews. On the other hand, the availability of participation in the new cultural activity, in the absence of any other choice, did much to ease the tension and to make the lives of many people easier, if only for a very short time. The questions, however, still remained in our minds.

Unsurprisingly, it turned out that the cultural center was yet another German tactic to deceive the Jews, clearly aimed at easing the tension in order to forestall any uprising, to counter the desire to organize resistance between the aktions, to prevent the Jews from fleeing, and to make it easier for the Germans to assemble the Jews for transports.

As far as I can remember, the cultural activity was geared primarily toward adults. But what were all the children to do? After all, the houses in which we lived were not really ours, and each apartment was overcrowded with a number of families. There were also not many toys around, and there was of course no school. What remained was the street of the ghetto.

The fact that Szefska Street did not cover a very large area meant that I again met up with my friends from before the war, most of whom had survived the first aktions. We created our own world. It was dangerous to be outside, and my teacher Chedva, whom I loved and admired, disappeared. Perhaps she tried to return to her hometown of Wroclawek, or maybe she had been taken during the first or second aktion. For me, her disappearance meant not only that I missed her from the bottom of my heart, but also that I was no longer being tutored.

My friends and I learned new games and made up our own out of boredom. Despite the atmosphere of the ghetto and the constant fear, our worries as seven- and ten-year-olds were worries typical of normal children of that age. In the evenings, I would usually go to a certain friend's apartment, in which two families lived in close quarters. At the home of this friend, we taught ourselves the fundamentals of knitting using sticks. We had no knitting needles, even though our home with the Zubermans held all the merchandise they had cleared out of their notions store (which they had been given two hours to vacate.) Along with the buttons, the zippers, and the colored thread in their apartment, there were also knitting needles of all sizes. There were also crochet hooks. I had a terrible urge to rifle through all the merchandise, but the door was usually locked, and they did not even let me peek inside. We spent a lot of time trying to figure out how to form a stitch on a makeshift knitting needle which was actually a stick that was entirely too big for the purpose.

After many attempts, we finally managed to form stitches, and, with a sense of victory, I ran home to show my mother that I had learned how to knit. Now that I already knew how to form stitches, I longed for a real knitting needle instead of a stick. One day I managed to sneak into the Zubermans' notions merchandise, and I stole a crochet hook, thinking that in the huge mess no one would notice that a hook was missing. I immediately began crocheting, so that people would know that I had mastered the skill, and it was then that I was caught red-handed.

68

The adults immediately realized that my explanations regarding how I had come to acquire the crochet hook were not believable. Taking the situation into account, they told me that I could keep the hook, but that I should not take anything without permission again.

I felt bad, and I was afraid that people would call me a thief. The experience of taking the crochet hook without permission has remained deeply engraved in my memory. I cannot explain why the story of the crochet hook still comes to mind and bothers me so much when I talk about the period. After all, I experienced things that were much more difficult and that had a much greater impact on my future.

Eventually, not only did the notions merchandise disappear, but so did the Zuberman family: they were murdered when our hideaway was discovered. There was Gittel Zuberman the small, energetic woman whom I liked so much, and Leibel Zuberman, who I also knew. There was also Sarah, the eldest daughter who was a redhead and who was nice, and seemed so very grown-up, and Mechel, the second oldest son, whose amiable personality remains engraved deep in my memory. There was also Itsche, who was the same age as my brother Shalom and who disappeared after the second aktion. I can still hear him telling his parents that he did not want to return to the hideaway and he wanted to leave Hrubieszow. After he left, all traces of him disappeared and nobody knew what happened to him. There was also Chana, who always complained that her stomach hurt. The grownups used to whisper to each other that perhaps she had cancer. Chana was a few years older than me, but we had a good relationship and sometimes played together. I mention each one by name here intentionally, because none of them are left. The entire family was swallowed up by the earth of Hrubieszow. But they did exist, and every family member had a name. Looking back on all of this, I wonder to myself again how important one crochet hook actually was.

On October 28th, 1942, just after the establishment of the cultural institutions, the Germans declared that Hrubieszow was to be Judenrein. In order to ease the task of gathering the Jews for transport and to prevent them from finding refuge with the Poles, they issued a proclamation meant for the Poles, which read as follows: Whoever turns over a Jew to the German authorities, dead or alive, will receive 5 zlotys and a kilogram of sugar. They also issued a warning that whoever hid Jews or helped them hide would be punished by death. Turning in Jews, they added, was the duty of every upstanding citizen. A just and proper civic responsibility indeed! These two concurrent orders undoubtedly made it easier for the Germans to complete the total destruction of the Jews of Hrubieszow.

Our hideaway had been ready since the second aktion, during which everyone had a permanent place, even though we only lived in it for a few nights. I remember the commotion that erupted in the street and the house that bitter, hurried morning. Everyone in the house was worried, and all I could see were frightened faces everywhere I looked. Each person packed something, and everyone started yelling that we needed to go into the hideaway. My refuge was the kitchen window and the view of the street and the events taking place outside, which I found most disturbing.

Outside, I saw people running back and forth. They looked terrified. Everyone was running. No one walked. People were looking for each other, and some held parcels packed in tattered fabric, women were crying, and there was a great deal of shouting Shema Israel. It was a scene I had witnessed before the second action. Three Germans, who did not look like ordinary soldiers, stood surrounding a Jewish man, plucking out his beard and his sidelocks. Shema Israel, the man shouted, clearly in pain. The spectacle frightened me to no end, and I fled to the inner parts of the house, where I was still able to hear the pleas and the shouts of Shema Israel. In my innocence, I asked myself a number of times why He, up there, did not hear the cries. Why did He not do something to help? Until that point, I had believed in an omnipotent God.

I had not been reflecting on these vexing questions very long when I was issued a panicked order to descend into the hideaway with everyone else. When they closed the hatch, I found myself with my back against the wall that faced the valley, sitting with my brother Shalom, my mother and my father. But he, and a few other men whom I cannot remember, spent most of the time whispering to each other while sitting next to the screen that separated the bathroom bucket from the rest of the room. This was the only place in the hideaway with enough room to seat a few people. Bella Gertel and her son Chaimke, my playmate, were also with us, as was the family with the baby. Unfortunately, I am unable to remember the rest of the people who were with us in the hideaway. I am sorry to say that I have even forgotten their faces.

Judenrein meant that Jews could not come out of their hiding places. Even eight-year-olds like us understood that the situation was serious, and we behaved accordingly. We did not engage in boisterous play, we did not cry out loud, and we did not demand anything from our parents. Like the adults, we sat tensely and in silence. We accepted events as they unfolded. Perhaps we thought this was the way the world worked.

However, we too had activities that were the center of our universe. As I said, the hideaway had a tiny window which was almost invisible from the outside due to a mound of earth covering it, but from which it was possible to peek outside, see a bit of what was going on in the street, and get a breath of fresh air. To reach the window, it was necessary to stand on a bench, which at night served as someone's bed. The bed was so high that it almost touched the ceiling. Of course, there was a line to stand in front of the window, and we children often had to push our way in, as the adults did not always allow us to stand there. Tense silence pervaded the hideaway until the moment that the sound of boots could be heard from the street. The sound was quite loud, because the boots the Germans wore had a kind of metal spur attached to them. Whenever German footsteps were heard, someone always whispered, Shh!

They're walking, in order to make sure that they would not even be able to hear us breathing, and therefore not find us. Whenever we heard their footsteps, we knew that they were not out for a stroll. They were searching for Jews in hiding, and in order to find them they had to go from house to house looking for Jews and their hiding places. We knew they would not pass over our house, and when they came in, we heard them moving and flipping over furniture. Once, we heard them throw marbles on the floor. Because marbles landing on a hollow surface make a loud, hollow sound, the Germans used this test to assess whether there was empty space beneath the floor that might be used as a hideaway. How much thought the Germans put into finding Jews in hiding!

Fortunately, the floor sat on a layer of dirt, and when the marbles hit it, they produced a dull, weak sound. During the entire time the Germans were searching the apartment, which usually lasted between fifteen and twenty minutes, we held our breath. We only allowed ourselves to breathe again when we heard the sound of boots leaving the house. The fear we might get caught gave me a stomach ache.

In the hideaway, we regularly ran out of drinking water and the bathroom buckets filled up. Volunteers had to be found to pour out the urine and feces and to bring back drinking water from the river, which was not very far from the hideaway. I remember that two men went out every night to perform this task and that they always took a few gold coins with them. The coins were meant to bribe a Pole or German that may have seen them on their way to the river. Every night someone else contributed a coin from what they had left. One evening, when we heard the sound of boots from a distance, the baby who was with us began to cry. It was as if all the people in the hideaway were driven insane by the tension. It was horrible. Her bottle was empty and there was no water. Then, someone suggested filling the bottle with urine in order to keep the baby quiet! This act must have shocked me a great deal, for whenever I tell my story and I reach the part about the baby, despite the many years that have elapsed, I begin to sob uncontrollably. After the Germans left the street and their footsteps could no longer be heard, the grandmother sat down next to her daughter, and I heard her say: I have lived my life, but you are still young. Give me the little one so as not to endanger all of the people in the hideaway. Toward morning, the grandmother took the baby, left the hideaway and returned to their apartment, which was on the slope of the house, and which had a wall that was adjacent to the wall of the hideaway.

Not two hours had passed since we listened as the German footsteps disappeared when the sound again filled our ears. From within the hideaway, we heard as they got closer and as they entered the baby's apartment. A short time later, we heard two gunshots, which killed the grandmother and the baby. Today, who can imagine what that German soldier was thinking at that moment, and how it felt to shoot an old woman and a helpless baby. Did he think at all? Did he feel anything? Did he even use the human part of his mind that we call emotion? Did he understand that the old woman and the baby were two innocent souls who never caused injustice to anyone? What kind of person was this German murderer? Was he married? Was he a father too? The baby's mother, who was with us in the hideaway, could not even weep for her mother and daughter. I loved the baby, but I did not cry either. We were not allowed to cry, because it could cause us to be discovered. This was something I understood instinctively.

Despite the unbearable tension in which the forty of us lived in the hideaway night and day, the days became routine, if such days can be thought of as routine. Everyone sat quietly in his or her place. Whenever we heard German footsteps in the street, we were terrified and immediately fell silent and held our breath. Sometimes we heard voices speaking in Polish. Nonetheless, in this unbearable, almost apocalyptic situation, we continued to hope that the incomprehensible evil would pass quickly. For without such hope, what was the reason for hiding in the first place?

I do not know the circumstances surrounding what happened next, but one night some of the people in the hideaway decided that the location was too dangerous. As the Germans had entered the apartment so many times looking for Jews, the adults suspected that someone had informed the authorities about the hideaway without knowing its exact location within the apartment. Father told us that we were leaving the hideaway and moving to another hideaway located on the edge of the Jewish cemetery, in a hut that in normal times was used to wash the dead before burial.

There, he told us, was an attic in which we could hide. We left the hideaway in the middle of the night – me, my father and mother, my brother Shalom, Bella, Chaimke, and a few other Jews whom I do not remember. It was a clear, cold, snowy night, and we were meagerly dressed. Father asked us to walk on snow that had already been walked on and that had already melted in order to conceal our footsteps. It was a quiet night. Nothing could be heard but a few dogs barking in the distance. We walked slowly in a single-file, taking cover behind the walls of Jewish homes, periodically stopping and looking around to make sure that no one was following us, and then setting off again at a quick run between the house and the next wall. In this way, we reached the corpse-washing hut at the cemetery, shivering from the cold and trembling with fear. At the entrance to the hut, right next to the door, stood a casket, and a ladder that father used in order to climb up and push aside a small board that served as an entrance to the attic. He entered, and we all entered after him without making a sound, as quiet as the dead themselves. The last to enter pulled the ladder up into the attic after them. There, we sat on the wood floor, with no cushioning, as a bone chilling wind blew through the cracks in the boards that formed the attic walls. For the rest of the night, we sat huddled close to one another in order to preserve some of our heat until morning.

At morning's light, we noticed a large pile of sugar beets piled in a corner of the attic. Because we did not take any food with us when we left our hideaway, we started eating the sugar beets. The adults told me I should eat it because it was sweet, and when the hunger started to bother me I did. During our first day in the attic, we could see through the cracks in the boards what was going on outside. A narrow path ran between the homes of the Poles and the beginning of the cemetery. We saw children with school bags on their way to school. They had no fear in their eyes, because they were permitted to live. People went in and out of houses very naturally, and were not in fear for their lives. They were free! But after the children returned home from school, they began to gather outside the corpse-washing hut to play some sort of game, as children do. This game, however, was different. While throwing stones at the wall of the structure, they yelled out repeatedly: Zhidy! Zhidy! (Jews! Jews!). This amazed us. How did the children know that at that very moment Jews were hiding in the miserable shack that usually housed dead bodies? We had snuck in at night, while they were all asleep, and we had been almost completely silent during the day out of fear, yet somehow they still knew we were there! We only stayed in that attic for three days, during which we had no water to drink and only sugar beets to eat. But it was not the lack of food that caused us to leave, but rather the shouts of the Polish children, which grew louder each day, making our presence there more dangerous with every passing moment.

This, the attic had become even more dangerous than our previous hideaway. So, after nightfall, we opened the door of the attic and descended into the hut. When we reached the purification room, the casket suddenly opened and a Jewish woman climbed out. She had been hiding there without food, how long, I have no idea. But when she heard us from inside the casket, she decided to expose herself and join us. I think my father actually knew her. She told my father about the camp the Germans had established in Hrubieszow.

We went back to our old hideaway, and we of course could only do so in the middle of the night! After all, would the German authorities permit a group of Jews whose lives were now prohibited to walk around in broad daylight?! It was a clear, freezing cold night, and snow covered the ground. We walked in a single-file, making sure to walk on the ground and not on the fresh snow, which made a squeaking sound. Our eyes quickly darted left, right, and behind us in order to be sure that we had not been seen by anyone. We did not walk close to one another. Only when the person in front found a wall behind which to hide would the next person in line begin to move. Suddenly, my father thought he heard a noise and that someone was following us. At that moment, the whole group managed to stop behind the wall of a house. My father, who was under an immense amount of pressure from the great responsibility of protecting his family, began to tell Bella, in deafening silence, that under the circumstances he could no longer protect them, and that the time had come for them to leave us. When I heard my father say this, I realized that he was no longer the courteous, kindhearted, and extremely well-liked man he had once been. Frightened that Bella and Chaimke would suddenly have to leave us, I began to cry, but not out loud. I felt terrible! I could not understand why they had to leave us now. For my entire adult life, this episode has remained stamped on my heart as evidence that you can never know what tomorrow will bring.

After this outburst, my father broke down and began to cry. In the end, he let Bella and Chaimke stay and told them that whatever will happen, will happen to all of us. We continued on our way to the

The house on Jatkwa Street

hideaway with Bella and Chaimke still with us. For the rest of the night and during the days to come, my father was particularly courteous to the two of them. The unbearable situation had caused him to break down and he apologized, because he knew that Bella had no other place to go and that she could not leave us as we were her only refuge. We returned to our hideaway and found that all the people we had left when we moved to the cemetery were still there. They of course asked us what had happened and why we had come back. In our old hideaway, life went back to normal. In today's world, a person who never experienced such normalcy cannot understand it. In the meantime, the Germans periodic visits to the Jewish homes ceased, because most of the city's Jews had already been killed.

One night, when the two men whose turn it was to bring water and empty the toilet buckets left the hideaway my father went out with them. I cannot recount the details, but I did know this: when we were in the corpse-washing hut at the cemetery, the woman who had been hiding in the casket told my father that on Jatkowa Street, where the Judenrat building was located, the Germans were assembling a group of Jews and establishing some sort of labor camp. As we know, everything the Germans did was calculated not only how to kill the Jews and to mislead them before doing so, but also how to strip them of all their property.

By this point, Hrubieszow was virtually Judenrein, with only a few hundred Jews remaining. All the homes that had been owned and occupied by murdered Jews stood unguarded along the empty street, as did the property inside. It was like a ghost town. The Germans assembled approximately 150 young Jews and ordered them to do the following: collect and sort the property from the Jewish homes in order to send it to Germany, and to establish a group of gravediggers to bury the Jewish bodies who were murdered after being discovered in their hideaways. The Germans themselves never buried any of the dead. They only did the killing. They left the dirty work of burial to the Jews, who were sometimes forced to bury their own loved ones.

The first group assembled on Jatkowa Street was organized thanks to the efforts of a few young Jews, including Julek Brand, a good-looking young man who was energetic and very active. A few young men had escaped from a train on its way to Sobibor by removing some of the boards on the side of the car after the train left Hrubieszow station. They had been captured and brought to the local prison, where Jews were taken before being killed.

Although the Gestapo chief in Hrubieszow was a German, presumably of flesh and blood, he was an evil devil incarnate. Ebner was his name, and he killed babies, children, adults, and the elderly. The stories circulating about him were horrific, and the mere mention of his name was enough to instill fear in every Hrubieszow Jew. When he saw the group of young Jewish men in the local prison, his initial plan was to murder them. To save themselves from the fate that surely awaited them, Julek Brand told Ebner that he knew the location of a substantial cache of gold. He promised Ebner to lead him to the treasure, in exchange for Ebner sparing them from death. The men were young and healthy and the Germans stood to profit from the deal both by acquiring the stash of gold but also by using these prisoners to collect the property from Jewish houses. For these reasons, Ebner agreed to the offer.

My father left the hideaway and joined the Jatkowa Street work camp. After speaking to the right person (and the details regarding this part of the story are unknown to me) he was assigned to work sorting shoes. From then on, he came regularly to the hideaway very early in the morning with bucket and broom in hand so that the Germans would think that he was going to clean the houses. In response to an agreed upon knock, we would open the hatch of the hideaway and my father would enter and bring everyone up to date on what was going on outside. On one such morning, Sarah Zuberman, who was then in her twenties, accompanied him. My father somehow also managed to have her join the work group at Jatkowa. After another few days, which to us in the hideaway seemed like years, they were joined by my brother Shalom, who was then almost sixteen.

Mother and I stayed in the hideaway, and Chaimke Gertel and his mother Bella were always by our side. Every morning, one of the three at Jatkowa – Sarah, my brother, or my father – managed to come to the hideaway and inform us about what was going on outside. Sometimes, they were able to hide food in the bucket they carried, and bring it to the hideaway.

"Cut!" said Carlos, apologizing and adding, "If you are tired, or if it is difficult for you to go on, we can take a break. I noticed that you got quite emotional when you talked about the baby. If you want to stop, even though you haven't yet explained how you got to Majdanek at such a young age, perhaps we can hear you tomorrow when we get there. What do you say?"

"I'm tired from the trip," I told him, "and it is an extremely emotional experience to tell the story of what I experienced as a child. Returning to the past has demanded a great deal of emotional strength. Although I sometimes feel weak, I would like to go on. If you and the cameramen still have the energy, despite the late hour, I'll drink a glass of water and continue. I would at least like to tell about my arrival at the Budzyn labor camp, how my brother was murdered, and how I was left alone when my parents disappeared."

Motti the cameraman agreed to continue.

"All right," agreed Carlos. "Drink some water and we'll continue, even though it is so late and we have to get up early tomorrow."

"Good," I answered, "Let's go on."

I cannot say how long we stayed in the hideaway. It was most likely a matter of weeks, and certainly not a matter of months. More than that, however, I simply cannot remember. This is because days and nights blended into one long, ongoing, unidentifiable tension-filled period of time. People only fell asleep at the moments when tensions subsided, and because of the tension some people were also unable to sleep at night. There was no place to walk around in the hideaway, and I do not remember any books. However, even if we had had books in the hideaway, no one could have had the patience to read. The major, if not primary occupation of the people in the hideaway was listening with great concentration to what was going on in the street outside, in order to hear if someone was entering the apartment. The words most commonly uttered were, shhh, someone's walking! Typically, these words were followed by a deathly silence. One winter night after falling snow had covered the street, the two men whose turn it was to empty the toilet buckets and fetch drinking water left the hideaway as usual. They generally made an effort to walk on the winding paths in order to prevent their discovery by the guards, who were usually Polish policemen patrolling the area at night to guard the property in the empty houses. The men on rotational duty always left the hideaway with gold coins in their pockets in order to offer a bribe should it be necessary. That night, after they had finished filling the buckets with water from the river and when they were on their way back to the hideaway on a path along which there was no place to hide, they encountered two Polish policemen. When they returned to the hideaway, they knocked on the hideaway entrance using the agreed upon knock and we were all relieved to see them back safely. Then, however, they told us in words that to this day remain permanently engraved my memory, that they had used the coins to bribe two policemen to get them to agree not to follow them. They believed that the Poles would keep their promise. The policemen had not laid a hand on them and seemed to have left the area. All the occupants of the hideaway were relieved.

However, the fact that the policemen made a promise in order to receive financial payoff did not mean that they felt obligated to keep their promise. At midnight of the next day we listened as footsteps above us in the apartment walked directly to the cabinet concealing the hideaways entry hatch. They even knew that they first needed to remove the drawer in order to get to the hatch. The hatch opened at once, and the barrel of an automatic machinegun was shoved into the hideaway. The occupants heard the shouts of Juden raus! (Jews out!) rather passively and without hysteria, as if they had been waiting for the moment to arrive. Our hearts beating with fear, we climbed the wooden ladder leading out of the hideaway one-by-one, in a single file. Me, my mother, Chaimke and his mother Bella were among the first to emerge from the hideaway, and we were made to remain in the room and to stand against the wall. We faced two Germans pointing machine guns at us. Until then, I had never seen such a weapon, which seemed bigger than I was. Trembling with fear, I held my mother's hand tightly, which caused me to whisper to her in Yiddish: Mommy, let's run away.

Shhshh, my mother responded nervously, apparently frightened that the German would see me talking and shoot me first, which would silence me on the spot. I was already almost nine years old, and I understood very well that our death was imminent. I was certain that once they got everyone out of the hideaway, they would kill us all then and there, in the room against the wall, with the machine guns they were pointing at us. I stared into the barrel of the gun, all the time expecting a bullet to be fired.

Once all the people from the hideaway were above ground, one of the Germans went down below to make sure that all the Jews had come out. Who would have judged them if they had left one Jew in the hideaway? Was someone watching their every move? They worked like cats with a natural instinct for catching mice. From what I observed, it is my belief that they were murderers by choice! After making sure that none of us had remained in the hideaway, we were ordered to move toward the door.

Just before we reached the door we were ordered to stand in rows of four. Then, we were instructed to exit the apartment. They brought us all out through the Zuberman family entrance to the apartment and had us stand on a sort of open balcony with a wooden floor. Once outside, we were also made to stand in rows of four. We were standing in what must have been the second or third row. After being inside for so long and having no idea what the outside world looked like, we now found ourselves stepping on fresh snow. When we got outside, I was standing at the end of my row, right next to the wall of the house, holding my mother's hand. Despite her repeated efforts to keep me quiet, I continued to whisper, Mommy, let's run away.

Except for the Germans who had found our hideaway, no one had stepped on the snow since it began to fall. The hill was covered with white snow and the sky was very clear. The snow lit up the night, and the stars lit up the sky. The visibility was almost like during the day. The dry cold caressed my cheeks. I breathed in the fresh air, which was something I had not done for a long time. A German with a machine gun stood by the exit facing the group of Jews, who were lined up in rows of four as ordered.

At one end of our row stood Bella holding Chaimke's hand. I stood on the other side with my mother. The Germans were shouting at us constantly, barking insults and orders pertaining to how we were to stand, how we were to keep quiet, and how we were to move. Every shout inevitably ended with the same words, as if they simply had to get it out of their mouths: Verfluchte Juden, Donnerwetter, noch einmal! (Dirty Jews, to hell, once again!) As the Germans screamed, I frantically began pulling on my mother's arm, and we suddenly started running along the wall of the house, which was not long, and immediately darted into the entrance of our apartment. We broke open the door, jumped over all

80

the upside-down furniture, broken glass, and the rest of the things that were scattered on the floor. As she ran, my mother yelled after me: Jump out the window onto the roof of the sukkah! I ran to the open window in the Zuberman's living room and jumped, just as my mother had told me to. However, the sukkah was no longer there and there was no roof to jump on, and I fell one story and landed in the snow. Faygeleh, are you alive? My mother shouted when she saw that I had fallen. Yes, I answered, and she jumped down after me! The high snow drift had saved us both. Had I broken a leg or sustained a head injury, my fate would have undoubtedly been completely different.

I have no idea why the Germans did not pursue us or shoot at us with their machine guns. Perhaps they thought that opening fire would cause pandemonium to break loose among the Jews standing before them and that they might not be able to regain control of the situation. That is the only explanation that makes sense to me. Certainly, it had nothing to do with having mercy on us.

We scurried down into the valley near the apartment in which the baby had lived. No one was there but the two of us, and we were both lucky to still be able to stand on our own two feet. It was then that my mother noticed that my nose was bleeding. She took a handful of snow and pressed it to my face, and said that we needed to start moving before someone began looking for us. She told me that a woman living in the valley once told her the location of their hideaway, and suggested that we go there. As we started running, we regretted not having eyes in the back of our heads, as we had to constantly look behind us to make sure that no one was following.

Ours were the only feet that had stepped on the fresh white snow of the valley that night, and we were of course the only Jews walking that night in the deserted valley. As we walked, my mother continued to press snow against my nose, which by now had stopped bleeding, but in the meantime had become swollen. As we continued our tense walk, my mother suddenly felt a pain in her leg that intensified with each step. Still, we had no other choice but to keep moving, as every moment we remained in the open and every mouthful of fresh air we gulped down made it more and more likely that we would soon meet our deaths

Despite the pain, the fear of being pursued and caught prompted us to keep walking and to continue looking for another hideaway.

At the end of the valley stood a large house which, like most formerly-Jewish houses, was in a state of total chaos, complete with upside-down furniture, as a result of the repeated Germans searches. We heard voices coming from under the ground, and my mother called out to the occupants of the hideaway and begged them to open the door for us. She explained to them who she was, but received no response. The occupants did not open the hideaway for us, and we did not know where the opening was located. After remaining in the house for some time and making countless pleas to the occupants of the hideaway, my mother explained that we should give up on that location, because the people were undoubtedly too frightened of being discovered. Fear now dominated all else. In the meantime, many hours had passed since our hideaway had been discovered, and my mother said that we could assume that the Germans had already left the site with the Jews discovered there. Indeed, we ended up returning to our hideaway, as we had nowhere else to go and as continuing to walk around outside would have resulted in our eventual capture.

The trek back to our hideaway took a long time, as we walked around houses and between walls to avoid being seen. By the time we got back, it was almost morning.

When we reached the entrance to the hideaway after re-entering our house, it was no longer necessary to open the cabinet drawer to find the hatch underneath the cabinet.

The Germans who discovered us had moved the cabinet and the cover of the hatch when they removed us all from the hideaway. When we re-entered the empty hideaway all we could do was to pull closed the cover of the hatch, because we were unable to move the cabinet back into place from the inside. We were hoping that someone from the Jatkowa group would come and check up on us, and that is precisely what happened. It was Sarah Zuberman, who arrived carrying a bucket, a broom, and a few rags, as if she were coming to clean the house, as usual. She had hidden a bit of food for the occupants of the hideaway underneath the rags in the bucket. When she approached the hideaway and realized that the cabinet had been moved and the hideaway hatch was exposed, she immediately understood that something had happened. When we heard the agreed upon knock, my mother climbed up the ladder to the hatch. Rivka, where is everyone? What happened? Sarah asked.

The two Polish policemen who had seen our men on water duty returning from the river at night followed them and alerted the Germans about the hideaway, my mother explained. The Germans did not even have to search for the hatch, because they knew exactly where to find it. The Polish policemen were the only people who could have told the Germans the location of the hideaway and how to enter it. What do we do now, Sarah? my mother asked, visibly stressed and in utter despair.

It's not a good idea to stay here in the hideaway, answered Sarah. I'll give the girl my jacket and the broom, and we can walk through back court yards to the apartment on Jatkowa Street where Mendel, Shalom, and I are now living.

When we had briefly returned to the hideaway, everything was in disarray. Clothes were strewn around. The benches on which we slept had been flipped over. The water had been poured out on the floor. It appeared that someone had gone through each and every piece of clothing in search of valuables. I suspect that the two Polish policemen who informed the Germans of the location of our hideaway were the ones who had searched the hideaway for valuables. Two days after the Germans found the hideaway, the two Polish policemen who often went to Jatkowa Street, told my father, that when the occupants were taken out of the hideaway, two figures had been spotted in the valley but it was decided not to open fire on them, as their fate was sealed. When they told this to my father, the policemen were unaware that those two figures were his wife and daughter.

After the Germans declared Hrubieszow Judenrein, after the hideaway was built and before we entered it, my father took our entire family into the hideaway and showed us where he had hidden a package containing pictures of our family and other important documents, the contents of which I was unaware. It was a relatively large package, wrapped in what looked like x-ray photographic paper and held closed by a rubber band. The ceiling of the hideaway was reinforced by blocks of wood. Years later, after the war, I searched for that package but was unable to find it.

Even today, I am convinced that it is still there, somewhere between the beams and the ceiling, despite any structural changes the Poles have likely made since then.

But when my mother and I returned to the hideaway, we did not check to see if the Germans or the Polish policemen had found the package of pictures. As we did not find them scattered on the floor, we assumed they had not. We did not search for them either, as at that moment all we had on our mind was our immediate need to survive.

Sarah Zuberman removed the short jacket she was wearing, put it on me, and handed me a long stick with a brush at the end. She then gave my mother the broom and kept the bucket for herself. All this was aimed at concealing the true nature of our dangerous walk through the Jewish alleyways, out in the open. That way, a person spying us from a distance would think we were three Jewish women cleaning Jewish houses, and no one would suspect that one of us was a young girl.

Again, we left the hideaway. It was now the early hours of the morning, and no one was outside yet. We tried to walk through courtyards and behind walls in order to avoid being seen. By means of a long circuitous route, we managed to get to my father's apartment on Jatkowa Street without encountering anyone, and this alone was a great accomplishment. The apartment was located along a narrow corridor with a few doors leading into extremely small apartments. Sarah knocked on the door, and asked us to wait outside for a moment so she could tell my father about the discovery of the hideaway before he saw us. When he opened the door and let her in, he immediately understood from the expression on her face that something terrible had happened. Dos kind! (the child) he yelled, before he even saw us. At home, I was always 'the little one.'

She's here, Sarah said to him. After a moment, my mother and I went inside, only to find my father on the verge of collapse as a result of his fear that we had been captured as well. He looked pale. He had just gotten out of bed, and when we entered the apartment he hugged me and burst into tears. It was only after he stopped hugging me that he realized how swollen my nose was. Mother had not yet shown him her broken leg when someone entered the apartment to warn us that the German camp commander was going apartment to apartment in search of 'illegals'.

Within a matter of seconds, my father had put me in Sarah's bed against the wall, covered me with a down blanket, and covered the bed with a bedspread in order to make it look as if no one was underneath. Because my nose was swollen, I had barely been able to breathe when I was outside in the fresh air, let alone under all the blankets where there was no air to breathe. Moreover, during those moments, I was not even allowed to breathe, for if I did, someone might hear me and find me hiding in the bed.

My mother was then in her early forties and could pass for a legal occupant. Despite her broken leg, she remained standing. Within a few minutes, a German entered the apartment. I, of course, was unable to see him. I was later told that he had entered the apartment quickly and suddenly, looked at each person inside, blurted out a few curses, and then climbed onto a chair in order to check behind the high fireplace, which stood adjacent to the wall and almost reached the ceiling. In the middle, there was a niche that was typically used for storage. All around, above the niche, were large blocks of laundry soap that had been placed there to dry. He touched the blocks, muttered another curse against the Jews, stepped down from the chair, and left just as suddenly as he had appeared. As soon as he was gone, my parents quickly uncovered me. They were afraid that I would suffocate, and I was, in fact, on the verge of passing out. After opening a window to let in a bit more air, they put me in the clothes closet, next to the wall of the closet. I was again covered – by clothes, this time – but there was more air and it was easier for me to breathe.

Between hiding places, they placed a wet rag on my nose to reduce the swelling. After some time had passed and the wind had died down, before Father left for work, we learned that the rest of the occupants of our hideaway had been brought to the prison to search their bodies for valuables. From there, it appeared, they were brought to the cemetery where they were shot to death, one after the other. The entire Zuberman family was murdered, except for their son Itsche, who had disappeared earlier and whose fate remains unknown. Itsche Zuberman was only sixteen years old when he disappeared. He was a beloved son born into a good, kind family, and only I remain to attest to his existence. The people in the hideaway who were murdered included the baby's mother; and Bella Gertel with her son, Chaimke; and the thirty-some other Jews who lived there with us, but whose names I am, to my sorrow, unable to recall. But the Jews at Jatkowa had no time to mourn, and, in any case, how much could we mourn?! More hideaways were found with each passing day, and in the end, almost all of their inhabitants found their way to the killing field that had once been a cemetery.

At my father's apartment, life fell into a routine of sorts. Each morning, my parents would place me in the niche of the fireplace, give me a few slices of bread, and leave the apartment. There I would sit, in the otherwise empty apartment, all day long, hunched over so that my head could not be seen. The door was locked from the outside, and I had the entire day to sit and imagine what would happen to me if I were caught. As a result of my father's efforts, my mother became 'legal'. In the morning, my father left for his regular place of work in the shoe warehouse which stored shoes taken from Jewish homes, as shoes were his area of expertise. My mother worked in a garment warehouse that stored clothes from Jewish homes, as well as clothes removed from Jews before they were shot to death. Both Mother and Father sorted goods to separate those that were suitable for shipment to Germany, which included everything that was new or in good condition. There was also a warehouse that stored furniture. However, because no one from my family worked there, I know nothing about it.

"I'm sorry, Carlos. Could we please stop here?," I asked. "What time is it? Oh my, it's very late!"

"All right, Cipora. We'll film for another fifteen minutes, and then we'll stop, even if you don't manage to tell us about Majdanek. Maybe you'll talk about it when we get there," he answered.

"I need some water," I told him. "Then we'll continue."

After taking a few sips of water, I felt better and I continued my story.

I seem to remember that my brother Shalom went to work with a few other young men emptying out homes. However, I cannot recall exactly what he did. I stayed in the niche of the fireplace all day, every day. In Yiddish, my parents referred to the niche as pekalik. I had neither a book nor anything else with which to occupy myself during the day. All day

86

long, I listened tensely for footsteps. Across from the fireplace was a window with a view that I no longer remember today. Although the window was covered by a curtain, I was forbidden to lift up my head in order to prevent anyone from seeing me from the outside. All I had to occupy myself was my imagination. As a nine-year-old girl, what did I have to daydream about under the circumstances? I daydreamed about what would happen if they caught me, how I would escape, and how I would scream. Would I scream? I also daydreamed about what I would do after the war. If I managed to survive, I thought, I would catch a German, cut out a piece of his flesh, cover it with salt, and put it right back into the place from which it had been cut. I suppose the adults talked amongst themselves about how they would take revenge on the Germans after the war if they survived, and that I imagined similar things after hearing their conversations. When I imagined the piece of flesh, it came specifically from the thigh and was extremely realistic. In my mind's eye, I could envision its exact shape and the part of the thigh from which it would be removed. In addition to listening attentively for footsteps and imagining what I would do if I were caught, such daydreams kept my mind busy for most of the day, until my parents returned. By that time, I understood exactly what was expected of me and I accepted it as a normal part of life.

This routine of spending days lost in surreal daydreaming did not last long. My parents were soon ordered to move to a different apartment at the end of Jatkowa Street, in a building that faced the valley along the river. Although the only possessions they had to move to the new apartment were beds and a cabinet, the process was very complicated. In truth, I was the problem. How could I go outside and risk someone seeing me? After discussing the matter, they decided to move the cabinet, with me inside of it, late at night, when almost no one was around outside.

When the cabinet arrived at the new apartment, they first locked the door and only then allowed me to come out. The new apartment was larger than the previous one, and in addition to my parent's beds were those belonging to three other occupants. They had simply added us to an apartment in which other people had already been living: Reiseleh Zilbermintz, her daughter, and her niece. We all crowded into the large room. Thus, three more people learned of my existence. The apartment had a kitchenette with a stove that was almost never used, because the Jatkowa work camp had a public kitchen that prepared food for all the camp residents.

The new apartment also had a fireplace with a niche above the stove. As they had in the previous apartment, my parents again padded the niche with a thick blanket so that it would be a bit more comfortable for me to sit in all day long. The niche itself was more comfortable than the previous one had been, despite a small hole in the back wall that led to the neighboring apartment. The hole was a real source of concern for my parents, because of the risk of exposure. For this reason, my parents persuaded the neighbors on the other side of the wall to cover the hole with a piece of wood and to hang a curtain over it, so that they would not hear me. This niche was wider and deeper than my previous one, and I could sit up without worrying about someone seeing my head or about being seen from the outside. The best part about the new niche was the kitchen window, which faced the hill that ran along the ravine. It was a window that no one ever passed, as the house was the last house on the street and stood on the edge of the hill. When I peeked out the window into the valley, which was not very far from the bank of the river, I had a clear view of a Polish house and its occupants, children walking around freely in front of the house, and a gaggle of geese with their goslings waddling after them toward the river. This landscape enchanted me. In the new niche, I spent almost the entire day gazing out at the landscape before me. I was jealous of the Polish children who left home every morning with packs on their backs freely and without fear, while I was scared to even breathe.

Each morning, my parents left the house with the rest of the occupants, and my mother would leave me a bit of bread. I mostly remember the bread, which I generally was unable to finish because I was not hungry. Neither my preoccupation with the landscape outside the window nor the periodic necessity of holding my breath when I heard footsteps on the porch outside the door, put an end to my fantasies. What would happen if I were discovered, and what would I do to the Germans when the war was over? Despite the view, fear was at the core of my existence in the new niche as well. As busy as my eyes were looking at the view, my ears concentrated intensely on what was going on outside, which for me was sometimes dreadful and traumatic.

Located not far from the structure that was our apartment – actually no more than a shack facing the street – stood another structure with doors that also faced the hill. The wall of this nearby structure which faced the street was chosen by one of the Gestapo chiefs, Wagner – whom the adults referred to in Polish as 'Alex I Love to Shoot' – as 'the wall of death'. Every time the Germans discovered a hideaway or an illegal Jew, Alex would bring them to this wall and execute them. As I sat listening intently to what was going on outside, I always heard the pleas and screams of those about to be murdered, including mothers screaming: But he's just a child! Have mercy! Why?! And then, bang! When my parents would come home in the evening, I would always tell them how many shots I had heard, or, more precisely, how many Jews had been murdered that day. As time passed, I learned to distinguish between a bullet that hit a person and a bullet that was simply fired in the air. I learned that a bullet that hit a person made a dull sound. At such moments, I actually felt quite safe and protected where I was sitting. After all, they did not know I was hiding so close to the wall. 'Alex I Love to Shoot' would walk around Jatkowa Street and practice shooting just for fun, taking aim at anything in his path that moved with equal enthusiasm, whether it was a bird flying by, a passing cat, or a Jewish person.

One day, I think it was on a Saturday, my parents and the other occupants of the apartment had not gone to work. A rumor started spreading through the camp that a Gestapo officer was going house-to-house, searching the niches of fireplaces. This sent my parents into a terrible panic. What would they do with me now?! Someone suggested they hide me in the toilet that stood outside the house, at the edge of the hill. It was a small toilet consisting of only a wooden seat and a putrid smelling hole. With the door closed, there was barely enough room to stand inside. My parents took me there immediately, put me inside and shut the door from the outside. It was a wooden door through which it was possible to see what was going on outside through the slits between the boards, albeit with great difficulty. There I stood, inside the putrid-smelling toilet, tense with fear of what was to come and trying to see what was going on outside. My heart pounded as I saw the Gestapo officer walking back and forth outside, cursing the dirty Jews. He almost turned toward the toilet door, when one of the Jews accompanying him yelled to him that it would be wiser to look elsewhere, because the toilet smelled terrible

(Did the Jewish man know I was there? I have no idea). After the Gestapo officer left and my parents were certain that he was no longer nearby, they brought me back home and placed me directly in the niche, as they knew the Germans would not search there again.

This is how I spent my days and nights. With every passing day there were fewer and fewer Jews living in Hrubieszow. In the evenings, my parents would take me down from the niche, and we would sit around the table together and eat food that had been collected from Jewish homes. At night, I slept in bed with my mother, my father, and my brother. One day, Dr. Orenstein – the head of the camp – came to our house, and told us that they were adding another young couple to our apartment. Until then, the couple had been living in a nearby village, but someone had informed on them and the Germans caught them and brought them to Jatkowa. They had not shot them on the spot, as they usually did when they caught Jews in their hideaways. They were a young couple and they looked physically healthy. The woman did not even look Jewish. She had blond hair and light colored eyes.

That was the first time I realized that there was something interesting that went on between members of the opposite sex. Because I was so young, and because children were not given sex education in those days, it is understandable that I did not know anything and that I could not understand the apartment's other occupants' reaction to what went on in the apartment after the new couple moved in. The others began joking about them, because every night the same peculiar sounds could be heard emanating from their bed. When Reiseleh Zilbermintz, who was the oldest occupant of the apartment, would have angry words with the couple in the morning, I thought she was simply getting mad at them because they were preventing her from sleeping, even though I heard them kissing and the creaking of their bed.

One morning, everyone except the young woman left for work. Suddenly, Dr. Orenstein, who of course had no idea that I even existed, showed up. After opening the door for him, the young woman went into the bedroom followed by Dr. Orenstein. I heard everything that went on in the room. He asked her to bring him a large bowl with hot water in it, and after some time passed I heard a restrained cry of pain and then the sound of Dr. Orenstein trying to calm and console her. Then, he told her that he was going to pour the blood in the toilet, which was located down below in the yard, at the edge of the hill. The woman continued to weep bitterly but quietly, so that no one would hear her outside. I heard everything, but I did not understand what was actually happening in the apartment. I did not understand that Dr. Orenstein was the only person who could ensure that the woman would not remain pregnant. She had just had an abortion. She cried the whole day, and although I heard her weeping, I was unable to help her, talk to her, or even understand why she was crying. I sat in the niche, but now, instead of daydreaming the whole day, I listened to her bitter weeping. All I knew was that she stayed home because she felt very bad. From where I was sitting, I also could see the white bowl, which Dr. Orenstein took outside. In the end, both of the couple died, I know not where but it is likely it was in Majdanck. No one would ever know for sure. And I cannot even remember their names.

"Cipora," said Carlos, "might there be someone from their family left who knows what eventually happened to them?"

"If only I could remember their last name, "I said. "Certainly I once knew their first names, but I have forgotten them as well."

They were rural Jews who were likely born in a village near Hrubieszow. They were young. Except for my memory of them, it is as if they never existed at all.

Life went on this way every day. The adults woke up early in order to report on time to the roll call that was conducted every morning. Roll call enabled the Germans to ensure that no additional Jews joined the camp, and that no one had escaped or disappeared during the night. Although the camp was not fenced off in any way, no one dared leave it in the light of day. The Germans had total control over the Jews. At some roll calls, the number of Jews actually present did not match the number of Jews that were supposed to be present, according to German calculations. Sometimes there was one-too-many people. In such cases, the Germans counted out ten prisoners and executed the tenth one in plain sight, in order to teach them that the number of Jews in the camp must be precise!

It was both strange and surprising when, one afternoon, I heard footsteps near our porch. This was something that did not happen often. When the footsteps came closer, I heard the voice of my mother weeping bitterly. She opened the door and wailed: Sholem, Sholem is no more, they killed him, my child, my precious child. When I heard what had happened to my brother, I also started to cry. All at once, my mother stopped crying and started yelling at me: Quiet! They'll hear you. You cannot cry! She ran over to where I was sitting and checked to make sure that there was no one on the other side and that no one had heard me crying. My older brother Nathan and I had been parted when I was just six years old. Since then, we had had no idea where he was or whether he was still alive. I no longer had any friends, but who could think about friends in such living conditions anyway? Under the circumstances, I had become extremely attached to my brother, Shalom. Now I was not even able to mourn his death. I was not allowed to cry over the loss of my dear brother!

My brother Shalom had been a handsome teenage boy with sparkling black eyes. He was also musical, and he had a wonderful voice. At home, I can remember the family talking about his future as a cantor. He was the middle child, and he was only sixteen years old when he died. I learned how he was killed by listening to discussions between my parents.

One day during roll call, the Germans announced that all sixteen year-olds in the camp would be assigned "interesting" work outside of Jatkowa. All they needed to do was to report to a specific location from which the Germans in charge would take them to work. After Shalom was murdered, a Jewish man who was a friend of my parents told them that when he saw Shalom walking toward the group of teenagers, he warned him not to go because the Germans were lying again. However, after seeing that most of the people his age were going, my brother did not listen to this warning. As soon as a large enough group assembled the Germans surrounded them, brought them to the Jewish cemetery, and ordered them to dig a hole. They never imagined the purpose it would eventually serve. After they dug the hole, the Germans pushed them in and cut them down with machinegun fire. The boys had dug their own graves.

"Carlos, wait." I said. "I need a few moments to calm down. I was very close with my brother, more so during the war than beforehand, and when he was murdered I was not allowed to mourn his death. I think

92

this is actually the first time I have been able to open up my broken heart and talk about him this way, and to mourn my loss. Back then, and particularly at my age, we never thought to commit dates to memory. That is why I don't know the date he died. I also do not know where in the Jewish cemetery those sixteen year olds were buried, and how many were killed."

"I know it's already late, Cipora," Carlos said understandingly, "but take as much time as you need."

Within a few minutes, we had resumed filming, and I continued to tell my story.

The death of my brother turned me into my parents' only child. One of their sons was supposedly in Siberia, but we had no way of knowing for sure what was his condition. Their other son had been murdered. Now, as far as we knew, the three of us were the only ones still alive.

As I sat in the niche, day after day – which in retrospect seems like quite a long time – I imagined my brother Shalom and tears came to my eyes. I wept in a controlled, restrained manner, without making a sound. At the same time, I continued daydreaming about how I would run if I were discovered. I think this marked the true beginning of my hatred for the Germans. Back then, usage of the term Nazi instead of German was not as prevalent as it is today. Whenever it was necessary to refer to the soldiers who were walking, searching, murdering, torturing, expelling, and perpetrating other horrendous crimes, they were referred to simply as Germans. In fact during the war, I did not hear the word Nazi used even once. My father also knew nothing of the party affiliation of 'Alex I Love to Shoot'. My father knew only one thing for certain: that the killer was a cruel German, murdering for Germany and fighting for greater Germany, which he was serving with unconditional loyalty. He was a proud German and not at all ashamed of his actions. Many such Germans survived the war and lived to a ripe old age, while all the time Germany continued to pay them a regular pension for their service to the nation.

One evening after I came down from my niche, my father reported that the police had released a young woman named Fela Shtecher and that she was now 'legal'. Fela, however, was older than I was, and I did not understand why the age difference was so important. I started to pester my father to do something to make me legal, as well. After all, I argued, she was a girl, and they freed her. Why was he not doing anything to free me? My father had become extremely sensitive about the issue even before I began pestering him about it, and after I brought it up a few times, he actually started to cry right there in front of me. He would do anything, he explained for me, but it was not up to him. I will never forget that moment, when I brought my father to tears.

"My dear girl, don't you understand that it is not up to me?" he pleaded, trying to explain the predicament to me. "You are only nine years old, and there is no chance in the world that they will allow you to be legal."

As he cried, he continued to explain that I was asking him for something that was impossible to obtain, and to stress the fact that no other living soul except the occupants of our apartment could be allowed to know about my existence. It hurt me to see my father cry. It was the first time in my life that I had seen his tears.

When a little girl sits all day long in a confined place in constant fear, she is simply not hungry. That is why I hardly touched the food my parents used to leave me for my whole day in the niche. One day when I was sitting in the confines of the niche, busy with my own fantasies, a tiny mouse suddenly appeared out of nowhere and crept toward me, or, to be more accurate, toward the piece of bread that was sitting beside me. I was not able to scream because someone might hear me, and I was also forbidden to leave the niche. Having absolutely no way out, I curled up in the corner of the niche until I was almost completely pressed up against the wall. Not daring to take a breath, and with a hand trembling with fear, I pushed the piece of bread to the other side of the niche, which was not very far. The mouse followed the bread, and in this way I was able to relocate the danger of the mouse to a more comfortable distance. The mouse had entered the niche from the opening into the other apartment, through the board covering the hole in the wall, and it left in the same direction. Every time I see a mouse these many years later, I am reminded of the mouse I encountered that day in my niche.

94

Every evening in our apartment, we ate a dinner consisting of food taken from the vacated Jewish houses. Usually, there was a tense silence around the dinner table, as everyone was either lost in their own thoughts or in conversation with their own family members. One evening after everyone had finished eating and was getting ready for bed, someone let out a muffled cry: Shhh! They're walking! We could hear the heavy footsteps of the German boots on the porch leading to the entrance of the apartment, followed immediately by a loud knock on the door. This, of course, meant that we must open the door at once, or they would force it open. I was no longer in the niche, as I always ate dinner at the table with my parents and the others in the apartment. The door was kept locked and shutters down.

The moment we heard the ominous words, my mother grabbed me and shoved me under the closest bed to the table. When they opened the door, I was already out of sight. In walked a Gestapo officer and a Jewish man. For some reason, I never asked who the Jewish man was. Both began searching immediately, based on the claim that they knew that an illegal child was in the apartment (it appears that someone had informed on us after all). During the search, my mother stood by one corner of the table and my father spoke with the Jew in order to distract him, explaining to him that there were no 'illegals' in our apartment. In the meantime, the Gestapo officer started looking under all the beds in the apartment with a flashlight. On top of the bed under which I was lying was a long bedspread that reached the floor. The German officer lifted the bedspread, turned on the flashlight, and lay down momentarily with the flashlight in his hand, shining it along the length of the bed. As for me, the moment I realized that the German was underneath the bed illuminating the area with a flashlight, I pressed myself up against the wall, willing myself to disappear into it. Of course, I also held my breath. It was clear to everyone that to be discovered would mean not only the end for me, but for all the apartment's occupants as well. I cannot explain how the German, with his bright flashlight, did not discover me. He ordered the Jewish man who had accompanied him to go outside and leave the location. How I was not found that day will always remain an unsolved mystery to me.

When the Gestapo officer left without finding what he came for, all the occupants of the apartment breathed a sigh of relief. Words cannot effectively describe the experience to someone who has never lived through a moment of such great tension. As soon as the Gestapo officer left the house, my mother, who was standing by the corner of the table, completely fell apart from the stressful moments during which she was certain that she was about to lose her only daughter, and she began to cry uncontrollably. As neither of my parents survived to explain what happened, I am still left with the unanswerable question: was it a miracle or just blind luck? Did the Gestapo Officer truly not see me, or is it possible that he decided to have mercy on me? Could the same man who murdered so easily also have mercy? Exhausted, all the occupants of the apartment climbed into bed as a tense silence fell over the room.

The following day was normal. Father left for work in the warehouse for shoes that had been collected from Jews. Before leaving for work, he never forgot to show me where he had hidden a few gold coins, which Jews referred to as lokshen (noodles). Mother left for work in the warehouse for garments that had been collected from Jews. The other occupants of the apartment worked in different places that I do not recall and that I may never have known in the first place. Every day, I heard the shouts and pleas of the Jews brought by 'Alex I Love to Shoot' Wagner to the wall next to the apartment. Their cries penetrated deep into my soul, and in the evenings I would tell my parents and the other people in the house the number of people that had been killed.

I learned of the mood that pervaded Jatkowa during this period from my parents' conversations around the dinner table. My parents and the others spoke a great deal about Alex Wagner, who walked around Jatkowa all day long with a loaded pistol in his hand. He really did love to shoot, apparently at anything and everything. It could be an empty bottle, a formal target, a bird that had not managed to take flight in time, a Jewish adult running away from him, or an innocent Jewish child.

I particularly remember an incident recounted in one conversation at the dinner table. 'Alex I Love to Shoot' Wagner had found a little girl holding a doll in a hideaway, and after immediately shooting all the other people he had found, he brought the girl to a more central location near headquarters. There, he looked once more at her, said 'nice, pretty girl', and then shot her with the doll still in her hand. It seems that he had intentionally brought her to the center of Jatkowa Street so that other

96

Jews could be present and witness this senseless murder. Alex Wagner also knew Yiddish well, most likely because either he or his parents had worked with Jews. He used his knowledge of the language to find and kill Jews who were in hiding. He would enter houses that had been vacated of Jews, to identify himself as a Jew on the run, and to plead for mercy or for water. Upon hearing the words mercy and water in Yiddish, the Jews would come out of their hideaway in order to help him, and he would then apprehend them and murder them. The inhabitants of Jatkowa pondered the same question over and over again: where did Alex Wagner learn Yiddish? And, who were the Jews with whom he had been in contact prior to the war?

One evening when my parents returned home from work, they told us that members of the Jewish Council – Rabinowitz (an attorney) and Julek Brand– had been murdered and that Ebner, the Gestapo officer who had promised not to kill Julek in exchange for the stash of gold, had shot him personally.

It was at this time that Dr. Orenstein was appointed as the official head of the Jewish camp, supposedly due to the fact that Gestapo chief Hans Wagner was said to have regarded him as an extremely professional and reliable doctor. As the camp's Jewish head, Dr. Orenstein was responsible for the distribution of food to the camp population, and also served as the liaison between camp inmates and local Gestapo commanders.

It was a hard winter. Many of the Jews who had been hiding in the fields and the forest and who heard about Jatkowa came to see Dr. Orenstein after nightfall, and asked him to help them join the camp and attain legal status. The terms 'legal' and 'illegal' were extremely important in the camp. It meant the difference between life and death. By bribing the Germans, Dr. Orenstein tried to gain legal status for as many Jews as possible. He was, however, unable to do so for adults over the age of forty or fifty or for children, because according to German policy these groups could not serve as part of the labor force. The Germans even used the Jatkowa labor force to construct a new building to house Gestapo headquarters in Hrubieszow

These relatively routine days in Jatkowa, did not last long. The Gestapo officers who counted the Jews each morning at roll-call found more

Jews than the Germans needed to complete the tasks of collecting all the Jewish property from the empty houses and burying the Jews found in hideaways, in the forest, and under haystacks in the fields. In February 1943, the Germans made their move.

With no advance notification, the Germans decided one morning to load a large group of the 'superfluous' Jews onto a truck headed for the train station in order to ship them to Majdanek. The group was relatively small compared with the mass transports of the aktions. Until this episode, illegal Jews discovered in hiding were either murdered on the spot or were brought to the local prison prior to ending up in a mass grave in the local cemetery.

For me, the day of the sudden transport began as a regular day. As was my habit, I listened carefully to sounds coming from the street, trying to identify and decipher who was walking nearby and where they were going. When my parents did not come home from work at the usual time, I began to worry. But it never crossed my mind that they might never come home. So I sat there in my niche and waited for them until it started to get dark and I started to get hungry. It was then that I was overtaken by a terrible fear that something had happened to them. An hour or two after they usually came home, I still sat tensely in my niche, alert, and worried, and completely helpless, unable to do anything about the situation. I suddenly heard someone outside the door shouting to open up and trying to force the door open. I of course did not dare leave the niche to open the door, because I did not know who it was. Eventually, the front door was forced open and a woman entered the kitchen and told me that something terrible had happened: they had taken my parents! The woman told me to stay in the niche while she went to tell Uncle Yitzchak (my mother's brother) where I was. I began to moan.

Shh!, the woman whispered, silencing me immediately. Be quiet, or they'll hear you! She then apologized for having to go and walked out. There I was, left alone, completely confused by the terrible news.

"Cut," I shouted to Carlos. "I can't go on. It's getting too hard for me and I want to go to sleep."

"I understand, Cipora. We'll all finish up then," Carlos soothed me. "We'll record the rest of your testimony at Majdanek. We still don't know and cannot understand how someone as young as you managed to survive until reaching Majdanek."

"There are two more things I want to talk about," I told Carlos. "Uncle Yitzchak and his family, and why, of all the people in the camp, the Germans took my parents, who were legal and who held jobs that the Germans regarded as essential."

"No problem, Cipora," said Carlos. "You'll tell me everything you can remember from your childhood. The camera crew has leased a car to carry all the equipment. You can ride with us in the car. We have a long trip tomorrow, and you can continue your story during the drive. When we get to the hotel in the evening, we'll show it to the kids. Does that sound all right to you?"

"I am so exhausted," I answered, "that I'll agree to anything."

"Okay," said Carlos. "Go to sleep, and we'll meet tomorrow morning for breakfast here in the hotel."

I left then, and walked toward my room, trying to take in the Polish surroundings.

In Warsaw in those days, tourist groups were required to eat breakfast and dinner in hotels, because aside from hotels, there were no restaurants whatsoever. Communist Warsaw was truly hungry – hungry for food, clothing, and just about anything else.

When I finally made my way back to my small room in the hotel, the clean bed inside was all I really needed. It was already very late, and the woman sitting by the samovar followed me with her large eyes as I opened the door and went inside. By the time I entered my room I was emotionally and physically exhausted. I locked the door, quickly got undressed, and got into bed. A hot shower, I decided, would have to wait until morning.

I dozed off immediately, but my sleep was not at all restful. I dreamed that they were chasing me and that they almost caught me, as if an arm that had been extended to snatch me up was just short of reaching me. I awoke in a sweat and a panic, and then I fell back asleep. Next, I dreamed that my father was sitting with me in the niche crying and that he suddenly disappeared, which woke me up a second time. This happened to me twice during the short night. When I awoke in the morning, I was tense and still very tired.

Surprisingly, the breakfast was delicious. It brought me right back to the Polish food of my childhood, which I had completely forgotten over the years. There was no factory-produced food, so the food contained none of the preservatives so overused today. The roll I ate reminded me of the rolls I used to buy on the way to school, and the salami reminded me of the wonderful taste of the salami my mother used to buy at the kosher meat store. The butter also tasted like it did back then, when farm women would sell it in the market wrapped in cabbage leaves. I really enjoyed the meal.

Carlos and his crew did not spend much time at breakfast, so I packed a sandwich, a thermos filled with coffee, and a bottle of water and joined the film crew in the car. The drive from Warsaw to Lublin took approximately six hours, and the driver drove slowly due to the fact that the road was narrow and in poor condition. As soon as Carlos told me they were ready, I picked up where I had left off.

I had already spoken about my mother's family, which was more like a large clan, most of which lived in Hrubieszow. By the time the Germans established the Jatkowa camp, almost all of them had been murdered, except my mother's brother, Uncle Yitzchak; his wife, Aunt Fayga; and their daughter, Tema. Tema had a boyfriend named Itsche. Uncle Yitzchak and Aunt Fayga had had four children. Their eldest daughter, Perl was already married when the war began, and she lived with her husband in the Ukraine, where she was killed, although where she and her family were buried is unknown. Their son, Nathan, tried to escape to Russia with my brother, Nathan, and since their escape, no one had heard anything further about them. Their youngest daughter Sonia, my cousin and playmate, was killed after a Pole reported the location of the hideaway in which she had found refuge with other family members. In the Jatkowa camp, Uncle Yitzchak and Aunt Fayga were left with only one daughter, Tema, with whom they lived together in one small room.

The same woman (who forced open the door of our apartment while I was still in the niche told me how both my parents had been taken.

After the Gestapo chiefs realized that the property in most Jewish homes had already been collected and that there were no longer many Jews left to murder and bury, they decided they no longer needed to leave so many Jews in the camp in Hrubieszow. At the morning roll call, the Germans announced that there were too many Jews in Jatkowa. They then went to the various work places to search for anyone who could be considered superfluous. Most Jews were then working in the warehouses that stored Jewish property, and that is where the Germans started to round up more victims. Their first stop was the shoe warehouse where my father worked. Because my father was a skilled professional, the supervisor requested that they not take him. The German asked my father's name, and he was told that is was Mendel Rozensztajn. Instead of taking my father, he took a group of other victims and headed for the garment warehouse. At the garment warehouse, the Gestapo officer asked the name of every worker, and my mother identified herself as Rivka Rozensztajn. What about your husband? he asked. My mother did not know that the German had already visited my father's warehouse. Frightened to tell them where my father worked in case they wanted to take him as well, she said that he had already been taken. According to people who were working with my mother at the time, the German went red in the face with anger when he heard this, and began screaming at my mother that she was lying. He took her back to the shoe warehouse at gunpoint, and as a punishment for her lie, he took my father as well. I never saw my parents again.

When my parents left the house that morning, they did not say goodbye any differently than they usually did, and the fact that they were so abruptly taken away by the Germans meant that I never had the chance to say goodbye to them. In the decades since they were taken, I have had endless dreams and daydreams about bringing them back to life, even for only a moment, in order to say goodbye and to tell them that their efforts to keep me alive were successful. It is a dream I have had my entire adult life, on happy days and on sad days alike. It is a dream that has become an inseparable part of who I am.

The evening my parents were taken away, I stayed in our apartment with Henia, Reiseleh, and her daughter. My aunt rushed back to the apartment. With great urgency, she tried to explain why she could not take me with her to their apartment because there would be no place for me to hide.

Their entire family lived together in one small room with nothing but four walls, three beds, a table, and two chairs. There was also a closet, but my aunt ruled out the possibility of hiding in there. How will you be able to survive standing up in a closet all day? she asked. But she also tried to reassure me, saying that they would not leave me all alone, sitting in my niche, moaning oy, oy.

When it was almost completely dark outside, I finally came down from the niche and crawled into my mother's bed, this time all alone. The bed was empty and cold. Reiseleh tried to give me some food to eat, but the disappearance of my parents was so crushing a blow that I couldn't eat anything.

The next morning, even before roll call, my cousin Tema came to see me and told me that the transport of Jews that included my parents had been sent to Majdanek. When I listened to the grownups talking, they often referred to a non-Jew who would come to Jatkowa in the evenings and pass on news. He was the one who said that my parents had been sent to Majdanek.

My situation appears to have troubled my uncle and aunt, because after the morning roll call, my Aunt Fayga came to see me. As I already told you last night, she began, we have no way of hiding you in our apartment, regardless of how much we would like to help. You would be vulnerable to anyone who happened to come knocking on our door, and your mere presence there would be dangerous for you and for all of us. Yesterday, we met with the woman who comes some evenings to trade belongings for food, she continued. I told her about you, and she said that because she knew your parents well, she would be willing to hide you with her. This is your best option.

I listened closely to her proposal, and although she tried hard to convince me, I knew deep down that I did not want to go. The only way I can explain my fear of going to stay with that Gentile woman was that I had heard of Poles who were paid to hide children but who would hand them over to the Germans once the money ran out. Also, the woman had neighbors who might inform on me to the Germans. I was afraid of the unknown. I was frightened of strangers. I was frightened of non-Jewish surroundings. And most of all, I wanted to stay with the few relatives who were still alive. My aunt tried to persuade me that it would be best for me to stay with the Gentile woman. I remember being determined not to go. I'm afraid to go there, I told her. I don't want to stay with her.

When my aunt saw how scared I was, she said, Faygeleh, whatever happens, we will do everything we can to help you. However, under the present circumstances, we must tell Dr. Orenstein about you. Perhaps he can help us.

All right, I said quickly. Go tell Dr. Orenstein about me. And she proceeded to do just that.

When my aunt returned, her face was more relaxed and, rather happily, she reported, I told Dr. Orenstein about you, and I asked him if I could add the Rozensztajn daughter as a worker in my kitchen.

So, what did he say? I asked anxiously, waiting impatiently for her response.

He said that in the meantime you should stay in the niche and that Reiseleh should look after you there. But the most important thing is, he said he would wait for a good opportunity to speak with the Gestapo chief about you, when he's in a good mood. He'll tell him that a young girl who knows how to cook well found her way to Jatkowa, and that it would be a good idea to add her to the kitchen.

My aunt continued, he also said that he could not make any promises, and that the Gestapo chief might want to see you first, before he allows you to become legal. If he demands to see you, Dr. Orenstein said that you will have no chance of staying alive. This is the only possibility he could suggest that he thought might help you. Then he went back to his other work, my aunt concluded.

I don't want to go to the Gentile, I told my aunt. I want you to tell Dr. Orenstein to wait until the German is in a good mood! I was emotionally prepared to die, but only among people I knew. As far as I can remember, my aunt was astounded by my answer and appeared to be convinced that something terrible was on the horizon. She thought that going with the Polish woman was much safer for me. She was visibly displeased. I could see it in her face.

Many years later, while reading the book, I Shall Live: Surviving Against All Odds, 1939-1945, written by Dr. Orenstein's brother Henry, I learned how Dr. Orenstein eventually told Gestapo Chief Hans Wagner, about but now without having to hide. In the morning, I would leave for work together with all the other occupants of the apartment and report with them on time to the morning roll call. My aunt found me a pair of shoes with heels and styled my hair so that I would look older. During the roll call itself, I never stood in the front row, always finding a place behind someone taller to make sure I would not be seen. As a result, the Germans who counted the Jews at roll-call never took any special notice of me. The kitchen was now the place where I spent most of the day, evading dangers and hearing about events taking place on the outside. Being in the kitchen under the supervision of my aunt was the best hiding place I had had up to that point.

My aunt made sure that I never left the kitchen during daylight in order to minimize the risk posed by Germans who might still be outside patrolling the area. I was to leave the kitchen only after darkness started to fall. Only then, could I safely scurry from place to place, like a mouse making its way to its den. She would ensure that I ate something before I left the kitchen, for in the apartment where I lived, there was no one to take care of me. I was the only one left out of my immediate family, and I was all alone. Within the camp, I was the youngest Jewish girl alive in Hrubieszow. There appeared to be a sense of collective responsibility for me among the remaining Jews.

One morning, I was running late for some reason and I did not leave for roll call with everyone else. Apparently, I was unaware of the serious danger posed by my tardiness. When I stepped out of the alleyway along which the house was located and stepped up onto the narrow wooden main sidewalk that ran along Jatkowa Street, I saw all the inhabitants of the camp standing at morning roll-call. They were actually at the beginning of the count that the Germans carried out every morning. There I was, a little girl, walking on the main narrow sidewalk by myself, along a completely desolate street, when out of nowhere, a Gestapo officer appeared before me, on the very same narrow sidewalk. He was very tall and had broad shoulders, and when he saw me he stopped in his tracks and stared at me wide-eyed with surprise.

He looked at me like a lion surveying his prey, as if he could not believe that such a young Jew still existed! I shook with fear as I stood before him, and felt that these would be my last moments. Almost instinctively, before he had a chance to say a word, I began to talk a mile a minute. I remember telling him that I was legal, that I worked in the kitchen, and that although I looked young I was really quite old. I continued to stammer, and the German continued to gape at me from above with amazement, seemingly shocked by what he saw and confused by my rapid speech. He asked me my name, and after I answered him he again stared at me with a penetrating gaze. Then, suddenly, he turned and continued on his way, and did not lay a finger on me. My fear did not subside immediately, but I nonetheless took a deep breath to make sure I was still alive. When the Gestapo officer got a bit farther away, I continued to walk, trembling, toward the inspection.

Only when I approached the people standing at the roll call, who were already about to break up to go to their different workplaces, did I realize that they had all anxiously witnessed my surprise meeting with the new Gestapo chief. (As it turned out, the new commander was not as bloodthirsty as his predecessor. Years after the war was over, I learned that his name was Waldner.)

When I got closer to the roll-call, many people began lecturing me about what had just happened, out of concern for my well being. Didn't I know that I could not afford to walk around in broad daylight, and that doing so meant risking my life? They were quite angry with me, and I tried to justify myself by explaining that I was just going to work. I said that I would try not to be late again and I wouldn't walk around outside in broad daylight for no reason.

As the days passed, I became part of the adult life in the camp. This was especially true in the evening, after working hours, when camp residents used to gather in one of the Jewish apartments. I listened to their stories about the homes they had emptied and the food they had found in the process. For some reason, the thing I remember most clearly from these stories was their discussion of the number of eggs they had eaten each day. In most houses, the Jewish workers found eggs that were still fresh. As other food was extremely hard to come by, they ate the eggs. I can still remember one particularly tall fellow boasting that he was then eating as many as ten eggs per day. In addition to those stories I also sometimes experienced the mood of the adults in the camp. Aside from me, Zalman (who worked with me in the kitchen), and Fela (Cipora) Sztecher and a few other teenagers, most of the people were in their twenties and thirties.

One evening, the conversation turned to relationships between the sexes, and who was "with" whom. During the conversation, they also jokingly pointed out the fact that there was only one virgin in the room at the moment, and the mischievous eyes of everyone in the room turned to me. I was only nine years old, and completely ignorant. I did not understand the label that had suddenly been pinned on me and why! All I knew was that when they said what they said about me, everyone laughed and then dodged my questions on the subject.

In Jatkowa, everyone carried, at all time, a military-style mess tin, including a fork and a knife. Since for us, everything was temporary, the adults also talked about how the mess tin had become essential personal equipment for everyone in the camp. We never knew where and when we would find food. I also heard some people say that because we were going to die soon anyway, we might as well enjoy every moment of our lives, until we met our certain death. The threat of death hung over our heads at all times.

During the day, I stayed close to my Aunt Fayga in the kitchen. In addition to looking after me, she was also busy cooking food for the people of the camp. Before going to bed, I sometimes spent evenings with the few extended family members I had left: Uncle Yitzchak, Aunt Fayga, my cousin Tema, and Itsche, her boyfriend.

After the disappearance of my parents, Tema had told me that the entire transport with which my parents were expelled had been sent to Majdanek. After more time had passed, Tema told me that at Majdanek, the men and women had been separated from each other. The men had stayed at Majdanek while the women had been sent to Trawniki.

Soon, the winter started to recede and the camp inmates enjoyed slightly warmer weather. Since becoming legal, I had always worn the same dress in which I first arrived at the camp, along with the only winter jacket I had. By this time, the mass murders had stopped, as had the transports and the aktions to send people to the death camps. Most of the Jews of Hrubieszow had already been killed. Only rarely were new hideaways found, and when the pitiful refuges were uncovered, the victims were typically brought to the Jewish cemetery, where they were murdered and where camp residents were forced to bury them.

Now, however, this was not happening as frequently as it had in the recent past. The contents of the homes of the Jews who had been deported to Sobibor, Belzec, and Chelmno had already been collected, and the Germans in Hrubieszow had less need of Jewish hands to labor on their behalf. The regular work of collecting and sorting property from empty Jewish homes and burying Jews, had slowed down so the Germans ordered a group of the Jews to construct a new building for Gestapo headquarters in the center of town.

There was never a dull moment on Jatkowa Street. Each new day brought tragedies of its own. A roll call was held every morning, and the fate of those in attendance depended on the whims of the Gestapo officer doing the counting.

There were also the interpersonal problems typical of normal life particularly, romantic relationship problems. I remember one day standing by the bridge near the Huczwa River, waiting for my cousin. She was visiting a friend who was having problems with her boyfriend. As I stood waiting, two young men appeared. They were standing nearby so I could hear what they were saying. One told the other what was happening in the Warsaw ghetto with a sense of pride in the Jews' ability to stage a revolt. He also said that he knew that some of our people in Jatkowa had pistols, and that perhaps they would organize something. The other young man responded with skepticism regarding the acts of heroism, and said that he hoped no one in Jatkowa would mount a rebellion. If they did, he explained, not only would they be killed but we would all be killed. I stood on the side and listened. I was very interested in what was happening to we Jews. I remember the conversation well, and today I know that it took place in April, around the time of Passover. Although we spoke about Passover in the camp, we certainly could not celebrate.

The Germans went to great lengths to ensure that many of their atrocities were carried out on Jewish holidays. Practically no holiday went by without a tragic event taking place. If they were not putting someone to death on a holiday, then they were murdering someone on the Sabbath, although they had no problem with committing murder on weekdays as well.

At some point in May, the Gestapo unveiled another exercise in torture for the Jewish community at Jatkowa. Each day after work, the camp residents who had been taken to work outside of Jatkowa were brought to a large field with a lake surrounded by low hills. The Germans would order the Jews to disrobe, so they would think they were going to kill them, and to get into the water. Then, after some time had passed, they would order them to put their clothes back on and would return them to the camp. The Germans carried out this exercise for a few weeks, and never explained their actions. Perhaps it was only a training exercise so the Germans would be skilled in murdering Jews with as little effort as possible.

By late July, almost no work remained for the Jews of Jatkowa. The day everyone was dreading finally arrived in August, when a large group of young Jews was sent to a hitherto unknown camp known as Budzyn, located near the city of Lublin. The Jews who had been selected for the transport were loaded onto a truck and disappeared. Those who remained in the camp feared that those Jews had been killed before they even left Hrubieszow. It was only a few days later the remaining Jews learned that the group was in Budzyn, a labor camp with extremely harsh conditions. Upon learning that they were still alive, the Jews of Jatkowa rejoiced and took solace in the information. In the best case scenario, they said, this will be our fate as well.

During a roll call that took place about two weeks after the group transport to Budzyn, the Gestapo chief informed us that we were all going to be taken immediately to prison. After the roll call, all 150 of us were taken directly to prison. Many took off rings and other valuables that they had managed to keep secretly. I remember hearing women saying to each other that it would be better to throw it all into the prison latrines (crude open latrines with a hole in the center) just as long as the valuables did not fall into the hands of the Germans. And that is what they did. Who knows if the Poles later found a treasure in those old latrine pits? We did not know if we were going to be sent to Budzyn, or if we were destined to be killed in Hrubieszow.

Although I am no longer able to remember everything from that period, some incidents remain ingrained in my memory like a photograph that never fades. One of these incidents was the relatively short march of the handful of surviving Jews of Hrubieszow from Jatkowa Street to the prison. We were the last living Jews in Hrubieszow. The city, which had had a strong Jewish presence for hundreds of years, with its synagogues, the stieblich (prayer house), the slaughter houses, the Jewish stores, was completely depopulated of its Jewish inhabitants. All that remained in the city were the silent bones of the Jews buried in the ground. There were many such graves. From Jatkowa, we marched in rows of four through the main street, as Poles leisurely strolling along the sidewalk gazed in our direction. Some eyes were full of pity, and others full of what looked like pleasure at the misfortune of the last remaining Jews in the city, who had once been their neighbors.

Fortunately, when I left for the roll call that morning, I also wore a sweater with four gold coins, which my father had left in our apartment, sewed into the pockets, and a jacket, even though it was already mid-June. This was to be my last day in Hrubieszow, as it was for the other Jews. It was the day on which I was unwillingly severed from the familiar landscape of my childhood, from my home, as I had already been severed from my parents and siblings, and from what had shaped me into the girl I now was.

Only years later did I learn, from people who were with me at Jatkowa, how lucky I had been to be the only little girl among so many adults in the prison. After we left Jatkowa, and while we were still in prison, I realized that many other people in addition to my parents had managed to hide their children in hideaways. Only the people closest to them actually knew about it. I do not know how the Germans found the children, but they were brought to the prison as well and interrogated in an attempt to discover who their parents were. After no one acknowledged being the parents, the children were taken away by truck. It is likely they were brought to the cemetery and murdered. It is still difficult to comprehend the lengths to which the Germans were willing to go in order to find and murder a few helpless Jewish children.

When our turn came to be loaded onto the waiting trucks, the Gestapo chief told a frantic Dr. Orenstein that we were being sent to Budzyn as well. But in fact, the trucks began driving toward the train station, where we were then loaded like cattle into closed, dark freight cars. Inside the cars, there was only one small window, which had been covered by barbed wire. The car was crowded, the trip was long, and in the corner was a bucket to be used as a toilet. It was a difficult trip, and the air inside the closed car was not nearly enough for everyone to breathe. For the entire trip, I never left my aunt and uncle's side, and my Aunt Fayga at least made sure that I was allotted a place to sit down. We had no food, but once in a while, when the train stopped, we were given a small amount of water. This was my first train trip and oddly, I did not develop a hatred for this form of transportation. In fact, to this day, I actually like taking long journeys by train.

After we had been travelling for four or five hours, the train stopped. When I asked where we were, I was told that we were in the city of Lublin, from which it was possible to see Majdanek. In fact, we could actually see a group of people in striped clothing working on something in the far distance. I pestered my aunt, asking her if perhaps my mother and father were there. I could see a far-off figure that to my childish eyes resembled my father, but no one confirmed this.

I do not remember how much time the train spent in Lublin station. However, while we were there, we all pressed up against the cracks in the boards and the one small window in the car in order to see how things looked outside, to get an idea of the direction in which we were travelling, and just to breathe some fresh air. The trip took seven or eight hours, and when we arrived at the train station near the camp at Budzyn we were exhausted and frightened about what was to come. From the moment we left the train, we were surrounded by SS soldiers and a few Ukrainians with dogs. They ordered us to get into rows and they marched us toward the camp. The whole time, I never left my aunt's side.

4. Budzyn Labor Camp

We could see the camp's guard towers before we even reached the camp itself. Because I had so little energy, it seemed to me like we had been walking for a long time, and it is difficult for me to estimate the distance. From the moment we left the train station and began walking, I could feel my strength fading. Eventually, I began to stumble. My aunt and uncle were seized with panic that one of the SS men guarding us would see how weak I was and shoot me. After I almost fell down, my aunt told me to get rid of the red sweater I had been wearing, as that would probably make the walk easier for me. I apparently left my jacket in the train car, and when I tossed off my sweater the thought of the gold coins sewn into the pocket never crossed my mind. All I could think about was how to make things easier for myself so that I could continue walking. I was so tired that I was even a bit confused

Nonetheless, I clearly understood what was likely to happen to me if I continued stumbling during the march. The walking conditions got much more difficult as we made our way to the camp, and one of the adults picked me up and carried me on his shoulders. By now, I was so small and thin that I was effectively hidden by two people walking on each side of the man, and the guards did not even notice that I was being carried.

When we finally reached an area encircled in barbed wire, the guards told us to stop in front of the gate. We understood immediately that we had arrived to a difficult and frightening place. Leaning against the double fence were a few men who looked on the verge of death. They were known as 'musselmen'. When they saw us arriving, they put out their hands and asked for bread, but were hardly able to open their mouths. In comparison to the men leaning on the fence, we Jews from Hrubieszow were still well-dressed, and our relatively healthy appearance indicated that we had come from a place with enough food. The look of the 'musselmen' terrified us. When the gate opened, we noticed the words written above: Work makes you free, in German.

We were marched through the gate into the camp where Ukrainian guards awaited us. These guards often scared us more than the Germans.

Now, however, it was not only the fear of being killed on the spot, but fear of being tortured, beaten, and abused in general. Standing with the Ukrainians, we also noticed a few guards in Polish military uniform. One of them, who had a large mustache, began screaming at us and ordering us to perform humiliating physical exercises. It all frightened me to no end.

First, we were led to a reception barrack that looked like a laundry room and ordered to leave any belongings that we still had. However, what remains most deeply engraved in my memory from our arrival at Budzyn is the way we were searched by one woman in particular. She was older and well-dressed, and her face radiated evil. She examined me internally to make sure I was not concealing any money or jewelry. Her search hurt me, and, although I was just a little girl, she was extremely cruel to me because I did not stand quietly. When we were ordered to get dressed, I was so frightened that I forgot to put my underwear back on, and I went out with nothing but my thin dress covering my skin. Outside stood a gigantic pile of clothing, and when I emerged from the barracks my aunt was waiting for me. When she saw I was wearing nothing but a thin dress, she grabbed a warm coat from the pile. Just after she grabbed the coat, they yelled at us to get into rows facing the showers. My aunt quickly dressed me in the coat, which was meant to fit a woman of medium height and which had a collar made of synthetic fur. It was this coat that not only saved me from the Polish cold but also prevented the discovery of my age and my childlike dimensions.

After the searches and the registration process, we were taken to the showers. Before we entered the showers, women and men were separated. The shower structure was a long barrack with a corridor down the middle; the showers were on the right, and directly across the hall from the showers was a dressing room. When I arrived at the shower barrack with the rest of the women, we were ordered to wait at the door of the showers in a straight line. As we stood there, they ordered the men, who were already in the showers, to exit and run naked into the dressing room. Because we were forced to stand there, we had to watch the naked men run by us, in great embarrassment, to the dressing room, covering their genitalia with their hands.

I distinctly remember a hysterical sound that sounded something like a half-laugh, half-cry being emanating from both the men and the women. To me, the men looked miserable and thin. This was because they included not only the men from Hrubieszow, but other men from the camp as well. It is difficult to forget such a disturbing spectacle. When the order was finally given for the women to enter the showers and disrobe, we expected to be accompanied inside by the female guards of the camp. But the women were accompanied into the showers by the male SS commanders, as if this was completely normal and routine. They circulated among us and drew our attention to the way we looked, checked our hair for lice, and simply walked around freely, as if it was normal for relatively young men to be milling around through a crowd of naked women.

The arrival process, the search for valuables, and showering were all carried out to the sound of guards yelling, Schnell! Schnell! When these activities came to an end, we were brought to a barracks where cloudy water – which they called soup – was being given out: a mess tin of salty water with an unidentifiable green leaf floating in it. It was then, while the soup was being distributed, that we first met the people from Hrubieszow who had been taken from Jatkowa earlier. This group included the father of the baby that had been with us in the hideaway. He was very happy to see me but he was shocked by what he saw. He asked me a long list of questions about how I had managed to stay alive until that point and about the fate of mutual acquaintances. He had already been there for quite some time, and he had learned how to get by in the camp. When he saw me hungrily eating the soup and even finishing it, he offered me another mess-tin of soup that he somehow managed to procure, although acquiring a second serving of soup in the camp was no simple matter. When he gave me the soup, he made it clear that he was serving me an extremely valuable commodity. Survive here, he instructed me.

The struggle for more soup was usually difficult, and I had received it without struggling at all. The soup was distributed across from the kitchen, where rows of wooden tables stood. Immediately following the soup, they again separated men and women. The women and I were led to an enormous barracks adjacent to the barbed wire fence facing the guard tower. As a child, I thought that the view through the fence was wonderful: densely packed trees with never-ending green covering the ground between the trees. The barracks stood on posts, and the hall was long and wide. In the barracks, I found other girls, both my age and older, who had been brought from other cities in Poland. In the enormous hall were two levels of bunks, each consisting of a wooden board padded by a straw mattress, and a coarse, grey blanket.

Two to three people slept on each bunk. My aunt, my cousin, and I were given a bottom bunk at the end of the hall. The bunks ran the length of the hall and stood in a long, crowded row that almost reached the door. The women of Hrubieszow found bunks throughout the hall, wherever one was vacant. This is how we got to be bunk-neighbors with women brought to Budzyn from different cities in western and eastern Poland, including Warsaw. Most of the women spoke Yiddish as their native language. However, all of them knew Polish, and some of them spoke only Polish.

The hall had a few windows, and by one of them stood a wood-stove that was used to heat the barracks. However, lighting the stove was not always possible because fuel was rare. There was usually a long line of women waiting next to the stove in order to heat up water to wash their hair. When we entered the camp, the Germans made sure to shower and disinfect us, they said, because Jews are always dirty, and to ensure that the dirty Jews did not infect Germans with illnesses and lice. As time passed, however, they seemed to have forgotten this need, and washing our hair became a monumental challenge.

The barracks also had one (and only one) bowl that could be used for washing hair. The barracks housed hundreds of women, and the line to wash hair with the little water they managed to heat up was quite long. In those days, more than ten women used the same water to wash their hair, and the last women in line washed their hair in water that was black with dirt. Among the women of Hrubieszow was the wife of Rabinowitz, the attorney, who had originally come to Hrubieszow from a big city after she married her husband, a Hrubieszow native. I remember how she cried when it was her turn to wash her hair. During our time at Budzyn, she came to be covered with sores, and when she saw the black water in which she had to wash her hair, she burst into tears! I remembered her

114

from Jatkowa. She was an impressive looking woman and had always been meticulously dressed.

We got to Budzyn in the middle of the summer, when it was still possible to wear only light clothing. Because I had forgotten to put my underwear back on after they undressed us, I walked around without any underwear on, wearing only my dress. The barracks was a lively place, teeming with life. It housed so many different types of people: fractured families of mothers, daughters, and nieces who were often the only survivors of entire families; friends from home towns, and girls from the same city who formed even stronger bonds in the camp. Each group looked out for its own interests in the camp, such as securing food, safeguarding garments, and even acquiring water. Some women fainted, and others fell ill and needed to be treated without the Germans discovering that they were sick. It was a world with a great deal of suffering.

Because I had not yet started to menstruate, I was thankfully free of this burden. As a result of the harsh living conditions and the malnourishment in the camp, a large number of other girls either menstruated late or ceased menstruating altogether. Still, many women had no hygienic means of absorbing the blood from their menstruation. Nobody explained to me what blood they were talking about. All I understood was that there was some problem having to do with blood and that nothing could be done about it. Back then, women did not discuss such subjects in public. I have no idea how they dealt with the issue. My problem, however, was different: I had no underwear, and neither my dress nor my large coat could help in the places where underwear usually served that purpose. I had to run to urinate a great deal. During the day I somehow managed to get by, but at night the need to urinate became a menacing nightmare.

The Germans were so concerned about the possibility of escape attempts from the camp that an SS soldier regularly patrolled the barracks at night, walking between the beds with a flashlight and shining it on our eyes to make sure we were asleep. The Germans thought that if we were not asleep, we must certainly be planning an escape. If they found someone awake, they were pulled out of bed and punished for not sleeping. I never knew the inspection times during the night, and this, in conjunction with the cold and my lack of underwear, made me wake up many times during the night to urinate. Our bunk was at the end of the barrack, and the toilet buckets were located in the hall. It took me time to make it from our bunk to the hall. Because I was frightened to leave my bed before the inspection and risk getting caught not sleeping, I would hold it in with all my might and pretend I was sleeping until the inspection passed. I had already learned how to appear as if I was sleeping heavily when the flashlight illuminated my eyes during the inspection. But as soon as the S.S. officer left the barrack and I was certain he was nowhere nearby, I ran quickly to the hall to urinate. This sequence would often repeat itself two or three time each night.

When my Aunt Fayga became aware of my situation, she decided to take a coarse blanket from an empty bunk and use it to sew me a pair of underpants. I do not know where she got a needle and thread, but one day she presented me with a pair of underpants made of a blanket. Instead of elastic, I used a piece of rope to tie it around my waist. And although they were extremely itchy, they kept my lower body warm.

Two Jewish women had been placed in charge of the women's camp as Ordnungsdienst, or Jewish order guards. The less kind of the two was also the one who used to count the blankets each day. The number of blankets in the barracks was supposed to match the number of blankets on the order guard's list. When she got to the empty bunk, she noticed that one blanket was missing. After a short investigation, she learned that it had been used to sew me a pair of underpants. One day, while I was lying in our bunk alone, she sternly reprimanded me and gave me a formidable beating, and said that she was likely to pay for the theft with her own head. But she also appears to have realized that I was nothing but a young girl trying to explain why a blanket had become a pair of underwear. In any case, I never heard another word about the theft, and the underpants my aunt sewed me lasted until I reached Majdanek.

At Budzyn I developed relationships with the other children and we became a group. Despite the atrocious conditions, and despite how hungry we were, we managed to pass some of the time singing and playing. After all, we were still children.

All the children were assigned the job of peeling potatoes. The peeled potatoes could not have been intended for the Jews of the camp, as there was no trace of potatoes in the soup we ate. The Budzyn camp was intentionally placed in close proximity to a German air force spare parts factory that was located in the forest approximately six kilometers from the camp. Even before the war, the factory was engaged in military production. Under the Germans, the factory manufactured spare parts for their air force and used camp inmates as a labor force. Although I do not know for sure, I can only surmise that the potatoes were fed to the factory laborers, which included not only Jews but Poles, Volksdeutsche, and Ukrainians. It was a select group whose energy had to be maintained in order to ensure the provision of essential parts during the war

Life in the camp had settled down into a regular, albeit threatening, routine of hunger, fear, and forced early awakenings, usually accompanied by shouts of Schnell! Camp prisoners were given only a very short time to run to use the toilet. At the beginning, there were buckets for this purpose in the hall of the barracks in which we lived. Water for washing faces was provided by a faucet located rather far from the barracks. Roll call attendance was mandatory, and the lives of those who failed to attend or arrived late were always at risk.

At the center of the camp was an extremely large plaza that was used for inmate assemblies. During our time at Budzyn, I learned subsequently that the camp contained some 4,000 Jews from all over Poland, as well as a few Jews from Germany

During roll call, the men and women stood separately from each other, with men on one side and women on the other. Every barracks was counted separately. Every female barracks had a kapo who was charged with counting its inmates and reporting the number of prisoners to the camp commander. The number always had to be exact, down to the last female prisoner. If just one prisoner was missing, or if the count was inadvertently off by only one prisoner, there would be hell to pay.

The two female kapos whom I remember were both from Germany. One was a short woman and quite large. She always wrapped her head in a kerchief and wore a special ribbon indicating her position. Nevertheless, she was very kind, and when she was able to help a fellow female prisoner or warn her of impending danger, she did so without hesitation. After all, if she failed to carry out the orders issued by the German rulers, she was likely to pay with her life.

The second kapo, whom I really liked, was Mrs. Schwartz, who was a native of Germany. They even allowed her to keep her young daughter in the camp, although I never knew exactly where. Despite her position, I have fond memories of her. This was because when she was not on duty, she treated us like friends. I even saw her daughter from time to time. I always found the whole issue of German Jews in Budzyn puzzling. In fact, because of their prominent position and the fact that they looked better than everyone else, I was never certain that they were really Jews. As far as I can recollect, they all held positions of authority, such as being a kapo. Of the entire group, I only remember the two women. After the war, I learned that those Jews had been taken from the city of Stettin to Belzice and from there to Budzyn.

Roll calls could last for quite a long time – an hour or two and sometimes longer – regardless of the weather. The length depended, first and foremost, on the prisoner count. The number of prisoners present was not always consistent with the number appearing on the German lists. If the numbers did not match, the count would be repeated from the beginning. During roll call, prisoners were not allowed to move. We would stand at attention until the prisoner count finally matched the number on the list of the German commander. Then, that number would be reported in military fashion to the camp commander. Another difficult part of roll call was the punishment meted out to prisoners who broke the rules. In some cases, people were even hung to set an example. The crimes committed by prisoners included stealing potatoes and/or bread, disobedience during work, tardiness to roll call, and so forth.

One day during roll call, a young man (who I believe came from Warsaw) was punished for stealing three potatoes and hiding them in an empty can he had filled with water. This was a typical route by which prisoners stole potatoes from the kitchen. The poor soul was caught in the act, and he received his punishment at roll call. First, they lashed him, hands tied, to a cart without wheels that was tethered to a horse, and then, they put him in the middle of the plaza and made the horse run around the plaza as the other prisoners looked on. The prisoners stood at attention and were forced to watch as the life slowly drained out of him, all in order to demonstrate to the other prisoners what happens to someone who steals potatoes.

Weather was never taken into consideration while we stood at roll call. We arrived at Budzyn in late summer, when it could already be quite cool in Poland. In December 1943 there was a heavy snowstorm, and the temperature dropped below freezing. But the only things the Germans regarded as important at roll call were accurate head-counts and the punishments they meted out.

At roll call, my aunt would always make sure I positioned myself behind taller girls and stood on something that made me look taller, such as a brick we happened to find lying on the ground or something else. She also made sure I always wore a kerchief on my head, as this also helped make me less conspicuous. After every roll call, when the count was finished and I had passed the inspection, I was always relieved. The prisoners split up to go to work. I cannot remember exactly when the small meal they referred to as 'breakfast' was distributed before or after roll call. I do remember, though, what it included: a cup of coffee, which was really just dark water containing no coffee whatsoever, a thin slice of bread, and sometimes a bit of jam or margarine. The prisoners who lived solely off the food that was distributed and were not able to supplement it in one way or another gradually became 'musselmen'. These poor creatures were usually Jews from Warsaw, who were already in terrible shape by the time they reached the camp. They were often alone – that is, without anyone whom they had known from home. The people from Hrubieszow who were still together in the camp, tried to look out for each other. Because I was the youngest prisoner from Hrubieszow, I was cared for by many different people.

The prisoners who worked in the German air force spare parts factory had an easier time in the camp, because they could barter for food with the Poles who worked with them. Sometimes they received bread, and sometimes, if they had something to trade, like a garment, they might even receive some salami. Once, my cousin managed to obtain an apple, which we split among the three of us.

For the Germans, morning inspection was not sufficient. The inspection spectacle repeated itself in the evening. Also, when prisoners left to go to the factory, they were marched out in rows, like soldiers, and were usually counted many times both when they left the camp gate to work and when they returned. The prisoners who worked in the camp's service branches (kitchen, sanitation etc.) were not subject to this ordeal. Budzyn had a German camp commander named Feix. I don't know how long he had been there. Feix was a money-hungry, bloodthirsty German sadist from the Sudetenland who imposed a regime of torture and tyranny in the camp. His appetite for cruelty was insatiable, and he was eventually transferred out of the camp because, it was said, he once even shot a German citizen. Still, his brutal personality left its mark on the camp for a long time.

Before we had come to Budzyn Feix appointed the Jewish head of the camp from among the ranks of Jewish prisoners of war who had been sent to Budzyn after being captured from the Polish army. His name was Stockman. He wore a different kind of uniform, not that of the SS but of the Polish Army. During roll call, Stockman always stood next to the German commander, who appeared to speak to him as an equal and not as a "dirty Jew", the derogatory name with which the Germans typically referred to Jews. Stockman made a great impression on me as a child. Always dressed in a Polish army uniform, he was a slim, tall man who always seemed to took great care to look respectable.

The German camp commander ordered Stockman to handpick his own assistants, and most were selected from the group of P.O.W. Aside from a single incident involving one of Stockman's assistants, which I will discuss later, I do not recall any malicious acts perpetrated by Jews who were appointed to senior positions within the camp. At the time, I did not understand exactly who was responsible for what. However, I did understand that we had to obey these Jews. I also noticed that, in comparison to us, they were well dressed, looked good, and ate better food. We had learned what food they ate because some of the older children worked cleaning the barracks of the Jewish commanders. After lunch, these children were given the mess-tins to wash, and the bones of the chicken that had been eaten were plain to see. We children often took turns chewing and sucking on what was left on the bones. We eagerly waited for it to be time to wash the mess-tins. We would say to one another, look at what they get to eat!

120

Although Budzyn camp is not as well known as Majdanek or Auschwitz and is only rarely discussed, it was one of the cruelest camps run by the Germans. It occupied a huge area within a virgin forest, of which one could see only the first line of trees visible around the barbed wire and the guard tower, and dense vegetation between the trees. From inside the camp, nothing else could be seen, not even the horizon! The camp had a large number of prisoner barracks, for at its height the camp held a diverse population of some 4,000 Jewish prisoners from all over Poland

In addition to the residential barracks in which males and females were housed separately, there was also a clinic, a shower barracks, and a barracks with water faucets and a basin for regular washing. The two open-hole latrines were located relatively close to the barbed wire fence, and one of the guard towers was located directly across from the women's barracks. There were also workshops, a kitchen, and a yard with wooden tables. They had established a sort of small town, but not every place within it could be freely accessed by prisoners.

One day, I took the risk of going on my own initiative to visit my uncle Yitzchak, without telling my aunt. The men's barracks held approximately 700 Jewish male prisoners. My uncle's bunk was located far from the barracks door, and was hidden by rows and rows of bunks that stood between it and the doorway. I was sitting on my uncle's bunk talking to him when the door suddenly opened. Completely unexpected, the SS commander entered to carry out a surprise inspection. My uncle's face went pale when he saw who had entered the barracks. Not only would I pay with my life if we were caught, but so would he. Without explaining anything, he threw me under the bunk and stood in front of it, so that no one would see me. Fortunately, it was quite a cursory inspection, and after checking a few bunks, he left as suddenly as he had entered. It took a few minutes for my uncle to allow me to come out from under the bunk, and even more time passed before we both recovered from the shock of the incident.

Immediately following this episode, I returned to my barracks, but via an indirect route. During the time I was absent from the women's barracks, my aunt started to search for me. I do not remember how she found out where I had gone, but when I returned from my visit, still trembling from the trauma, my aunt did not try to calm me down. Instead, she started yelling at me, with some justification. Her tension had been building from the moment she learned where I had gone, until my return. She was scared to death that an SS man would see me in the men's barracks. The women in the barracks, particularly those whose bunks were close to ours, were extremely curious about why my aunt was yelling at me. One woman even told me that if I was having trouble with my aunt, I could sleep with her in her bunk. Deep in my heart, I knew that my aunt was right to be angry with me. I had risked my life by deciding on my own to go to a forbidden place. And, I had put my uncle's life in danger, as well. Although I found the kind offer of the other woman touching, I did not respond to the questions of my bunk-neighbors and I did not complain about my aunt. How could I be angry at her under such circumstances? She meant so much to me. I had so little family left.

My cousin Tema was a young and pretty girl. One morning during roll call, the Germans were looking for a female to work in the home of a German SS officer who lived near the camp with his family. Tema was selected for the job. Not only did she clean their house, but sometimes she also had to cook for them. This enabled her to eat without endangering herself. I remember her being happy with her new job. According to what she told me, she did not have to work very hard. One day, the family gave her a bowl of sweet pudding, which she brought back to the barracks and hid in her bunk under the mattress. To me, this was not only real food, it was heavenly food, food fit for kings. The next morning, after everyone had already left for work and I was still in the barracks for some reason, I happened to come across the bowl. Without thinking too much about it, I hungrily pounced upon the pudding and finished it off. By the time I realized that that the bowl was empty, it was too late. When everyone returned from work and my cousin saw that the pudding had disappeared, she knew immediately who had eaten it, and she was quite angry at me.

She had been saving it for uncle Yitzchak, who had grown much too thin, and being thin in Budzyn meant being in danger of death. I was very sorry about what I had done, and I sorely regretted my lack of self-control when I discovered the pudding. I wept not only because my aunt was angry at me, but also because I had not left even enough for my uncle to taste.

122

Not a day passed without a tragic event further embittering the lives of the prisoners. One day while we were working peeling potatoes a girl entered the kitchen, and it was clear by her face that she had some terrible news. A selection was going on in barracks 12, she told us, and we were shocked by the news. Still, we were forbidden to leave our work. All we could do was to worry as we finished peeling the potatoes. A half-hour later, a man entered the kitchen and told us that a selection had in fact taken place, and that the victims had been loaded onto a truck naked. When we got back to the barrack in the evening after work, we heard the screams and the weeping of the relatives whose loved ones had been taken away and murdered. This selection marked the beginning of the sudden selections carried out in the camp, which were sprung on the prisoners as a complete surprise.

A few days after that selection, when the women were again peeling potatoes in the kitchen, we received news of another selection. This time, a Jewish man rushed into the kitchen in a panic and told us that everyone had been ordered to leave work and report to the roll call plaza. All the potato peelers, and especially my aunt and I, were extremely frightened. Why were we being told to report to the plaza in the middle of the day? We were certain that it was another selection, but we had no choice but to go. We left the kitchen in one group and reported to the plaza together. As it turned out, the entire camp had been called to the plaza without exception, including sick prisoners who had been lying in their bunks. At the roll call, the SS officers instructed us to stand in rows of two, and then began conducting drills. As we followed the orders of the German officers, the camp commander himself appeared with two dogs and two locks in hand. He was followed by two low-ranking soldiers marching on both sides of two miserable, frightened-looking Jews, who walked with their heads down. With all the camp prisoners standing at attention, the camp commander explained the reason for the unusual mid-day assembly: Before you stand two criminals, who stole two locks while at work, he announced. They are Jewish criminals and the punishment they deserve is a bullet in the head! You, he said, addressing the group standing before him, were brought to this assembly to see and to learn that such criminal acts are unforgivable. After you witness the punishment, he concluded, you will not repeat the crime.

123

I was standing in the second row, behind my aunt, and I trembled with fear. I did not see how they had tied the hands of the poor men, stripped them, and shot them. After the ceremony, we were ordered to disperse. The Germans ordered two other Jews to take the bodies of the victims away and to leave them by the fence. After this terrible spectacle, the camp inmates left the plaza, each going back to work as if nothing had happened.

"Cut!" I said. "One moment, Carlos. I want to explain something to all of you to make sure you understand it. When all this took place I was a child of almost ten years, and the war ended many years ago. It's already hard for me to remember what happened each day back then. As you know, not a day went by without an upsetting event. What I am recounting here are the events that stood out in my memory for one reason or another, and that I, therefore, still remember. Back then, I did not keep track of dates. When I was a girl, I didn't consider dates important, and I tend not to remember them. I remember seasons, what I wore during one period or another, and whether it was raining or snowing. I hope you understand."

After my brief explanation, I returned to my story.

One day, I was walking behind the camp warehouses and I noticed a tree that was in bloom. Behind the tree, we suddenly saw three men hanging upside down by their feet from the roof of one of the barracks. Close by the men stood a sentry with a rifle, who appeared to be guarding them to make sure they remained there, in that position. We, of course, were afraid to pay too much attention to them. All we could do was feel sorry for them in our hearts, and to continue quickly on our way, terrified and sickened by what we had seen. We immediately ran to the barracks to tell the others about the incident, but it turned out that the other prisoners already knew about this punishment. It had happened while the men were at work in the factory. In exchange for food, they had given clothes to the Poles with whom they worked. When they returned to the camp after work, the German guards at the gate found the bread underneath their coats, and this was the reason why they were killed in such a barbaric manner. And so the days passed, in an atmosphere of fear.

It had been a normal grey day, like all the others in the camp: long hours of standing at the roll call yard; the routine work of peeling potatoes; the familiar waiting from one meal to the next similar meal; roll call in the evening; and then the regular gathering in the barracks before going to sleep. It had already gotten dark when a few men stole into the women's barracks, where their wives were either already sleeping or were starting to doze off. All of a sudden, the sound of machine gun fire rang out outside the barrack. When the men heard the shots being fired nearby, they removed a board from one of the walls and disappeared. The shots were loud and close to our barracks, and woke us all up in a panic.

Suddenly, black-clad soldiers in pursuit of the men burst into the barracks, followed by the camp commander, who carried a sub-machine gun and proceeded to spray bullets indiscriminately in all directions. Then he screamed at everyone to lie on the bottom bunks and not to move, looking completely hysterical. We lay there trembling next to one another. Some women cried, and a few panic-stricken women even shouted, Enough! Let's take our leave already! We will be together with the people of Israel!

In the meantime, gunfire continued to ring out within the barracks and throughout the camp, as if a real war was being fought. Shouting in German could be heard from every direction. It was all taking place in the vicinity of our barracks, and we could hear moaning just outside the door. The chaos lasted for about an hour, during which time no one in the barracks knew what was happening or what had set off the incident. These were moments of terror I will never forget. Gradually, the gunfire grew weaker, and the German who had been shooting in our barracks left. Fortunately, no one in the barracks was injured.

We got out of our bunks and ran to the door to see what had happened outside. When we opened the door, a few dead bodies fell inside. Apparently, they had been killed while trying to take refuge inside our barracks and were shot right on the threshold, up against the door. We spent the rest of the night speculating, and no one slept. When we went outside early the next morning, we saw human bodies scattered all around our barracks and along the path to the toilets. Then, a few men pushing a wheelbarrow filled with bodies passed our barracks and told us about the night's events. A number of young men – mostly from Hrubieszow, including two brothers whose mother was with us in the barracks – had heard about the liquidation of nearby labor camps such as Poniatowa, and about the murder of thousands of Jews at Majdanek. They guessed that our camp was next on the list and decided to try to escape. They stole large shears from the German air force spare-parts factory to be used to cut the fence behind the latrines across from our barracks. That is why we heard shooting so close by, and that is why the armed German chose to burst into our barracks. It was not clear whether the guards in the tower had seen the men cutting the fence or whether the men had had some other mishap.

The next morning was very cold, and the tension within the camp was running high. The prisoners feared that we would all be punished for the escape attempt, so when we were called to roll call as if nothing had happened, we were terrified that they would kill us all during the head count. That morning, we stood at roll call in the freezing cold for much longer than usual. They also brought the dead to the roll call to be counted. After counting everyone over and over again, the Germans told us that if anyone else dared to try to escape, they would kill all the occupants of that prisoner's barracks as a punishment.

Everyone believed that the Germans would keep their promise. Although the men did not go to work that day or the following day, we women continued to report to work in the kitchen as usual. The tension remained high. We could not believe that the Germans would allow the escape attempt to go unpunished on a larger scale. The Germans also did not behave as they had before the incident. Now, we saw an unusually large number of Ukrainians walking around the camp in groups, as well as additional armed German soldiers. Speculation ran rampant as to what it all meant. Some thought that the Germans were about to kill us all and were just waiting for the order from above to do so. Others contended that if the Germans had wanted to kill us, they would have already done so.

Two days passed since the escape attempt, and the men had not returned to work in the factory. We were scared at night, fearing that they might kill us in our sleep. We assembled for roll call as usual, and the day went by like any other day. But the men did not report to the factory. Perhaps they did not plan to kill us after all, we speculated. Only a few days had passed since the rumors of the camp liquidations near Budzyn had begun to circulate. One morning at roll call, we were instructed to return to our barracks on a pretext that seemed very flimsy: the partisans operating in the surrounding woods were about to attack us, so for our own safety, we needed to stay inside our barracks and not come out. We were ordered to lie on the floor in the event that we heard gunfire.

We remained locked in for three days. Through the cracks, we could see large numbers of German soldiers surrounding the barracks in the camp. Any unusual movement within the barracks incited hysteria inside. The overwhelming tension caused many of us to remain completely silent. Others talked incessantly about our bitter fate. We all wanted an end to these agonizing conditions.

On our third or fourth day in the barracks, with no prior warning, the Germans suddenly opened the barracks door. It was only years later that I learned what the Germans had originally planned to do to us while we were locked in our barracks. The story is as follows: The German headquarters, which at that time was located in Lublin, had issued an order to liquidate the camp at Budzyn as had been done to all the other camps in the area, such as Trawniki, Poniatowa, and Majdanek. But our camp was different, it was supplying workers to a key German war plant of the Heinkel aircraft company. When the Heinkel factory management in Budzyn heard that the camp was to be liquidated – along with all of the prisoners who worked in the factory – they contacted the German Air Force Command for assistance. The Air Force command contacted Goering, the commander of the German Air Force. They asked Goering to rescind the order or else they would be unable to supply the necessary spare parts for the German planes, which were crucial to the war effort. Goering immediately ordered the camp liquidation plans to be canceled. This is how the Budzyn camp prisoners were spared the death sentence at that time, making Budzyn the only such camp in the Lublin district.

When the doors of the barracks were reopened, my cousin Tema went out to talk with another girl, a seamstress from Hrubieszow. Thanks to her skill with the needle, she had apparently survived the exterminations at Trawniki. The Germans had brought her to Budzyn to sew clothing for female SS soldiers. I am not sure how my cousin found out about the seamstress' arrival, but the two had been friends in Hrubieszow before the war. When the seamstress learned that Tema was in the camp, she arranged to meet her by the fence. The seamstress did not enter the camp. I have a vivid memory of what Tema told my aunt and me when she returned to the barracks from the meeting: the seamstress had been at Trawniki with my mother, and when my mother heard that I was alive and at Budzyn (I have no idea how she learned this) and that the seamstress was being sent to Budzyn, she wrote me a letter and sent it with the seamstress. It was quite clear that she had given the letter to the seamstress before the liquidation of the camp at Trawniki. The seamstress was unable to make contact with my cousin as soon as she arrived at the camp, and by the time they actually met she had lost the letter. When Tema told me that the letter from my mother had been lost, knowing as I did that the Trawniki camp had been liquidated along with all of its inmates, I began crying hysterically. Though the seamstress survived the war, I was unable to learn anything more from her about my mother. My mother's lost letter remained with me like an open wound.

After this, life reverted back to how it had been before we'd been locked in the barracks. The roll calls, the head counts, the hunger, and the lice continued to take their toll, and the musselmen continued to drop like flies. People died almost every day, usually from starvation. But despite the tension, the fear, and the terror that permeated life in the camp, our will to survive remained strong. At one point, someone came up with the idea of putting on a play, although I was not privy to the discussions and the work put into the project.

In order to survive, people needed some sort of relief. Putting on a show under such conditions seems like an impossible idea. Nonetheless, actors and actresses were selected from among the prisoners, including some women from Hrubieszow. We took special pride in the fact that one of "our" girls, Chanka Orenstein, was going to be among the stars. Chanka had been our neighbor in Hrubieszow. She was the same age as my eldest brother Nathan, and she had been in his circle of friends before the war. We impatiently awaited the show, as a ray of light in a world that usually contained nothing but darkness. The play was put on in Yiddish and was performed on a stage erected in an empty barracks. On the day of the show, we were so impatient to see the play that we arrived early, and therefore managed to get the seats closest to the stage.

When the play began, it was like a dream. They were magical moments during which I felt as if I were floating on air. I listened particularly closely to Chanka, whom I knew so well. I was amazed by her beautiful singing voice. I cannot remember the subject of the play, but I have never forgotten the melody and the first two lines of the song. It is hard to believe that at that low point of humanity, we were able to lift our heads high and to enable people who were hungry, freezing, in constant fear for their lives, and mourning their loved ones to enjoy themselves, even if only for one short hour. In this way, we managed to distance ourselves from the horrors and to take pride in our culture. What great sacrifices people made back then! I think it was that play, that apocalyptic moment, that sparked my love for the theatre. Years later I dreamed of becoming an actress.

5. Budzyn Concentration Camp

In late January or early February 1944, after the failed escape attempt in the camp, we were told that we were moving to a different camp not far away. It was a concentration camp, and it was located closer to the Heinkel factory. We were taken from the camp in groups and told that we would need to walk to the new camp by foot. It was early February. The sun was up and had melted the snow, and I did not find the walk particularly difficult. As usual, I walked with my aunt and uncle, and this time I did not stumble along the way. We walked in fear of what awaited us in the new camp. We already knew what a concentration camp was, and we knew a great deal about Majdanek, which was very close to Lublin. When we arrived at Budzyn katzet (concentration camp), we found it to be very similar to the last camp. It, too, had two rows of barbed wire and guard towers, and the structures inside were also similar. When we arrived, we were taken directly to the showers. When I reached the shower barracks along with all the other women, we entered a long corridor and were instructed to wait there until the men got out of the shower. Then, we were told, we would be able to enter. Here, too, we experienced the spectacle of the men being forced to leave the showers naked in order to humiliate them before the Jewish women.

After everyone finished in the showers, both the men and the women were assigned the same identical uniforms: striped concentration camp prisoner garments, with prisoner numbers glued to the left side of the jacket, and wooden shoes with wooden soles that were made of two pieces attached to one another by nails and a piece of leather. When you walked, these two-piece soles made a clicking sound. Fortunately, February was not as cold as the months that had preceded it, the height of winter. Nonetheless, in order to keep their feet warn, many people wrapped them in scraps of paper they found here and there. We were again separated by gender, and in the women's barracks I again shared a bunk with my aunt and my cousin. On the first night, I found myself unable to fall asleep because of my anxiety about what would await me in the morning.

We feared that we would face even more horrifying situations than those we had already lived through, but after being assigned to our barracks and getting through the first night, we were surprised the next day to receive a larger portion of bread with jam than was usual. It was a completely unexpected and somewhat pleasant surprise. Lunch was also more substantial. The soup we were served this time even had a few potatoes in it, which made the liquid a bit thicker and took the edge off our hunger. It was amazing! It took two or three days for life in the new camp to become routine. At the roll call, we were pleased to see that Stockman was still with us, and that he was the Jewish head of the camp here as well.

The new camp offered a wider variety of work for the adults. This was especially true regarding jobs for men. These were not just at the plane factory. In the new work sites, the prisoners met more Poles with whom they could trade money for food. Some prisoners had still managed to keep money hidden, in some cases, in the more intimate parts of their bodies.

Some managed to get food from other sources. My cousin Tema's boyfriend was an electrician who worked in a place from which he was able to acquire extra food from time to time. In the Budzyn concentration camp, the children continued working peeling potatoes in the new kitchen.

The new camp had an enormous kitchen. At the entrance was a peeling room, where the potatoes sat in a huge pile on the cement floor. We, the peelers, sat on the floor next to the pile and peeled the potatoes into a bucket of water that sat next to us. A row of huge pots stood further down the hall. Although they distributed slightly more bread at the new camp, people were always terribly hungry. And, despite the great risks, the potato thefts continued. As time went on, methods for stealing potatoes became more and more sophisticated. We girls also managed to find time to meet. We often talked about our lost homes and what we would do if we survived. These were the hopeful conversations of children taking refuge in their fantasies.

The relations among the Jews of Hrubieszow, which were extremely close when we first arrived in Budzyn, weakened somewhat over time. We met many people in the camp, even women from Warsaw. My memories of most of the women with whom I lived are vague, except for the few whose bunks were located close to mine. In the camp, your bunk was your home, the only place that belonged almost to you alone. I remember the neighboring women, already knowing that I had no parents taking care of me now and then. I also remember Mina from Warsaw, who lost her boyfriend whom she loved very much. When he was killed, she had an emotional breakdown. The other women from Warsaw looked after her and did everything they could to conceal her unstable psychological condition from the guards. For me and the rest of the other children, she became a subject of gossip. We were often unable to understand her behavior. Not only did she speak incessantly, but she spoke a great deal about sex, which we did not yet understand.

The camp and the barracks were not the only things that were new. So were the SS men, including the camp commander. We did not know if he would be as cruel as Feix, the previous commander. Morning and evening roll call in the new camp lasted as long as it had in the old camp, and we were given dinner in our barracks: a portion of bread with some sort of topping (a spoonful of jam or a cube of margarine). Overall, our conditions had not particularly deteriorated as we had initially feared. In truth, they had even improved somewhat, at least in terms of nutrition. This was in February 1944. The grownups continued to talk among themselves, expressing hope that our suffering would soon come to an end. We children naively listened to their conversations and started fantasizing about what would happen if we would finally be freed.

During this period, there was a significant reduction in the punishments meted out in the camp, even though the SS commander was always stern and frightening. At Budzyn concentration camp, Jews were shown a small degree of mercy. This may have stemmed from the fact that the Germans were now interested in retaining at all costs, the prisoners working in the air force spare parts factory, in light of the deteriorating situation on the front. The fact that Goering himself had extended us his protection may also have played a role in our improved treatment. It is also possible that Hitler's henchmen began to think about the possibility of punishment for the acts they committed during the war. And, perhaps it was simply that the highly respected Stockman, the Jewish commander of the camp, had some influence with the German commanders.

"Carlos," I said. "Cut please. We're getting very close to Lublin. I'll tell only about the events leading up to my arrival at Majdanek, and once we are at Majdanek, I'll explain how I got there and how we were also able to leave."

"That's fine, "he agreed. "But please keep going. We are extremely interested in your story. So, how did you get from Budzyn to Majdanek?"

When the Russians started closing in on our location, the Germans knew their time was limited. They decided to gradually liquidate Budzyn. In order to prevent prisoners from sensing what was really going on and mounting a rebellion, the Germans announced that they were in need of educated professionals to be sent elsewhere for 'interesting work.' Such professionals were instructed to register in the office. This was in March-April 1944. Again, many of the camp prisoners, believing German lies, along with others who did not sign up by choice, were added to the list. In this way, more than 100 people were assembled and sent to Majdanek.

It was only as an adult, long after the war had ended, that I learned the story of how those sent to Majdanek actually survived. It seems that a few high ranking Germans who wanted to evade serving on the Eastern front concocted a story about a unit of Jewish scientists who were ostensibly assisting in the German war effort. This group was eventually transferred first to Majdanek and then to the camp at Plaszow, where they established a small project working on fabricated mathematical and chemical equations ostensibly meant to develop a secret weapon. That is how the group, which included a few people from Hrubieszow was saved.

In late April 1944, emotions again ran wild within the camp. Something was about to happen, and the prisoners could feel it in the air. One morning, roll call was held as usual, and during the head-count, the German commanders informed us that we would not be going to work as usual. He stated that we were all about to be transferred to other camps, which he named. I do not recall all of them. However, I do remember that a group of men standing on the other side of the roll call was told that they were going to Plaszow. I also remember a German officer circulating through the other rows, pulling out young men and women, and having them stand close to where I was standing. Among others, they pulled out my cousin and her boyfriend. After assembling a large group of young prisoners, the German officer told them that they were being sent to Wieliczka (an ancient salt mine near Krakow). In the same breath, he also announced that the children and the elderly were being sent to Majdanek. Immediately after the announcement, my cousin took advantage of the fact that the German commanders were not standing nearby, and pulled my aunt and uncle into the group destined for Wieliczka, leaving me alone in the group designated for transport to Majdanek.

Even though it was already Spring 1944, those imprisoned in the camps remained cut off from the outside world. Nonetheless, we were aware that whoever was destined for Majdanek, children or 'elderly', would be sent directly to the gas chambers upon arrival. When the term 'elderly' was used in this context, it referred to people above the age of forty; by now, no truly elderly people were still alive.

The group that had been designated for Wieliczka stood right next to the group of children and the elderly. My aunt and my cousin began to cry because they did not want me to be sent to Majdanek all alone. After crying and deliberating over the crucial question of what to do, the entire family resolved to join me in the group designated for Majdanek, even though they knew what would happen to them there. This time, the SS officer did not notice them because he was standing far away. After a few minutes, the entire family, apparently rethinking the wisdom of their decision, returned to the group destined for Wieliczka. I urged them to return to the Wieliczka group, telling them that I don't want them to die because of me. I was only 10 years old at that time. This drama repeated itself three or four times: first they would join me, only to immediately return to the other group, leaving me alone with the group destined for Majdanek. Finally, during one of the moments when they were standing with me in the group destined for Majdanek, an SS officer with a baton in his hand ordered the whole family to remain where they were as punishment for attempting to decide on their own where they would be sent. Life and death was determined in a split second. By chance, their destiny would be to live.

It appears we were the last group interned at Budzyn. After thousands of people were sent from Budzyn to other camps throughout Poland and perhaps Germany as well, the camp was closed. As they had done in the other camps in the area, the Germans ordered that all the structures be destroyed and the ground plowed, in order to erase all evidence of their misdeeds.

6. MAJDANEK

Although I do not recall how we were transported from the camp to the train station in Budzyn, I do remember the ride in the train, the soldiers guarding us by the door, and the single window, which was covered by the crisscrossed barbed wire. I do not know how long the trip to Lublin took, but when the train stopped and the doors opened, we were given a frightening reception by a large number of German soldiers holding both machine guns and the leashes of vicious dogs.

Immediately upon disembarking from the trains, we were instructed to stand in rows, flanked by German soldiers and their weapons. The Germans announced that a truck was awaiting the children, and that we had to board it. All in all, we were eleven children between the ages of nine and thirteen. We boarded the truck, and, of course, we did it schnell. By that point we had learned to be extremely obedient. I managed to say goodbye to my aunt, and we all sat down. German guards also boarded the truck with us to prevent us from escaping. We were almost certain that the truck would take us directly to the gas chambers. Why else would they have separated the adults from the children and then loaded only the children onto the truck? After all, we knew that the Germans would never give Jewish children any special consideration.

"Cut, Cipora," said Carlos. "Stop here, and we'll hear the rest of your testimony inside the camp."

I let the teenagers get off the bus first, and my heart began to pound when I saw that terrible place again. Suddenly, I was looking at the same gate, the same hill, and the same barbed wire that I remembered from back when I was a child. The only thing that had not been there at the time was the giant monument. After concluding the necessary administrative business with the Polish employees, we were permitted to enter, with me leading the way. The day was cold and the wind was strong. The cameramen asked the kids to sit in a large circle by the entrance, and they sat me down in the middle of the circle and again aimed the camera at me. Once all the kids had been seated, Carlos asked me to continue telling my story.

136

"Girls and boys," I said, "the difference between me and you when we entered the camp is unfathomable. This is the second time I've returned to this place since I was liberated. The first time was just a few months after I was released from Majdanek. Then, I was in an orphanage in Lublin and the orphanage director decided to bring the children who survived to see the camp. At that time, the Polish authorities had not yet changed anything. Everything was just as it had been when we left the camp, just as the Germans had left it. The hair, the brushes, the pile of thread, the pile of glasses – they were all was still sitting next to the gas chambers. Now, this horrible place has become an organized, categorized Polish museum, completely different from the way it was. When you walk through the gates of this place, you try to imagine how human beings were treated here, but not even the wildest imagination is capable of comprehending how prisoners were humiliated, the cruel methods used, the way they were murdered. How could human beings be so cruel to other human beings, human beings who were innocent of any wrongdoing? When I enter the camp now, as a free person, I am overpowered by the unforgettable memory of those days, when the only crime committed by most of us prisoners was the fact that we had been born Jewish. Today, despite all the remnants from the war on exhibit here, it is still impossible for you to visualize what it was really like. This, unfortunately, is the difference between me and you."

We were taken off the truck at the entrance to the camp. Notice that we are now sitting in front of the showers, and that the shower building is slightly higher than where the camp's entrance gate had been. On this very same hill, across from the gate, stood a German officer with a riding crop in his hand. Apparently, he had been waiting for us. As we were ordered to go to him, we saw a long line of disabled people, some missing legs and others missing arms, walking behind him. I remember one of them in particular. The sight of this man, who had no ears and almost no nose and walked with a pair of crutches, was particularly terrifying to me. Each person held a towel and a bar of soap, and the line moved toward the showers in rows of four. Even in Budzyn, we had already heard that when the Germans brought people to the gas chambers, they lied to them and told them they were only going to take showers.

Rumors about these practices had already spread widely in many camps. When we saw the group of disabled people walking toward the showers,

137

with smoke coming out of the chimney, we were convinced they would be killed first, and that we would be next in line. We knew we had reached the end. The German officer who awaited us was meticulously dressed, with tall, polished black boots and the type of riding pants often worn by German officers. We immediately dropped to our knees at his feet and began begging him, insisting that we were strong and that at Budzyn we had worked in different types of jobs, and that, here too, we want to prove that we can work just like the adults. The German officer stood with the riding crop in hand like a statue, and his face revealed no emotion, neither mercy, nor hatred, nor contempt at our begging. But, he also did not beat us. The officer standing before us was like a frozen statue. We dared to touch his boots, yet still, he did not move. There was no change in his facial expression as we kneeled before him, begging for our lives. As we begged, the line of disabled prisoners passed us, continued moving toward the showers, and disappeared inside. Only later did we realize that these were Russian prisoners of war. When the last prisoner entered the showers, the officer suddenly ordered us to get up. We were also given a towel and soap and were ordered to walk in rows of four to the same showers. Most of us were girls; as far as I remember, there was only one boy among us. When we entered the grey, damp showers where death awaited, we noticed that the walls were lined by wooden benches. Immediately, an old German woman ordered us to get undressed. The women who worked in the showers then made us run schnell into the other room. We ran over a cement floor covered with boards, with spaces in between. There, the women ordered us to stand beneath the showers. We stood under the pipe which we feared would begin to release gas at any moment, holding one another's hands and trying to hug each other. Every passing moment during which nothing happened seemed like an eternity! We no longer cried, we were not hysterical. By now, we had seen so many corpses and had experienced so much death that death no longer frightened us. It had become almost as natural for us as life itself.

We were also cold standing under the shower. There we stood, shivering, waiting for the gas to finally be released. Then, all of a sudden, water started gushing out of the pipe! Finally, the unbearable tension to which we had been subject since setting foot in Majdanek was released. Water! we shouted joyfully, Water!

138

We wept tears of joy and laughed uncontrollably at the same time. Although only moments ago we stood facing what we believed to be certain death, life had now returned. We were stunned at the fact that we were still alive, and that instead of being choked by gas, we were under a stream of life-giving water. We were not able to enjoy this sense of euphoria for very long, for immediately after the first rinse we were ordered to run into the third room schnell, which was similar in size and appearance to the first room; it also had cement walls that had grown dark, wooden benches, and boards that had been placed over a cement floor. We had left our clothing on the benches in the first room, and in the last room the female German guards gave us the infamous prisoner uniforms. All the uniforms were the same size, although I cannot recall if they were too big for us. As we put on the uniforms, we were told that later, the children would be allowed to wear regular clothes.

As soon as we finished getting dressed, we were ordered to go outside, which we did with great enthusiasm. After all, we were not dead! We had left the showers alive. Then, the order raus, again accompanied by the word schnell, was shouted by the guards, whose expression was always frightening. The tone convinced me that if I did not move quickly enough, I would receive a baton blow to the back. Fear had made me perfectly disciplined.

Of course, we children neither knew nor thought about what had happened to the adults who remained at the train station after we were loaded onto the truck. We had neither the time nor the presence of mind to do so. We, the erstwhile victims, had been certain that we would never again see all those who had remained behind at the train station. When the adults saw us disappear into the truck, they also believed we would never meet again. No one seriously thought that the Germans had suddenly decided to display a modicum of mercy towards Jewish children or that they had wanted to make things easier for them by driving them to the camp by truck, instead of making them walk. At the time, such an act of kindness seemed unthinkable. Actually, I still cannot understand this unusual event, which was extremely atypical for Majdanek. The only possible explanation I can think of is that perhaps the commanders of Majdanek, surmising that their defeat was imminent, knew that they might soon face punishment. This is my own theory, for I have no proof.

139

When the shower doors opened and we walked outside, the adults from Budyzn, who were waiting right outside the door, could not believe their eyes! Suddenly, out of the building that they, like us, thought held gas chambers, stepped the children, who were still alive! The reunion was very emotional. Everyone wept. Mere words cannot describe the reunion, the taste of the air we breathed in during those moments, and the burst of emotion. You're alive you're alive, they mumbled. My aunt and my cousin hugged me and cried. The fact that we were still alive gave them a glimmer of hope that perhaps the camp was not as bad as we thought it would be.

But the emotional reunion did not last long, and the Germans immediately started pushing the adults into the showers, as they had done to us. And again, shouts of schnell echoed in the air.

After showering and the search for valuables in our clothes and bodies, including our mouths, our intimate areas, and our underarms, we left the showers and were brought to the offices where they recorded our names, where we came from, and other details. Only after all the bureaucratic procedures had been completed did the guards bring us to the barracks in the area in which we were to be housed: Field Number One.

As your teachers have already told you, the camp at Majdanek was extremely large. It was divided into six fields that were separated from one another by internal barbed wire fences. Each field, or camp, had its own entrance gate guarded by a German sentry. When we began walking in the direction of our camp, the sentry standing at the gate ordered us to sing. Looking back with an adult's perspective, it seems to me that the Germans felt the need to abuse us both physically and psychologically. Ordering us to sing when we were in such a heightened emotional state seems like psychological abuse to me. We did, in fact, sing, although I cannot remember the song. We finally reached our field, which was a kind of fenced-off piece of land that held two enormous barracks facing each other, which were separated by a large space for roll call. This is where inspections were carried out. To the left, behind our barracks, was a fence. As time passed, we noticed that the area on the other side of the fence was regularly filled with a large number of Polish families, sometimes including children. We were forbidden to speak to them. Based on their appearance, it appeared that they came from the city. In those days, there was a difference between urban dress and rural dress. They seemed to be from the upper class. Despite the ban on communicating with them, we managed to speak to them for a few moments from time to time. To the left of the Polish camp, was a double fence that separated us from the other prisoners. There, from afar, we could see only men. I later learned that they were political prisoners who had been sent to Majdanek from various parts of Europe.

When we arrived at our field, the women were assigned to a barracks in which there were already another approximately 150 Jewish women from Holland. At first, we were surprised. As Poles, we were unfamiliar with Dutch Jews, who looked so different from what we thought Jewish women should look like. Most of the women at Budzyn had come from the cities and small towns of Poland, and were primarily Yiddish-speakers. Most came from traditional or Orthodox homes, and very few were assimilated. Most of us had brown eyes and dark hair. The Dutch women seemed to many of us like non-Jews: tall, light-colored eyes and light-colored hair. They still looked presentable. But the biggest surprise was the fact that these women had no knowledge of Yiddish, so communicating with them was not a simple matter. Some of us were not even certain if they were Jewish at all. Nonetheless, relations between us warmed up slowly but surely. A few of the Dutch girls knew German.

During the morning roll call on the day after we arrived, the new female prisoners were issued explicit instructions regarding how to behave in the camp and the punishments we could expect for failing to carry out an order. Then we were instructed to walk to Field Number Three, where the laundry room was located. At home, in our pre-war lives, we washed our clothes in tubs with special laundry soap. In many places in Poland, water still had to be brought to the house in buckets and laundry water was heated on the stove. The life we had grown up with was very simple in many ways. Here at Majdanek, ironically, we were sent to work in laundry facilities with gigantic modern washing machines, modern dryers, and industrial flatbed ironing presses. For us, it was all amazing. Today, I cannot estimate the quantity of laundry that awaited us in those mountainous piles. The Germans not only murdered the Jews; they thoroughly dispossessed them as well. Garments, sheets, towels, and other items that were found intact and looked relatively new, were transported by train to Majdanek from all over Europe. Here, they were washed, dried, ironed, and folded by Jewish women, and then loaded onto trains heading directly to Germany. My aunt and my cousin worked inside the laundry facilities, while I worked with most of the other young girls sorting the pile of clothing. We placed good garments in one pile and bad garments in another pile. Climbing to the top of the pile was a challenging undertaking in itself.

We did not sort clothing all the time. Some days, we were charged with hanging up clothes to dry in the gas chamber, of all places, which were no longer in operation. We knew what they had previously been used for, and we felt extremely uncomfortable inside them. While we hung the laundry, our complicated feelings found expression in cruel practical jokes that served as an emotional outlet and enabled us to keep working. We would try to scare each other by pretending we were going to lock the door from the outside.

The gas chamber, which you will soon see, consisted of one large room with four dark cement walls, a ceiling that was not particularly high, and a smooth cement floor. It had no window. The ceiling was similar in appearance to the floor, and the room as a whole was large, empty, and cold. The door was made of metal and was wider than a large commercial refrigeration door. It had an iron handle that could be locked only from the outside. On the inside, the door had no handle, and we were haunted by the fear of being locked inside whenever we were hanging the laundry. Although the idea of the game was to scare each other by pretending we were going to close the door from the outside, we never dared to actually do so. Outside the door, at the entrance to the gas chamber, stood large piles of sewing thread, spectacles, toothbrushes and other brushes. The amount of money and manpower which the Germans invested in their industry of death is incredible and disturbing.

As had happened with us before, life in the camp soon became routine. For us, the last prisoners to be interned in the camp, it was no more difficult or cruel than Budzyn. The food we were given at Majdanek was very similar to what we were given at Budzyn: a piece of bread, sometimes with jam and sometimes with margarine, and the same meal in the evening. The hot soup was brought to our field in large, military-type thermoses, and was distributed in mess-tins in the area between the two barracks where we lined up to receive food. A portion of soup never filled you up. However, during the war, my small body may have very well gotten used to eating small amounts of food. I was also very thin, and I assume my stomach had shrunk. So the daily ration was more or less enough for me.

"In addition to our women, political prisoners worked in the large laundry facility as well. We also sometimes met our men from Budzyn there. This allowed people to see their family members from time to time, and it enabled my aunt to see her husband, Uncle Yitzchak, and my cousin to see her boyfriend. Such meetings were also an opportunity to relay news. I remember my aunt telling me that Uncle Yitzchak had told her that he was working in the crematorium, and that every day he put thirteen or fourteen bodies of Poles into the oven. I seem to remember him saying this with a sense of horror and sorrow.

"My aunt said again and again that they were no longer burning Jews, because there were almost no Jews left to burn. I later learned that the Germans had started burning Poles, primarily the Polish intelligentsia. Indeed, we noticed that the population on the other side of the barbed wire fence changed regularly. Faces we saw yesterday would suddenly disappear, only to be replaced by the faces of new people. Our workplaces became a site of integration for the prisoner population as a whole, and a meeting place for the Jewish women and the political prisoners. According to Nazi ideology, every population was classified according to either the race to which it belonged or a specific class. For this reason, the camp at Majdanek was divided into separate fields according to the type of population in each. The Jews, of course, had the lowest status, followed by the Gypsies, the homosexuals, the Poles, and the Russian prisoners. Political prisoners were sent to Majdanek and they enjoyed the highest status among all the camp inmates. They were treated differently. They received letters and packages from home, and the packages contained real food. I believe that the laundries were also the site of transactions and exchanges between the sexes (that is, deals made to trade food for sex but I am unsure of the details, as I was still so young and relatively unaware). Somehow, the political prisoners were able to enter our camp. At night, they would jump over the inner fence and disappear into our barracks. They were not able, however, to find any privacy, and couple after couple lay on the floor of the barracks corridor. In the middle of the night, when I had to use the toilet at the end of the hall, I used to jump over them, although I did not completely understand what they were doing. During the day, when I asked my aunt why men were coming into our barracks at night, she offered only a smile and a vague response, but no explanation. It was only much later that I came to understand what had been going on.

Among the women from Hrubieszow were two sisters from whom my mother used to buy hats. They had even sold her a hat for me before the war. One of the sisters was deaf and mute, and the group from Hrubieszow tried to protect her and often spoke on her behalf while we were in the camp. The most important thing was to prevent the Germans from discovering her disability. Most of the women from my town slept near one another. One night, we awoke to the sound of banging at the window, where we saw a man trying to break into the barracks. The deaf-mute woman, who clearly understood what went on in the barracks at night, had apparently feared being attacked by a man and not being able to scream. She therefore prepared a bowl of water next to her bed, and the moment she saw the man enter the barracks through the window, she poured it on him. The screams could be heard throughout the entire barracks and a major commotion ensued. Girls from the other rooms crowded into ours, and the men in the hall were frightened away. It was the first time in quite a while that I had seen people laughing in the barracks, as everyone praised the woman for her brave act. But the yelling quickly subsided, the laughter died down, and the commotion ended, all out of fear of the guards at the gate. Everyone went back to their bunks.

According to my recollection, no men ever broke into our barracks again after this incident. The deaf-mute woman earned the appreciation of the other women, especially those who looked askance at the behavior of the Jewish women who were trading sex for food. Although at the time I did not understand why, I often heard one woman in particular sighing, and saying Oy, look what the daughters of Israel have come to.

One day during work when I was walking to the garment-sorting barracks, I noticed a balloon-shaped piece of rubber lying on the path, and I immediately bent down to pick it up. Tema, who was with me at the time, saw that I was picking up something suspicious and came closer to take a look at what I had found. I was about to touch the opening of the balloon to my mouth to blow it up when Tema suddenly grabbed my arm and began insisting that I discard it immediately. Yuck! Put it down, now! she screamed. It's not a balloon, it's something dirty! As far as I was concerned, I had finally found something entertaining. Moreover, I had no intention of giving it up. Finally, with no explanation and without giving me another opportunity to make my case, she snatched the piece of rubber from my hand and threw it in a trashcan located close to the path. I later learned it was a condom.

Usually, the children in the camp could be found together. However, one day when I was walking alone between the laundry and the electric fence, I noticed a group of Russian prisoners-of- war working on the other side. We typically had no interaction with the Russian prisoners at all. However, when they suddenly saw a little girl walking around by herself, one of them threw two small packages over the fence. They contained a quarter-loaf of bread and a piece of salami made from real meat, food I had long ago given up hope of ever seeing. Kosher dietary laws no longer played a role in my life or that of the others in our group, and I grabbed the rare finds and blew the soldier a kiss. Back at work, I told no one about what I had found and what I had hidden in my clothes. When I returned to the barracks in the afternoon, I showed Tema and my aunt the treasure the Russian soldier had given me. At that time, the living conditions of the POWs were quite reasonable, and they were often taken out of the camp grounds to help area peasants with their agricultural work. Back in the barracks, the three of us shared the food, and the wonderful taste of the salami we felt so lucky to have received. It was a heavenly delicacy, and we chewed it slowly so that the flavor would last as long as possible.

The children did not go to work in the laundry every day. One day, we were ordered to clean the windows of the other adult barracks, which was empty at the time and which faced ours. We were joined by Mina, the woman from Warsaw who had an emotional breakdown after her boyfriend was murdered. The group from Budzyn tried its utmost to protect her by preventing the Germans from discovering her condition. That day, it was arranged that Mina would stay with us girls. Her unstable condition and uninhibited behavior had a negative effect on us all. Tell me, we started to ask each other, am I talking like Mina too? It also seems that Mina was often sexually inappropriate and the most horrible stories tended to circulate about her. Most important to us, however, was the fact that when we were with her, we were afraid that her psychological condition would rub off and that we would also start speaking as if we were crazy.

One day before we left for work, I sustained a heavy blow to my left eye, which swelled up and looked terrible. Surprisingly, even in Majdanek there was a clinic of sorts relatively close to our barracks. My aunt was worried about me, and I was somehow taken to the clinic. At the clinic, they told me to keep a wet cloth pressed against my eye and not to go to work. It is probably difficult for you teenagers to believe that although perfectly healthy people were burned at Majdanek, there was also a clinic for the camp prisoners. It was true, however. When I returned to the barracks, I could not find any other girls except a short, stocky Dutch girl who was also sick at the time. She had a sore throat because she had swallowed a coin when she was first brought to the camp, before she was searched. The coin got caught in her throat, and she could neither swallow it nor regurgitate it. She also could not tell the people at the clinic why her throat hurt. In any case, she, too, had stayed back that day. But because it was forbidden to stay in the barracks during work hours, we were sent to join a number of Dutch girls who were working outside in the fields.

I am unable to explain where they were working. Nonetheless, my impression was that the field in which they were working was located far from our barracks. At the edge of the field, not far from the fence, was a sort of stable full of hay. The sick Dutch girl and I were told to sit in stable, along with another Dutch girl who was sent to join us for some unknown reason. We were guarded by a German soldier of the Luftwaffe, who regularly peaked outside to check on the work of the other girls. I mention that the soldier belonged to the Luftwaffe for two reasons. The first is that I distinctly remember him talking to us and stressing the fact that he belonged to the Luftwaffe. I usually regarded all Germans in uniform simply as German soldiers, and I did not distinguish between the different corps, primarily because I was extremely frightened of all of them. However, I was able to distinguish between German soldiers, Ukrainian soldiers, and Polish policemen. The second reason is that, for some reason, he was a bit more humane. He spoke to us more or less as equals. While we talked, he moved closer to the second Dutch girl who had been sent to join us, and asked her something while making a relatively obvious body motion and pointing to the straw on the ground beside us. The Dutch girl refused, and the girl with the coin in her throat smiled, but did not tell me why. She just sat on the side and said nothing. As it turns out, the German soldier wanted to sleep with her, and she, a Jewish girl dared to say no, which was quite courageous. At the time, I was curious to know what they were talking about, and I wondered why the girl sitting next to me was smiling. In retrospect, I am surprised that the soldier took her refusal so calmly and did not push the matter further. He behaved like a gentleman, in great contrast to the way most German soldiers acted toward Jewish girls in Majdanek.

Another Dutch girl with curly blond hair, who was very tall and extremely healthy-looking, became the slave of the Gestapo chief in the camp. Out of all the Dutch women in the camp, she is the only one I still remember clearly. As I recall, this beautiful woman was the only female, aside from the children, who was allowed to dress in civilian clothes. She was also the only prisoner who could walk from our field to the German headquarters barracks on the other side of the fence, where the senior German camp commanders lived. She was the focus of a great deal of extremely critical gossip, and she was disliked by all the women.

After a short time, neither the Dutch girl nor I could afford to continue being sick and not at work any longer. We returned to work, even though

Watchtower at Majdanek Concentration Camp

147

our symptoms had not improved much. At Majdanek, even at this late stage, it was dangerous to be sick for a long period of time.

One morning during roll call, while the Germans were counting us and issuing instructions, we were informed that the children would not be working in the laundry that day but rather would be taken out of the camp for different work. We all panicked, as we did any time such changes were made.

At the end of the roll call, the Germans gathered all the children together and marched us out of our gate. The sentry at the gate ordered us to sing and instructed the girls to wrap their heads in the white kerchief that was part of the prisoner uniform. As I already mentioned, the children were permitted to wear civilian clothes. In a subsequent, incomprehensible context, which I will discuss in more detail later, the white kerchief would be used during our evacuation from the camp to protect the lords of the land against Russian shelling. We walked a considerable distance and passed through a number of inner gates until we reached a large field of vegetables from where we could see the crematorium, which stood adjacent to the end of the field. We crossed the field and were not permitted to dawdle. Plumes of smoke billowed from the crematorium chimneys into the sky above the camp, and we were sickened by the pungent odor of the burning corpses. The Germans guarding us directed us to the left, to a patch of strawberries close to the vegetable field. This was where the Germans grew fresh vegetables and strawberries for the German camp administrators. It was an open field close to the crematorium, which enabled them to use the ashes from the burnt human bodies to improve the soil. In this way, the fresh vegetables and strawberries consumed by the camp administrators were literally cultivated on land fertilized by the ashes of human beings

We were all still hungry, and the sight of real red strawberries after years of hunger made us virtually incapable of withstanding the temptation to pop some into our mouths. The German guarding us warned us from the outset that anyone who dared eat even one strawberry was taking her life in her own hands. We knew that he was not just trying to scare us, but that he would undoubtedly make good on his threat. Nevertheless, we were still children and our hunger made the temptation difficult to resist. We had long forgotten the taste of ripe strawberries, and our desire to eat one was equaled only by our fear of death. We were given baskets in which to collect the strawberries and instructed to pick only the red ones.

I cannot remember how many days we worked picking berries and what happened on each day of the harvest. However, I do remember that we really enjoyed working outside. Still, it would be inaccurate to say that we were working outside in the fresh air, as the stench emanating from the crematorium filled our noses each time the wind blew in our direction. During breaks, we would compete with each other to see who was brave enough to sneak a strawberry into their mouth, despite the great danger involved. I also recall that during our breaks we would tell each other about our homes before the war. But most of all, I used to tell the other children that I had not eaten even one strawberry, as strawberries were not something I was willing to die for. The children who did not dare take the risk of eating a strawberry regarded those who did so as true heroes, even if they ate only one. The whole time, we were guarded by only one armed Wehrmacht soldier. It seemed to be difficult for him to closely supervise children who were regularly bending down to the ground, and in any case he stood too far away from us to be able to determine if someone had eaten a strawberry or not. Some of the children took advantage of this opportunity by eating one or two strawberries and were not caught. In the end, none were shot for eating strawberries, and we all completed the harvest in one piece.

At the very same time, only approximately 50 meters from where we were picking strawberries for consumption by German officers, the corpses of innocent Poles were being burned in the crematorium.

Today, it is difficult to give a truly accurate account of camp life and what we did each day. The schedule of the camp included an early lights-out; getting into our bunks; night inspections to make sure we were actually sleeping and not planning an escape; an extremely early wake-up for the head-count; and the march to work. We had soup in the afternoon and a piece of bread with some sort of spread in the evening, and then we started it all over again. In conversation after conversation that I overheard, the adults told each other that they could already sense that it was coming to an end. Here and there, when the Germans were not looking, Poles on the other side of the fence told Jews in the camp snippets of information regarding recent developments. Our feeling, however, was that the Germans would never leave us alive and would be sure to kill us before their defeat.

Some things I still remember well, while others, apparently simple and obvious, have been lost to me. For example, I often wonder where we showered, if at all, after our first showers in the camp. I also wonder how we combed our hair, as we did not have combs. Our lives were based only on what we had on our persons. We were never allowed to bring even the smallest package from place to place. I do remember, though, that we always strived to look good at roll call. I can also remember the face of the SS commander who counted us every morning. To my eyes, this German officer seemed young and relatively handsome. Sometimes, roll call was attended by a female officer as well. She was much more strict and stern, and she almost always had a ruthless look in her eye. I remembered the face of the male SS officer for a long time. Once, after our release, when I was already living in the Jewish orphanage, we traveled by train to Silesia. At one of the stations along the way we saw German POWs working next to the tracks, and I thought that, among them, I recognized the man who counted us at Majdanek. But, before I was able to point him out and scream, I know him! the train had continued on its way. I sorely regretted the fact that the train did not stop long enough to allow me to confirm his identity, as perhaps he could have been apprehended.

7. FLAMES IN THE CAMP
AND THE MARCH HAS BEGUN

When we woke up that morning, everything was different. Morning roll call did not take place as usual and officers rushed in and out of our field with worried looks on their faces. When we ventured out of our barracks, we saw thick black smoke billowing out of giant flames burning in the direction of Lublin. The German commander who usually counted us announced that all men and women were to assemble for roll call by the fence closest to the gate leading out of our field. I no longer remember exactly what happened, but I can piece it together from things I later learned after being liberated. Some of the children with whom I was in the camp seem to have been taken away by ambulance (this I learned from other survivors months later in Lublin) while I walked with my aunt and the other adults. (I was later to be reunited with the children from Majdanek in an orphanage in Lublin. I was happy that they had survived when it probably had seemed at the time that they were being taken away to be killed.)

In order to make sure that everyone had assembled and that no one had run off or was hiding in the barracks, the Germans brought out another commander. The new commander was short and meticulously dressed in a military uniform and a long coat, even though it was already mid-July. He was extremely irritable and easily aggravated by every movement of the prisoners in the ranks. If someone moved, he would beat him with the riding crop he held in his hand. He first ordered a head-count, and when he was not pleased by the results he ordered another one. As we stood there being counted over and over again, we could see Germans removing an immense quantity of paperwork from the command barrack on the other side of the fence. They placed the papers in a large pile and set it ablaze, which meant that now there was a large fire burning in our field as well. Apparently, these papers were documentation of the prisoners who had passed through Majdanek over the years, and they were being burned because the Germans did not want such incriminating evidence to fall into the hands of the Red Army.

We stood at inspection for a long time, in fear of the furious commander who we believed might very well murder us on the spot. All of a sudden, we heard him issue an order: Raus! Schnell!, he barked. With my aunt and cousin by my side, I walked out of the field. Today, I am not sure if they marched the men out first and only then the women, but that is how I remember it. I was lucky to have been wearing a civilian dress with a small apron, which I had selected from a pile of clothing when I worked in the laundry. Around my neck I wore a dog tag bearing my prisoner number, which had also been sewn into the front of my dress. The very next day, I was already in hiding with a family of Polish peasants. It became clear that the civilian dress I had put on that morning, completely by chance, had saved my life. But first, I must recount how I got to the home of the peasants.

Field number one was located relatively close to the entry gate of the camp itself. It is difficult to identify its location today because the Poles dismantled most of the barracks after the war. We walked toward the main entry gate, leaving behind the flames that were quickly devouring evidence of the crimes committed at Majdanek. We passed the showers which had frightened us to no end when we first arrived. Then, we passed huge piles of human hair, spectacles, thread, and brushes of different types. Everything was organized into heaps. After we exited the gate, we realized that the Jews were not the only ones on the road, and that we were being followed by a long line of other prisoners. At the time, it looked to me as if the Germans had evacuated all the prisoners of the camp, and that the Jews were leading the march.

When we left the main gate, we heard the sound of airplanes overhead and saw that an aerial battle was being fought directly above us. With joy in their voices, the adults shouted that it was a battle between German and Russian planes. When we reached the main road, we realized that we were marching along with the masses of retreating German soldiers. The Germans positioned us right between their tanks and their other vehicles, which, in turn, were flanked by two lines of soldiers. German soldiers with packs on their backs marched along each side of the road, as vehicles drove amidst them. And, we were right in the middle.

Despite the German soldiers marching alongside us and despite the fact that the Germans were in a desperate situation, the camp commanders were still behaving as if we might escape. They never left our side, walking alongside of us with guard dogs. When the soldiers saw the aerial

152

battle, they ordered the women to wrap their heads in the white kerchiefs and to jump into the ditch next to the gate that ran between the road and the barbed wire fences of the camp. As we were ordered, we lay down in the ditch, only to find that it was already filled with German soldiers who were using it to take cover from the air strikes. We had been ordered to lie down on top of them to serve as human shields against the Russian attack. The white kerchiefs were supposed to serve as the sign of a concentration camp for the Russian pilots, who were already familiar with this signal, to prevent them from bombing us. The moment we lay down in the ditch with the German soldiers, the situation became surreal. The German soldiers themselves laughed at how it looked: the mighty Germans using a group of miserable Jews to defend themselves against impending danger.

As we lay there in the ditch, I pondered the ridiculous situation, in which we Jewish women were defending the German soldiers with our own bodies. In our hearts, we hoped that the German plane would be shot down. After we saw a fireball in the sky and heard a great explosion, we were ordered to get out of the ditch and to get back into our rows. Although we did not know for certain which plane had actually been shot down, the faces of the German soldiers seem to betray the fact that it had been the German plane.

When we resumed the march, I tried to remain next to my family, particularly my aunt. Every once in a while, I nibbled on the piece of bread in my hand that I had managed to take with me from breakfast. In Poland, rain often falls in the summer and soon, the rain did indeed begin to fall. The light garments we wore were soaked and the road grew muddy and slippery, and I started to walk into puddles. I do not know how long we had been walking when I started to stagger. By the time we reached a sort of pedestrian sidewalk that ran alongside the road, I was unable to focus on anything around me except for looking for a place to rest for a few minutes. But everyone kept on moving.

The German vehicles dispersed somewhat, and I stumbled and sat down on the edge of the sidewalk. I had only been sitting for a few seconds when I suddenly saw a German officer bend down above me, draw his pistol from its holster, and press it to my temple. I will never forget the sensation of the cold iron of the pistol barrel against my head. It enabled me to muster the strength to get up and start running. But I was unable to catch up to the Jewish group, and I lost contact with my aunt. With great difficulty, I continued to walk among a group of men who were unknown to me. I have no idea how long I walked after the German officer threatened me with the pistol. I grew weaker and I thought it was the end for me. I suddenly fell. I was totally drained — both physically and emotionally. I no longer could continue to walk. All my senses were foggy.

8. My Anonymous Saviors

Death no longer frightened me. To be honest, I wanted to die. My strength had finally run out. Suddenly, I could feel someone pick me up and put me on his shoulders. I was confused and everything seemed blurry. I was certain that I was being taken somewhere to be shot. Finish me off here, I begged the man who was carrying me on his soldiers, and who I now noticed was walking with someone else. I have no strength left. Where are you taking me? I asked. Finish me off here. Enough! Finish me off here!

But all he said was, Shhh Shhh. I begged to be allowed to die. At one point, the man carrying me put a cube of sugar in my mouth, and again said, Shhh Shhh. It had already gotten dark, and I was unable to see the faces of the men, including the face of the man who was carrying me on his shoulders. Suddenly, I heard the sound of knocking. We were standing at the door of a hut, and when the door opened, in the dim light of the oil lamp burning in the kitchen, I saw the face of my savior, as well as the faces of a peasant and his wife.

They certainly were not expecting guests such as ourselves, and undoubtedly, they knew it was forbidden to hide Jews. I heard the men telling them that I was a sick Jewish girl, and that they must care for me until the Russians would come to occupy the village. We are partisans from the surrounding area, the men lied, and if any harm comes to her while she in your care, we will make sure that you pay for it.

The man said nothing more about me, just stood in the doorway until the peasant's wife showed him where to put me. They laid me down on a wooden bench that stood by the wall and that also served as a storage chest. The bench was the width of a single bed, and was generally used by rural Poles as a piece of furniture. The men quickly disappeared and neither I, nor the peasants ever heard from them again. It is likely that they were political prisoners who had been marching with us at the end of the line. After the war I was told by a number of other survivors from the same march that the men may have been Czech political prisoners who had been marching behind us during the evacuation from Majdanek. Perhaps when they saw me lying exhausted on the road, they simply picked me up on their shoulders and escaped. How did they manage to leave the ranks of the march and put me on their shoulders without the Germans noticing them? We had been so heavily guarded. After the war, I was told that whoever had stumbled during that march was shot on the spot. I learned that another girl from Hrubieszow had been marching with us, but was murdered on the way.

"Cipora, even though we are wearing warm coats, we are freezing here. How did the prisoners withstand the bitter cold they had to endure in addition to their terrible mistreatment?," the students wanted to know.

"I have no logical answer to your question," I responded. However, the fact of the matter is that they did withstand it. I stood at roll call in Budzyn in below-freezing temperatures without any underpants on, and I did not get sick.

"Now, without the cameras rolling, we'll begin our tour. I'll take a break and the guide will tell you about the camp. I'll continue my story when we meet back on the bus, but without any cameras," I told the group.

The next part of my story, the part when I was brought back to life, always makes me sad. My sorrow does not stem from my suffering but rather from the fact that I was never able to thank the people who actually saved my life.

A months later, when Lublin was already in Russian hands, I was living in a Catholic Polish orphanage, which I will tell more about later. One day, as I walked through the city streets, I thought I saw the men who scooped me up and brought me to the peasant's house, standing in a huge, densely packed crowd. I remembered their faces from when I had seen them in the peasants hut in the light of the oil lamp. I tried to make it over to them and to introduce myself. It's me, I would have told them, the sick girl you saved! I'm alive and the peasants took good care of me. I had truly been hoping for an opportunity to thank them, but I was unable to get close to them despite my attempts to reach them through the crowd. When they disappeared from my sight as I pushed my way through the mass of people, I was certain I would have the opportunity to meet them again, but I never did. Since that day, I have always had painful regrets about not trying hard enough to reach them. Even today, I still know nothing about the men who saved me. Ever since I saw them in Lublin, I have searched unsuccessfully for some kind of lead that would enable me to learn something about them. Despite the many years that have passed since then, missing this opportunity has always haunted me and will most likely continue to haunt me for the rest of my life.

I also regret that, during my stay with the peasant and his wife, I never asked their names or the name of their village. I never addressed them by name, but rather as Mrs. and Sir. As a result, once I left the family and the village, I was unable to explain who had cared for me and where I had been hiding. It troubles me that because I did not know their name and because of the little information I had to go on, I was unable to thank them for treating me well.

When I was brought to the peasants hut, I was extremely confused and only half-conscious. I found it impossible to move and it was even difficult for me to open my mouth and to chew.

I fell asleep quickly. I remember nothing from that night except the moment I was carried inside. The next morning, I woke up early. The peasant had already left to start his work, and his wife brought me a cup of hot tea to drink. Not only was I unable to sit up, I could barely even open my parched lips. In the end, she fed me the tea, spoonful by spoonful. Fortunately, when she bent down to help me she noticed that I was still wearing the dog tag with my prisoner number around my neck, and she took it off. Suddenly, two little girls with wild blond hair walked into the kitchen. One looked about my age and the other looked about three or four years old. They were surprised to find an unknown girl in their home. After standing and staring for a few seconds, they went outside. I eventually fell asleep again, only to awake to the sound of knocking on the door.

When the peasant's wife opened the door, she found herself face-to-face with none other than a German officer. He walked right in. I can imagine the fear she must have felt when she saw him enter her home, knowing that she was hiding a young Jewish child with a prisoner number on her dress and her sleeve! The officer sat on a small stool across from my bench and asked for some water and whether he could rest there for a few minutes.

157

Trembling with fear, the woman ran to the water pump next to the entrance of the house and served it to him in a tin cup. After a short time, during which the officer drank the water and rested, the officer asked the woman in German if I was her daughter and why I was so pale. Because I knew Yiddish and a bit of German by now, I understood his question. The woman limited her response to mumbling in Polish, My daughter is sick, my daughter is sick. The officer saw that I was ill and came over to me. I took my hand out from under the blanket. He asked to see my tongue, and then he grabbed my hand and took my pulse. Fortunately, the rest of my body was covered, and the officer did not see the prisoner number on my dress.

After taking my pulse, he told the peasant's wife that he was a doctor and offered his diagnosis: She is very sick, and she has only a slim chance of living, he told her. Run quickly and find a doctor, he continued, and tell him to come right away, urgently! Her life is in danger! I understood every word the German doctor said to the woman. Still quite frightened, the woman told the officer she would do as he said. The German doctor gulped down the rest of his water and excused himself, saying that he had to rejoin the retreating German soldiers who were marching down the road.

The peasant's wife, who was still shaken from the incident, told me she was going to look for a doctor and left the hut in a hurry, leaving me alone on the bench in the kitchen. I was clear-headed enough to assess my immediate surroundings, but I was unable to do anything else, as I was still unable to move much. In addition to the bench on which I was lying and two other chairs that stood in the kitchen, I saw a stove to the left of the door with a large steaming iron pot on it. It appeared the peasant's wife had already started cooking lunch.

I lay there for quite some time while the peasant's wife was out looking for a doctor. In the meantime, the older daughter entered the hut and looked at me, communicating with me only through facial expressions. As I lay there, drifting in and out of sleep, the peasant's wife returned. I did not find a doctor, she said, but a woman I met in the village said that the medicine my husband took when he was sick, may help you as well. There's still a bit left in the bottle. Until the woman motioned with her head toward the bottle of medicine standing on the shelf above me, I had not even been aware that there was a shelf hanging above my head. She then stood on the chair and took down the bottle and poured me a spoonful. She fed me the medicine and I swallowed it at once. Of course, I did not ask her the name of the medicine, and even if I had, I would not have known if it would help me or hurt me.

I lay there on the bench for a few days, but I cannot remember exactly how many. Most of the time, I was still unable to sit up or eat on my own, and the peasant's kind wife had to feed me like a baby. Out of all the food served to me while I was staying with the peasant family, what I remember the most was a delicious mushroom soup. After years of hunger and consuming only bread and watery soup, this was the first time I had tasted real hot soup with mushrooms and potatoes. I remember complimenting the woman on the soup, and this pleased her.

Although I did not know it at the time, the medicine that had been in the bottle was Valerian. The peasants had it in their house because the husband suffered from heart disease. The medicine had possibly raised my blood pressure, which may be why I felt better. Luckily, it didn't make me even more ill.

I used to wake up early with the members of the family. The peasant usually left early to work in the field and returned home late. He barely spoke to me. When he left the house, though, he used to look at me, and sometimes he would ask me: How are you today? Nevertheless, I can still conjure up his image. He always wore dark pants tucked into a pair of leather boots up to the knee and a white thick cotton shirt covered by a black vest. He was medium height and had a dark face, and his upper lip was covered by a small moustache. The girls always wore the same dresses, and I noticed that their hair was never combed.

Most of the time, I just lay on the bench half-asleep, alone in the kitchen. The peasant and his wife told me that the Russians had almost reached the outskirts of the village. They also told me that the Poles killed a Jew whom they had found in a nearby village. So, even in this warm family home with people who took such good care of me, I did not feel completely safe.

One morning as I lay there on the bench alone in the house, I suddenly heard the whistle of a bullet that had been shot directly into the baking oven above the stove. It was immediately followed by another one, which also hit the oven and grazed the top of my head. I shuddered and quickly understood that the front lines now ran through the village itself, and that the bullets of the German and Russian armies were now flying through the village at random. When my hosts heard the sound of the bullets coming from all directions, they ran into the kitchen in a panic, and I told them where the bullets had landed. Following that incident, the peasant decided that it would be best to move me into the stable. There, he reasoned, I could lie on straw on the ground, which would be lower and therefore safer. I was not happy about the move. As I was still not strong enough to move to the stable on my own, my host carried me there and told me there were no animals at the moment. When we entered the stable, which faced the door of the hut and was located just a short distance away, my bed – a tall mound of hay – was already arranged, and he lay me down on it.

The stable door was left open during the day, and that is how I knew when it was daytime and when it was nighttime. The mound of hay that served as my bed was separated from the stable door located a few meters away by a cement floor. In order to prevent the pile of hay from dissipating, they placed a wide wooden board next to the mound, which served as a divider between me and the entrance.

The battles in the village continued to rage and the bullets continued to fly, finding their way into the stable as well. I remember being relatively indifferent to what was going on around me and no longer fearing anything, not even the bullets whizzing over my head. When my hosts came into the stable to take care of me and sometimes just to visit, I told them that bullets were flying in here, too.

The reason why the peasants decided to move me into the stable was a mystery. Looking back, it may have been their fear that the Germans might rally their forces and reenter the village. If they found me inside their house, the Germans would likely have executed the peasants. Alternatively, it could have been that having me in their house, lying hidden in their kitchen, the life hub of a peasant household, may have overwhelmingly infringed on their limited privacy. However, it is remotely possible that they truly believed I would be safer in the shadows of the stable. I will never know.

I was so weak that I could not move. I was almost totally indifferent to my surroundings. Most of the time I could not even ask for help and I was forced to defecate and urinate where I slept. One late morning an unfamiliar woman from the village visited me. Showing concern for my well being she sat on a small stool and stated that she was; "a friend of the family" who had "come to see how I was doing?" After a short conversation she left, but the woman returned every day. She never brought me anything, but she continuously asked questions about my life. At times she would tell me strange stories that really frightened me. I listened, but never commented on her stories.

This woman was my only human contact, other than my interactions with the peasant wife. I began to look forward to the woman's daily visits. During one of her visits, after I had told her about some of my experiences, she said "After all the terrible things you have experienced in your short life as a Jewish girl, I have to ask you why want to continue being Jewish? As soon as you are stronger you can come live with me. We can adopt you and you can go to Church and convert to Christianity. Jews are smart, so when you get older I can send to you study and you can become a teacher."

Listening to her I got goose bumps. I could not comprehend what she was talking about? Me? Convert to Christianity? I told her that I want to remain Jewish. My mother and father may still be alive, I told her, or so I hoped. I then turned to her and asked whether she wanted to convert to Judaism?

Despite my impertinence, the woman persisted: "Why continue being a Jew after suffering so much because of your Judaism?" Finally, she started getting angry and stated: "You are a foolish girl."

Once she left, I was scared that she would not give up easily. She did indeed come back the next day. This time instead of trying to convince me to convert, she threatened me by saying: "If you don't agree to come live with me, my husband will come and cut your head off with an axe!" she said.

I had been hidden in closets in a ghetto and a concentration camp. I even lived through the hell of Majdanek. Now, after all this, with the Germans seemingly gone, a new and unexpected threat had appeared. When the peasant's wife appeared in the stable to feed me, I immediately told her about the threats made by the women who had introduced herself as "a friend of the family". The kind peasant woman tried to calm me down, saying that I had no reason to fear her, but I was inconsolable.

As I already alluded to, the state of my hygiene was indescribable. My hair had not been combed. It was full of lice and itched terribly. I know that I smelled horribly, but I was too weak to do anything about this. Days and possibly weeks passed, while I slowly regained my strength. Eventually I was strong enough to stand up and take a few steps on my own. I was not aware of the military situation. I did not know that Russians had taken control of the village from the Germans, so I was very careful.

One day I was finally strong enough to move from the stable to the hut. While making the walk, I was able to see, for the first time, that there was a well in the middle of the yard. There was also a vegetable garden (growing mostly carrots) on the far side of the hut. I also saw an old man, who was the peasant's father, sitting on a bench in the yard. This was the first time that I learned of his existence.

Having regained my strength, I was able to feed myself and could urinate and defecate in a hidden part of the yard. I cannot describe my happiness at regaining these most basic human skills. As timed passed I became friendlier with the peasants' two daughters. The girls seemed to enjoy my company. After I told the peasant's wife about the scary women who was visiting me had said, the woman never came back.

One day while I was sitting on the packed earth floor of the kitchen, there was a knock on the hut's door. In entered a woman who was clearly not from the village. The peasant's wife told me this unfamiliar woman was the owner of the village estate. She added that this woman had come to help me, which she immediately proceeded to do. She asked the peasant's wife for a bowl of hot water. Then she bathed me, washed me. She combed my hair. I remember she removed countless lice from my hair, which to the best of my recollection was not very long. When she was done, I almost felt reborn. Unfortunately, I was still wearing the same dress I had been wearing since we left the camp.

The woman who spoke very gently asked questions about what I had been through. It was clear that it was difficult for her to hear about my experiences. I felt a kinship with the woman, but soon after finishing cleaning my body and hair she left, promising to return. Much to my disappointment, that was her only visit.

As I became stronger I began to help the peasant's wife with her work in the garden. I enjoyed seeing the rows of carrots grow, and tasting a fresh carrot immediately after picking it. One morning the peasant suggested that I help to herd the cows in the pasture. I was amazed that he trusted me enough to put his precious cows in my care. However, although I was now somewhat stronger, I was afraid that I was not strong enough to walk to the pasture by myself, as the pasture was located a substantial distance from the house. I was also fearful that some of the village children might attack me while I was all alone in the pasture. My greatest hesitation was due to the fact I had no idea how to herd cows in a pasture. I told the peasant that I had never herded cows in a pasture before, and that I also had no idea if I have the strength to walk that far. The peasant politely accepted my refusal. He shrugged his shoulders, as if to say, he should know not to have any real expectations of me anyway. Then he went on his way.

During the whole period that I was sick, I knew nothing about my hosts. Once I was better the peasant wife invited me to see their living room. She told me that, in addition to working the field, her husband was also to the village dentist. I asked where his office was located. She indicated that his office was right there, pointing to a long rope with one end tied to the handle of the living room door, and the other end sitting on a shelf against the wall facing the door. Also located on the shelf was a pair of blacksmith pliers. The pliers constituted his only "medical instrument". She explained if a tooth of a villager hurt, he would tie it to the rope with a piece of string and pull on the handle, and it would come out. If it didn't come out completely the first time, he would use the pliers.

I was horrified by the peasant's wife's description of her husband's procedures, despite my complete lack of knowledge of proper dentistry practice. I remembered the time my father took me to the dentist, right before the war, because I had a baby tooth that was loose. That was the only time I had seen an actual dentist's office, and it, of course, bore no resemblance to what I saw in the peasant's living room. Obviously, I refrained from expressing my opinion of his office or dental expertise. During the entire time I stayed with them I never saw a patient come for an appointment.

One morning while I was standing by the well the peasant approached me and said that he had something to tell me. He told me that he had heard that the Germans were about to return to the area. He added: "and you know what is likely to happen to you and us if they find out that we are hiding a Jewish girl." Still, without knowing what was happening on the military front, I found his story unlikely, especially after he had told me a conflicting story he had allegedly heard claiming that there were Jews living in Lublin on the 3rd of May Street. The peasant further stated that perhaps in Lublin, I would be able to find a Jewish person I know. Then the peasant walked away. Why the peasants had picked this moment to convince me to leave I do not know. It is possible that other villagers were not comfortable with the fact that they were harboring a Jewish girl and had pressured them to get me to leave.

The very next morning, my hosts packed me a few slices of fresh bread and a few slices of blood salami in a small pack wrapped in cotton cloth. This is so you have something to eat until you find Jews, they said.

When the time came for me to leave, the whole family assembled to bid me farewell. As I said goodbye, I felt a distinct need to give them something, even something small, to express my deep gratitude for the kind way they cared for me. I had a small colorful apron tied to my dress when I left Majdanek. As we stood facing each other I took off the apron and handed it to the older daughter as a small gift. You don't need to do that, said the peasant's wife, but I insisted until the girl eventually reached out her hand and took the apron. I had nothing else with which to thank the family, and that small gift served to express my immense gratitude, even if only symbolically. They were the family that nursed me back to life.

After I said goodbye to the entire family, including the peasant's elderly father, the peasant picked up my small pack and took me back to the road that I must have been walking on when I fell during the march from

Majdanek. I discovered that that road was indeed close to their hut. The peasant showed me the direction that I could try to catch a ride to Lublin. Then he left. There I stood, a ten-and a half-year old girl, wearing a thin flowery dress, carrying a small pack of bread and salami wrapped in cotton cloth, all alone on the road to Lublin. I had no information as to the fate and location of my parents or any other relatives and I was headed to a city that I did not know. Majdanek was actually located in Lublin. My sole knowledge of the city was what I could see through the camp's electric barbed wire fence. Standing on the road I had no idea how I would find the 3rd of May Street, or if the story that there were Jews on that street was even true. But I was free and alive, and I was a Jewish girl in Poland who no longer had to fear the Germans.

9. In Lublin

I had not been standing on the road long when a truck stopped beside me, its wheels making a terrible screech. A large number of Red Army soldiers were packed into the back. The driver got out and, in Russian, which I understood only slightly, asked me where I was headed. I immediately bombarded him with all my basic information: I am a Jewish girl who wants to go to 3rd of May Street in Lublin, I told him. I was told that there are already Jews there. I spoke to him in Polish, which he somehow understood, and he lifted me up onto the truck. Do you know where 3rd of May Street is? he asked me once I was sitting down, and I told him that I did not. I sat on the floor of the truck with the Russian soldiers who smiled when they saw me. I noticed that the driver had not at all been concerned by the fact that I did not know the location of the street to which I was headed. He got back in front of the wheel and started the engine, and we began to drive.

I do not remember how long the ride lasted, but it took long enough for me to take notice of the fact that one of the soldiers would periodically remove his military coat. This type of jacket was filled with cotton wool in order to keep the soldiers warm in the winter, and it was covered by a crisscross pattern of stitches, which also happened to provide lice with convenient paths along which to stroll. The soldiers cleaned the lice off their coats during the ride, taking off their coats and picking off each louse, one by one, and crushing it between the fingernails of their two thumbs. In addition to delousing their coats, they also sang during the trip. They didn't ask too many questions, probably because of the language barrier. The truck finally came to a halt in Lublin next to the police station. The driver got out of the cab, walked around to the back of the truck, helped me down, and told me that we had arrived at 3rd of May Street. If I did not find any Jews there, I could go to the police station and ask for help, he said, pointing to the building.

The truck continued on its way, and I stood on the sidewalk and pondered what I was to do. After a few minutes, I started to walk around, searching for Jewish-looking faces among the people passing by. I walked a bit, and then retraced my steps. After failing to recognize any Jews, I decided to continue walking along the road. I was tiring quickly and I was also getting hungry. After finding an entryway with a wide threshold into what was either a store or an apartment building, I sat down, opened the food the family had given me before I left the village, and ate.

Many people passed by and looked at me, and then continued walking. As I sat there, I noticed that I was sitting close to a large square lined by a burned car, wrecked trucks, and a tank. These were, no doubt, the remnants of battles recently fought in the city.

I sat there for a while. In the meantime, the sun had gone down and evening was approaching. Where would I sleep? What would I do at night? The fear of not having a place to sleep started to take hold of me, and I decided I would start knocking on the doors of houses to ask for a place to sleep for just one night.

The first door I knocked on was opened by a young woman, who stood in the doorway looking at me curiously, surprised by what she saw. What do you want, little girl? she asked me.

Good evening, I answered without hesitation. I am a Jewish girl. Could I possibly sleep in your house for just one night? She immediately told me that I could not, because her husband was in the army and without him she could not host me, even though I repeated the fact that it would be just for one night. Wasting no time, she slammed the door in my face. I knocked on many other doors until night had truly fallen and I had still found no place to lay my head. The thought of spending the night on the street of an unfamiliar city in which no one knew me was extremely frightening for me.

I continued to walk the streets, alone, tired, hungry, and weak. Fortunately, I happened to notice a rather large woman with broad shoulders and pinned-up hair standing nearby. I do not know why I approached her to ask if she would be willing to let me sleep at her house. Again, I explained who I was and that I desperately needed a place to sleep for just one night. Come with me, she said, as soon as I finished speaking. I have room in my apartment, but only on the floor. I live alone now. My son is a soldier in the Polish army, and I have no idea where he is or how he is doing. Come with me, she said again, and took my hand. I was elated by the fact that I would not need to spend the night on the dark and unfamiliar streets of Lublin.

Her apartment was located in a large apartment building relatively close to where we had met. You must also be hungry, she said when we got inside. Indeed, I had eaten nothing since I finished the food I had taken with me from the peasant's home. I told her what I had eaten the entire day, and that I was indeed very hungry. I do not remember exactly what I ate when I was in her apartment. I do, however, remember the fresh bread, the kind I used to eat in my parent's house. The woman also took food for herself and then sat down beside me. As we sat and ate, she began to ask me many questions about my past. Every once in a while, she interrupted me with a heavy sigh: Oh, she said, look what those damn Germans have done during this terrible war! She also told me again about her only Polish army son, saying that ever since Lublin had been liberated by the Russians, she had been searching unsuccessfully for him. He is the only person I have in the world, she said.

She apologized for not being able to offer me a bath because she had no hot water. That's all right, I told her. I was so pleased to have found shelter for the night that I kept thanking her hospitality.

When the woman decided that it was time to go to sleep, she took me into her spacious living room and spread a large white fur on the floor near the table where we had eaten, and gave me a small blanket with which to cover myself. Again she apologized, this time for not being able to offer me a bed. Don't worry, I told her, everything has been so nice that I really don't need a bed. I told her that after being in the concentration camp, I was no longer used to sleeping in a proper bed. I have not slept in a regular bed for years, I explained, lying down on the fur, still wearing the same clothes I had worn during the day. Finally, I was sleeping in an apartment and not in a stable. I crawled under the blanket and immediately fell asleep. We were both awakened by the first morning light. I got up and tried to put the fur back in its place.

You don't have to do that, she said. And if you would like to, you can stay here for a few more days, she offered. I am all alone, and it is no bother at all if you want to stay with me.

My entire goal at that point was to find Jews, so though I again thanked the kind woman for her generosity and warm hospitality, I told her that I wanted to go back to 3rd of May Street because I had been told that Jews could be found there. In the meantime, she served us breakfast, and all I can remember about the meal is that it was very tasty.

For someone like me, a person who for almost half my life had neither eaten at a table nor eaten from a normal plate, the breakfast we ate at the table in the woman's apartment was a luxury that I savored. Aside from her gracious hospitality and her sincere concern for me as an abandoned child, I know nothing else about that generous Polish woman. As I write about her, I am overcome by a sense of longing and profound regret that I cannot go back to see her, to thank her with all my heart for the kindness she showed me during those dark times. I would also have liked to know whether that kind-hearted woman eventually found her son. I spent only one night and a single morning with her, but she will always have a place in my heart.

I do not recall exactly when I went back outside. Before I left her apartment, I asked the woman if we were far from 3rd of May Street. She told me that the street was close by, and told me how to get there. Then I was alone again, on the street where I was supposed to find Jews. My eyes scanned each passing face. No one looked Jewish to me. I walked up and down the street until I got tired, and I stopped next to a gate that was so large that even a horse and wagon could pass through it.

As I stood by the edge of the gate and examined the passersbys, I noticed a fruit store with red currants in the display window. I loved red currants, and I momentarily turned my back to the street and looked at the fruit in the window. I must have been standing by the window for quite some time, because the moment there were no more customers in the store, a short and skinny woman dressed in a dirty old apron emerged from within and asked me what I wanted. I quickly told the woman my prepared little speech about who I was and what I was seeking. As soon as I fell silent, she opened the door, went into the store and came out after a moment with a handful of red currants, and gave them to me.

I'll find the Jews for you, she said, I know who they are. I did not ask her how she was able to identify Jews. Eventually, she came out of the store again and stood on the street beside me, pointing out the Jewish people among those walking by.

Do you see that woman with the hat and the bag in her hand? she cried suddenly. She's Jewish. As she spoke, she ran over to the woman, pointed to me, and addressed her: That's a Jewish girl. She's looking for other Jews. Under no circumstances would I ever have picked out such an elegant woman, dressed in such fancy clothing, as a Jew. Nonetheless, the Polish woman introduced me to her. Surprised, she walked over and started bombarding me with questions. As it turned out, this was her first meeting with a Jewish child since the liberation of Lublin. I answered her questions as best as I could, but begged her to take me with her. The woman began to apologize. She was willing to give me money, she told me, but in her current situation she could not take me with her. She was still using Aryan papers and living with a Polish family who had no idea that she was Jewish. As she apologized, she opened her bag, took out a small purse, and tried to shove a coin into my hand. Take some money, she said, so you will at least have enough to buy something to eat. I took a few steps backward and refused.

I don't want money, I explained, I just want you to take me with you. In my childlike naiveté, I hoped that the first Jewish woman I met would immediately take me to live with her. Please take me, I continued to beg. She still held the coin in her hand and again asked me to take the money, but I refused. I was frightened of the street. What would I do in the street all alone, I thought to myself? To me, this woman looked like the only lifeline that could rescue me.

Looking back on it today, I can think of no good reason why I refused to take the money. I can only remember the immense sense of disappointment I experienced when she tried to give it to me as I stood there by the gate in my tattered dress, with her refusing to take me with her. I did not want to feel like a beggar. I came from a comfortable, middle-class home, and I remembered how my mother always gave food for the Sabbath to the poor people of the city

Of course, I have no way of knowing exactly what she felt when she left me there whimpering. When she left me there in the street, I could see the disappointment in her eyes. I could not believe that she did not take

170

me with her. She did not even offer to help me in some way, other than financially.

When the fruit vendor saw through her store window that the woman had walked away without me, she rushed out of the store and asked, Why didn't you go with her? I told her what had happened, and she comforted me. Don't worry, she said, more Jews will pass by. That day, she had few customers. So, every time the store was empty, she joined me outside, scanned the people walking by, and made inquiries. I also kept my eyes on the pedestrians who looked at me, but kept on walking. Quite some time had passed since the Jewish woman had left, when I suddenly heard the fruit vendor yell: Here are Jews! She rushed over to me and pointed to three muscular-looking men wearing peasant hats and tall boots. She ran over to them and spoke to them with great excitement, all the while pointing at me.

They walked over and started asking me many questions: Who are you? How old are you? What city are you from? Finally, after these and many more questions, they asked: Do you want to come along with us?

Orphanage in Lublin 1943 Cipora, age 11, is highlighted in the upper right-hand section of the photo

Of course, I quickly answered. They said they would take me to meet an important Jewish man named Emil Sommerstein, who was a minister in the provisional Polish government that had recently been established by the Soviet Union. He would find me a place, I was assured.

Holding the hand of one of the men, I walked with them until we came to a flight of stairs and entered an empty apartment with a small wooden desk in the middle. Behind the desk sat a bespectacled old man with a short grey beard. Sitting in front of him on the table was a stack of sheets of paper. On one of the sheets, he proceeded to write down all my vital information. The moment we entered the room and he saw a little girl standing before him, he stared at me with wide eyes and said: This is the first young Jewish girl I've seen since I've been here. Then, after carefully writing down all my information, he explained: I have no arrangement for a Jewish girl, but I do know of a Polish orphanage that will certainly accept you until we come up with a different arrangement. I was a bit frightened, but what else could I do? When he saw that I was hesitant, he reassured me and called out someone's name. A young woman entered the room, and he turned to me and said: Do you see this woman? She will stay with you until you get to the orphanage. Don't be afraid. She will come visit you every day so we can be sure that everything there is fine for you.

After delivering me to the important man behind the desk, the three men said goodbye and disappeared, and I never heard anything about them again.

I have no idea who they were or how they survived the war. To my sorrow, I also never again saw the fruit vendor from the store near the gate.

After entering my information in a register and concluding a number of final arrangements the young woman and I descended back down to the street. When we got to the street, a black car with a driver in it was already waiting for us. Such a private car was an extremely rare commodity in Lublin in those days, and we both got into the back seat. The young woman was very nice to me and reassured me that I had no reason to fear living among Polish children, as she would come visit me often.

10. The Polish Orphanage In Lublin

The Polish orphanage to which she brought me occupied an entire floor of one of the street's main buildings. It was connected to another two large buildings, one on each side. The buildings were surrounded by a gigantic courtyard that was entered via a large brown wooden gate. We entered an apartment containing a few long narrow tables lined by wooden benches and were received by a relatively young, well-dressed woman with a pleasant smile. The young woman who brought me gave her the sheet of paper with the personal information I had provided earlier, told me that she was very busy and that she needed to get going, said goodbye and left. I stayed there with the woman, who I quickly realized was the director of the orphanage.

She gave me her hand and led me into her office. There, she told me where I would sleep and explained the rules of the orphanage. After a few minutes, another woman entered the office. This woman, the director told me, was the house mother of the orphanage. The house mother was the person who fed the children, made sure they had clean laundry, and ensured that the place was kept clean. She also sometimes functioned as a teacher.

At the end of our initial meeting, the house-mother served me something basic to eat, which I finished rather quickly. After that, she took me to another room that was extremely large and filled with many beds – some bunk beds and some regular beds. She then showed me my bed, and I was pleased. She also told me that I needed to bathe. She took me to a small room with a large white bowl, filled it with water, and instructed me first to wash my hair and only then to get into the bowl. I truly cannot remember if at this point she gave me clean clothes or if I had to put on my old dress from Majdanek again.

When the children arrived and saw a new girl, it never occurred to them that I was Jewish. As new children were brought to the orphanage almost every day, they tended not to notice and not to get excited. Sometimes, children were reunited with parents or other relatives and they then left the orphanage. Children also might sometimes leave the orphanage and be transferred to other facilities. For these reasons, the children did not tend to forge close relationships with one another. The food we were served was meager to say the least, and our diet was primarily bread-based. As the orphanage had no cooking facilities, volunteers had to walk from the orphanage to the nearby convent each afternoon carrying two pails, which the nuns proceeded to fill with soup they had cooked for us.

During my first days at the orphanage I had nothing to do when the other children went to school. I used to go down to the courtyard and wait for the young woman who had brought me there. I looked forward to her visit with great anticipation. I was so in need of a Jewish connection, and at that point the young woman symbolized just that.

I felt very different from the Polish children, much like a stranger. I felt as if nobody knew me and nobody was aware that I even existed, as if my life was empty. I believed in my heart that the woman would come visit me, for she had promised she would do so. For this reason, I grew increasingly disappointed with every day that passed without a visit. One day, the orphanage director asked me who I was waiting for in the courtyard every day. The woman who brought me to the orphanage promised she would visit me, and I am waiting for her, I explained. I am sure she will come. But after more time passed and she never arrived, I realized that she had actually been lying to me, and the resulting disappointment and insult lingered for a long time.

The orphanage had a regular schedule. We woke up early and got dressed. There was no time for brushing teeth and I do not remember if we washed our faces. However, thirty minutes after wake-up we all assembled in the large hall for morning prayers, which began after the director of the orphanage arrived. During the prayers, I always stood by one of the chairs, on which I also sat until the director arrived. I also did not stand up when everyone else stood up to pray. For many days, none of the children commented on the fact that I did not pray with them. One day, I began to realize that both the house-mother and the director liked me. I not only volunteered for all the required rotational duties, such as walking to the monastery to fetch the afternoon soup and cleaning the tables after meals, but I was also relatively quiet and never got into arguments with the other kids. For this reason I was both frightened and surprised when I was summoned to the director's office, as such invitations were typically issued only to children who misbehaved. When I entered her office, I found her waiting for me quietly, with a smile on her face. You are a very nice girl. You behave well, and both the house-mother and I like you very much, she said. But then she took a deep breath, and continued, I know you are Jewish, and that is why we do not require you to pray. Still, all religions must be respected, so when everyone stands up to pray, you should at least stand up.

I'm sorry, I said politely. I didn't know I had to get up, but that won't be a problem. I'll get up every time they pray. The director sent me on my way with a satisfied smile on her face, and from that day on I stood up during the prayers. I stood, but I did not pray. I heard them praying so often that I learned the prayers by heart. As time passed, I also noticed that one boy in particular, who was often around me for some reason, always volunteered to go with me to the monastery to fetch the afternoon soup and was always very nice to me. Apparently, he liked me. One day, he asked me to take a walk with him on the street near the orphanage, and I accepted his invitation happily. As we walked down the street talking about other children in the orphanage, he suddenly turned to me and asked, Tell me, why do you stand quietly while we are praying? Why don't you pray with us?

Because I am Jewish, I told him, no longer frightened to identify myself.

That's not true! he said excitedly. You just don't want to be my girlfriend. That's why you're saying that you're Jewish!

No, really, I am Jewish, I told him, as sincerely as possible.

But how can you be Jewish when you are so nice? It can't be true!

Why not?, What, do Jews have horns on their head? I asked, clearly indicating that I had been insulted by his reaction.

We returned to the orphanage. It was my impression he remained unconvinced about my being Jewish. But he never invited me to go for a walk with him again. I was all of eleven and he was twelve.

After I arrived at the orphanage, the director decided that the time had come for me to begin attending school. She told me that a teacher from the school would soon visit the orphanage to assess the appropriate grade for me. Based on my age, I was meant to be attending the fourth grade. However, the entirety of my formal education amounted to two weeks of the first grade and another half-year of tutoring with Chedva.

When the teacher came to the school, he sat me down in the doorway of one of the rooms and tried to be friendly. Then, he asked me a few knowledge-based questions.

I cannot recall if I answered all the questions, but the teacher concluded the test rather quickly and immediately told the director that I was ready for the third grade. I was surprised but relieved that I would not be going back to first grade, where I thought I belonged. I had no school bag, but the next day I was given a notebook and pencil and was sent along to the same school as the other children.

I can still remember how one day during the third grade the teacher asked the class questions about Polish history and King Kazimierz the Great. When I was the only student who answered correctly, the teacher stood up and pointed at me. Aren't you ashamed that you Polish children are not interested in the history of Poland, and that this Jewish girl is the only one who knows the answer? he said, rebuking them. As the only Jewish child in the class that is just what I needed. Until that point, I had managed, despite everything, to make friends with a few of the girls in the class. But, following the teacher's comment, none of the other kids would even talk to me. After that, I remember losing my self confidence and sitting through the rest of the lessons without saying a word. I feared the reactions of my classmates.

As long as I was living in the orphanage, I was quite satisfied by the fact that I had a bed to sleep in, food to eat, and someone to care for me. Here and there, after someone found out that I was Jewish, they would compliment me on my Polish language skills. The nuns were particularly courteous and always paid special attention to me.

One day, I was again summoned to the director's office. This time, it was in order to inform me that the Mother Superior of the convent wished to see me. Apparently, the nun had heard a great deal about me and was very interested in meeting me. I went to the church by myself and walked inside uneasily. It was the first time I was ever inside a place that I had always been told belonged to non-Jews and was off-limits to me. Before the war, as a Jewish child I had been forbidden to enter churches, as it went against the Jewish way of life. As I stood inside the church entrance, the Mother Superior walked over to me, quietly greeted me, and began telling me how pleased the director of the orphanage was with me and what nice things she had told her about me. It would be a shame for you to suffer again as a Jew, she then told me, and as a sign of appreciation for my good behavior, she wanted to convert me to Christianity. It would be for my own good, she said. They would find me a good Christian family, and I would be very happy as a Christian. Thank you for your generous offer, I said, in an apologetic tone, but I am Jewish, and I do not want to convert to Christianity. The smile on her face quickly disappeared and was replaced by a look of pity. After leaving me for a moment, she returned with a piece of candy the likes of which I had not tasted for years, and continued with her efforts to persuade me, despite my initial refusal.

Every afternoon, I walked to the convent with another child carrying a large empty bucket, which the nuns would fill with soup for our lunch. The soup was not especially rich in content, and the children, who were always hungry, always finished every last drop. I cannot recall why on that day I ended up walking with the bucket to the convent alone. It was afternoon, and the street, which was usually full of people, was now empty. Suddenly, about twenty paces away as I walked in the direction of the convent, I noticed a Russian soldier with a large number of medals pinned on his uniform speaking with a tall, thin woman who was standing across from him. When I got closer, I realized they were speaking Yiddish. My excitement knew no bounds! Upon hearing the familiar sound of the language, I quickly ran over to them and said excitedly in Yiddish, I am a Jewish child! The soldier looked at me and immediately burst into tears, and the woman, who bent down toward me and stroked my head, also began to weep. The dam of emotions within me burst wide open all at once, and I started crying. There we stood, all three of us, on an almost empty street in Lublin, crying. I was crying because I finally found other living Jews, and they were crying at the sight of a Jewish girl. After the initial emotions subsided, the questions began. Where was I from? Where was I living now? How did I survive the hell we had been through? I told them where I was living and that I was all alone in the world. Again, I hoped in my heart they might take me home with them, away from the Polish orphanage.

Although the man was extremely happy and visibly moved by the sight of a young Jewish girl, he had no way of helping me. The woman immediately told me that she and her family lived close by and that she had two daughters, one of whom was my age. She invited me to come to her house every day for lunch, and she suggested that I come with her right away so she could show me where she lived. She wanted to introduce me to her daughters, and I was overjoyed. Other Jews had survived after all, I thought to myself, even Jewish children! And I could now go to their house and play and spend time with Jewish girls. That day, I was late bringing the afternoon soup to the orphanage, but when I returned with the full bucket,

I explained the reason for my tardiness to the house-mother, and she of course forgave me.

The following day right after school, I went to the family's house in heightened spirits. The girls awaited me with chicken noodle soup. I had not eaten anything like it since our home had been destroyed, which at that point accounted for almost half of my life. I ate the soup with great appetite, all the time saying how good it tasted. As I ate, I continued talking to the girls, who never ceased asking me questions about my past, where my parents were, and if I had any siblings. When I finished eating, I told them that I had a brother in Russia, and that I did not know where he lived.

The moment I said that I had a brother in Russia and that I did not know where he was, a guest came over to me and asked for additional information about my brother. I told him that he had managed to flee to Russia right after the death march from Chelm and Hrubieszow, and that since he fled to Russia I had received only one postcard from him, which was after we had already moved into the ghetto. I told him that the postcard had said that he was in Siberia, and that my mother had cried when she heard that. When I finished telling the man about my life, he told me that Stalin could help us locate my brother. All we needed to do was to send a postcard to Stalin, who would certainly be able to find my brother and tell me where he was. As I had nothing to write on and no stamp, I asked my hosts to provide me with a postcard and a stamp to enable me to find my brother. When I returned to the family's house the next day, a postcard was already waiting for me on the table. Because I did not know Russian, they found someone to write it for me. In Yiddish, I dictated the following words:

Dear Comrade Stalin: I, Fela Rozensztajn from Hrubieszow, am looking for my brother Nathan Rozensztajn in Russia. I very much hope you will find him, because he is all I have.

We addressed the postcard to: Comrade Stalin, Moscow, Russia. Back then, those who survived the war and were saved by the Russians regarded their liberators as omnipotent, particularly Comrade Stalin. As a young girl, I believed in our Russian heroes with all my heart. Nonetheless, I am still awaiting an answer to my postcard.

During that visit, the woman who was hosting me told me about an office that had been opened near their house in order to provide assistance to Jewish survivors. She was told that the office distributed sugar and soap, and she encouraged me to take advantage of the opportunity and to visit

From right to left: Gittel and Leibel Zuberman, Rivka, Fela, and Mendel Rozensztajn, aunt Chayele, (---), (---), Mechel. Standing: Chana Zuberman, (---), Itsche Zuberman

179

the office, where they would also put my name on a list of survivors. She complained that families were not receiving the same assistance, as most had returned from Russia and were for the most part managing to get by. They were not completely without possessions, like the survivors from Poland. During the days following the war, Poland lacked all types of commodities, including such basic things as food, clothing, and shoes. Under the circumstances, sugar was as valuable as gold. Not only had the Germans removed everything from Poland, but the commerce in which the Jews had played an active role prior to the war had also ground to a halt, as the Jews were no more. All the stores that had been owned by Jews were now closed and the Poles had not yet gotten back on their feet. Perhaps the Russians were also not permitting them to re-establish their economy. In those days, it was extremely difficult to find basic food.

The next day, I told the orphanage director that I would be eating lunch at the home of the Jewish family. After lunch, I went to the office that provided assistance to Jewish survivors. A long line stretched out in front of the office, and the place looked like a rowdy meeting place for Jews. I was surprised by the number of Jews who were there, as until that point I had not been aware of their existence. Dozens of people who knew Yiddish wandered around the courtyard, and I was truly astonished to see so many Jews in the same place at the same time. How had I not known that they were living in Lublin? How had nobody told me about them until I met the kind woman who invited me to her home? The man who sent me to the Polish orphanage, who I believe was Dr. Emil Sommerstein, also had not told me about the other Jews. I was extremely moved by the sight of so many Jews, and after I calmed down a bit, I took my place in line to receive my allocation of sugar and soap, just like the adults.

180

11. My Meeting with Rafael and the Turning Point

As I stood in line among the masses of other Jews, I noticed a man who appeared to be taking a special interest in me. He moved closer to me and looked at me and then moved away again. I was wondering what he wanted when he suddenly came over to me, turned me around so that I was looking directly at him, and stared at me wide-eyed. Tell me, he said, are you by chance from Hrubieszow?

Yes, I answered quickly, my heart racing now as I began to try to figure out the identity of this unfamiliar man who nonetheless knew me and was so excited to see me.

Tell me, he continued, are you by any chance the daughter of Mendel Rozensztajn?

Yes, I said again, more excited now, and much more curious to know just who this man was.

You don't know who I am? he asked.

No, I answered. Who are you? Instead of answering me, he began to weep hysterically. From my part, I was quite excited by the fact that someone finally knew me. Who are you? I asked again. Are you Uncle Hershel, back from Russia? I asked, wondering deep down if Uncle Hershel could have changed so much in so short a time. The man standing before me looked nothing like how I remembered my uncle.

Still crying, the man pulled me out of the line. We stood there for some time, with him crying and me just standing beside him. Emotionally moved but still unsure who he was, I repeated my question: Who are you? Again, he was unable to answer through his tears. Eventually, I grew impatient and demanded to know who he was with greater force: Who are you?! I repeated again. Tell me already! Still crying, he took my hand and we moved further away from the crowd and found an empty space by the door of a neighboring building, which had a wide threshold to sit on. We both sat down, and he continued weeping. All he could do in response to my repeated question was to ask me over and over again if I was sure I did not remember him. Finally, I too broke down and started to cry.

We sat there and cried until he finally regained his composure, wiped his tears, and asked: Do you remember Shmuel Gertel?

Yes, he's my friend Chaimke's father.

You don't remember that I used to work in Gertel's bicycle shop? he asked now, and I told him that I did not. My name is Rafael, he told me finally. I used to work in Gretel's store, which was right across from your shoe store. I was friends with your brother Nathan. I truly did not remember him, even though I used to go into Gretel's bicycle shop with Chaimke, who sometimes let me ride his tricycle. I assume I had no memory of Rafael because Gretel's store employed a number of boys, and at my age they were certainly of no interest to me. After I learned who he was, and after both of us recovered somewhat from our chance meeting, Rafael told me that he had just returned from Russia with Shmuel Gertel and that they were living in Hrubieszow. If I wanted to, he told me, he would be willing to take me there. Indeed, this is all I had been waiting for since I left the peasants house in the village.

Yes, of course! I cried, without hesitation, jumping at the opportunity. I can also tell Gertel what happened to his wife Bella and his son Chaimke, I told Rafael. My father made a promise to Gertel that if Gertel managed to escape to Russia, he would look after Gretel's wife and son until they were able to join him in Russia. And that's what he did.

When I told Rafael that I wanted to return to Hrubieszow with him, I also explained that I first needed to inform the Polish orphanage that I wanted to leave and why. For me, it was important to be up-front and honest with the people at the orphanage. I also wanted to thank the wonderful family I had met for taking me in and feeding me every day and for their kindness, and to tell them that I had found someone to take me to Hrubieszow. After we agreed on the various arrangements that needed to be made before leaving Lublin, I got back in line to get into the office of the Jewish committee. When my turn came and I entered the office, I found a man sitting behind a large wooden desk who wrote down my name and some of the things I had been through during the war. Then, they gave me the bag of sugar, which I, in turn, gave to the Jewish family that had taken me in. The soap, however, I kept for myself.

From there, Rafael and I went to the orphanage director to inform her that I would be leaving. It was then that I learned that she had another office in addition to her office in the orphanage, and that is where I was directed this time. When we arrived at her office, she received us from behind a large desk, elegantly dressed as usual. A warm smile appeared on her face when she saw me. After saying hello, I introduced her to Rafael and told her that I wanted to leave the orphanage in order to travel with Rafael back to Hrubieszow, my home town, where a friend of the family was now living. She turned to Rafael and began asking him a series of questions: who he was, how he knew me, and whether he could handle such a large responsibility. She then told him that she clearly could not let him take me without his signature. Rafael of course did not hesitate to sign his name and take responsibility for me. Then, I said goodbye and we left the office. I have nothing but fond memories of that orphanage director. She was a pleasant, sensitive woman, and even though she was a devout Christian, she never displayed even the slightest trace of racism toward me.

How Rafael managed to get hold of a coachman with a horse and carriage I will never know. In addition to the dress I had been wearing since Majdanek, I was now wearing a light sweater I had acquired at some point, although I cannot remember how or when. That afternoon we left Lublin, a city to which I would subsequently return. The narrow carriage was padded with straw, which made the endless bumpy ride slightly more comfortable. As it got late, after it was already dark, we arrived at a village. Rafael paid the coachman, who quickly disappeared. I was again surprised when it turned out that Rafael knew a peasant who produced laundry soap, and we spent the night at his home.

Initially, I wondered how he knew how to handle such arrangements as well as he did. However, as time passed I learned that he had made this trip a number of times, and that is how he knew where we could pay for a place to sleep in that particular village. The peasant and his wife lay a few jackets down on the floor, and that is where we slept. According to Rafael, the village was situated half-way between Lublin and Hrubieszow. We left early the next morning and walked a long way by foot. We then caught a ride with another horse and carriage, with which we continued until it got dark. When the coachman told Rafael that we had to get off, Rafael started looking for a place to sleep. I remember nothing about where we slept the second night. All I know is that it takes about an hour or an hour and a half to travel from Lublin to Hrubieszow by car, and the trip took us three days. When we reached Hrubieszow, it was already midday.

It suddenly hit me that I was in Hrubieszow and that I was no longer frightened to walk freely through the streets. Although the streets and the houses were all very familiar to me, it was strange when I realized that all the shops that once belonged to Jews were now closed and that new people, certainly non-Jews, now lived in the houses where Jews had previously lived. This was the case when we passed my house as well. As we walked, Rafael told me that only a few dozen Jews had managed to return to the city since it had been liberated from the Germans, most of who had advanced with the Red Army and entered the city with the soldiers themselves. Those Jews found places to live in a number of small apartments with a common courtyard. Actually, this was the courtyard where my uncle Yitzchak's house was located. It was a closed courtyard that could only be entered through an enormous gate, which was large enough to fit a horse and carriage on snowy and rainy days. Some of the Jews who returned to Hrubieszow, including the Orenstein brothers, found apartments in other areas.

12. Living with Gertel

When we arrived at the apartment in which Gertel was living, Rafael asked me to wait outside for a few minutes so he could tell Gertel he had found me. He was concerned about how Gertel would react to suddenly seeing me, without being forewarned. But I had not been waiting long when all of a sudden Gertel swung open the door yelling, Faygeleh! How did you survive? He examined me carefully from head to toe, unable to believe his eyes. For him, I was an incomprehensible miracle. Immediately, he blurted out the question that had preoccupied him throughout his long stay in Russia: What happened to Chaimke and Bella? he asked. Come inside. We'll go in, and you'll tell me about it. We were both quite moved and we both wept, as Rafael looked on, wiping the tears of emotion that he too cried while witnessing our meeting. Until I arrived, Gertel had been trying with all his might, but in vain, to discover what had happened to his family, of which there were no survivors. He was so impatient and emotional that it was difficult to answer all his many questions. Until I arrived, most of the Jews who had returned to Hrubieszow had come back from Russia, and the few Jews who had actually survived the Holocaust somewhere and returned to Hrubieszow did not know Gertel's family and knew nothing about the fate of his wife and son. Of the forty people who had lived in our hideaway, I was the only one still alive.

Despite our fatigue after three days of traveling the difficult route to Hrubieszow, and the great excitement that overcame all three of us, Gertel, Rafael, and I sat down together, and I started to tell Gertel the circumstances in which Bella and Chaimke joined us in the hideaway. I told him how we were all there together, how we sat close to each other, and how we had left the hideaway and spent two or three days hiding at the cemetery. Today, I can no longer recall if I told Shmuel Gertel everything that had happened while we were in the hideaway together, but I did tell him that Bella and Chaimke had definitely been killed. They were buried somewhere in the Jewish cemetery in a mass grave along with Leibel, Gittel, and Chana Zuberman, and another thirty people from Hrubieszow whose identities I can no longer remember.

In those days, during the period immediately following liberation, the number of Jews in Hrubieszow increased on a daily basis. They included

Jews who had survived the Holocaust without getting sent to the gas chambers and Jews who had returned from Russia. It started to get somewhat crowded in the apartments, and one day Shmuel Gertel's friend Yechezkel Drucker and his wife found a vacant apartment on Jatkowa Street. Once again, I was living in Jatkowa, where the camp had been located during the war. The house to which the Drucker family moved was located just across from the house that had served as Dr. Orenstein's office in the camp during the war.

Gertel, Rafael, and I moved into the apartment with them. It was located in a two-story structure in which the ground floor consisted of one large room, which was still occupied by Poles. The first floor consisted of one apartment with a bedroom and a very spacious kitchen. The Drucker family slept in the bedroom, and Gertel and Rafael slept on two small iron beds in the corner of the kitchen. The dinner table stood opposite the door. As a bed for me, they pushed the seats of two chairs together and padded them with everything soft in the apartment they could find. As a blanket, they gave me a coat they found in the house. There was no running water, and dirty dishes were washed in a bowl of water. There was also no place to bathe and no place for washing hair. Taking into consideration the extremely modest conditions in which we lived, we managed reasonably well. After a short time my head began to itch, as did my entire body. I never once even suspected that lice were running rampant all over my body.

One day, I was awakened by Mrs. Drucker, who was extremely kind and gentle with me. She told me that she had noticed that I had been scratching myself a great deal and that I had better check my dress, which I wore day and night, for lice. Indeed, when I took off my dress and checked it, I found that lice were having a field day in its seams: not one louse or a few lice, but rather a long, densely packed line moving along the upper seams of my dress. I was shocked by what I saw. When I told Mrs. Drucker that I had found masses of lice in my dress, she instructed me to wash the dress in water which she would boil for me. She took the bowl in which she usually bathed, filled it with water, and brought it to me along with some soap. It was the first time I bathed and washed my hair in a long time, and it turned out that my hair was full of lice as well. Mrs. Drucker took her time combing my hair with a fine tooth comb in order to get rid of the lice. I washed my dress a few times in boiling water, until I was certain that all the lice were dead. However, some time later, festering wounds appeared on my head and my body, and especially between my fingers. As it turned out, they were caused by scabies, which caused scars that remained with me for more than half a century, particularly between my fingers.

Gertel bought me a black cream that was very difficult to find in the pharmacy that before the war had been owned by Jews but which had now been re-opened by a Polish pharmacist. However, none of my health problems prevented me from making friends with the Polish children who lived in the neighborhood. When I first met them, they did not bother me because I was Jewish and I played with them like all the other kids. However, one day, in the midst of an argument about a holiday, one of the kids told me that the Jews had murdered Jesus. When the other kids heard this, they started to yell at me angrily: Zyduvka (Jew)! As I still did not know much about history, I was shocked to hear that we had killed Jesus. When I got home to the apartment, I asked Mr. Drucker and Gertel with great concern why the Jews killed Jesus. It was then that I learned that Jesus was actually Jewish, and this confused me even more. The next day, I went back to the kids, and told them that Jesus was actually Jewish, like me. They were shocked as well. Of course, most did not believe me. That couldn't be true, they said. In any event, we continued to play together.

As I already said, the house on Jatkowa Street in which I lived with Gertel and the Drucker's was located not far the river. One day, I finally got a new dress, which had been sewn for me by a Polish seamstress who had managed to occupy one of the vacant Jewish houses in Jatkowa and with which I was quite pleased. A few days later, the other kids invited me to go boating on the river. I initially refused to take part in the adventure, explaining that I did not want to get my new dress dirty. However, I did not realize that it was precisely when the kids saw me in my new dress that they decided to play a trick on the Zyduvka. We boarded the boat and once we had reached the middle of the river, they started jumping up and down in the boat and tipping it on its side. I was the only one who fell in the water while all the other kids remained safe and dry in the boat. When they saw me in the water, they burst out laughing. I was actually quite lucky that the water was shallow, because I did not know how to swim. Had it been much deeper, I could have drowned. Although

187

I was drenched from head to toe and upset that my new dress had gotten soaked in the river, I was most deeply hurt by the fact that I had trusted the other kids and they had betrayed me. I went home crying, and that was the end of my relationship with the Polish kids in the neighborhood.

Each day that passed brought new developments. In the meantime, the apartment on the ground floor had been vacated, apparently because the Poles living there did not want to live in an area completely surrounded by Jews. Rafael again disappeared, as he had many times before, and Gertel said that he apparently traveled to Russia from time to time for an unknown reason. It was only years later, after I was already living in Israel, that I learned that Rafael was in Hashomer Hatzair and had been serving as the movement liaison with members in Russia, and that that was why he traveled there periodically in such a secretive manner. For this reason, Gertel and I moved to the ground floor apartment without him. Because the apartment only had one bed, we both slept together in the same bed, like a father and daughter. One day, after we had become extremely attached to one another, he told me that he wanted to officially adopt me and he asked me to call him father. At that point, it was clear to me that I would remain with Gertel. After all, since the march from Majdanek when I was separated from my aunt, my uncle, and my cousin, about whom I still had no news, he was all I had. Nonetheless, I could not call him father. If I were to call you father, I explained, I would constantly think of my own father. I love you Gertel, but it would be difficult for me to call you father. Not enough time has passed since I saw him last. He repeated his request a few times, but I continued calling him Gertel, as an endearing nickname. I hoped with all my heart that my father was still alive.

Gertel made sure I had everything I needed. When the days grew cold, he found me a good, warm coat in a second-hand market. In time, he also decided that I should begin attending school. Mr. Golombek, the principal of the Polish school that my two brothers had attended before the war, knew my family well. He was moved by the mere fact that I had survived, and he was pleased to enroll me in the third grade. I was the only Jewish child in the entire school, which was no simple matter. I was also quite frightened to walk there alone. The school was located somewhat of a distance from Jatkowa, and at times I quickened my pace when I saw boys walking behind me so that they could not catch up with me. Despite the difficulties and distrust I felt for Polish children, I made friends with a few Polish girls who sometimes invited me to visit them in their homes. Once, during such a visit before Christmas, they showed me some colored eggs and some sheep made of sugar that their family had made for the holiday. It was just like in Bethlehem, in Palestine, the girls explained. I did not understand how the sheep and the colored eggs were connected to Palestine, and the Polish girls could not explain it either. It was the first time I had ever heard such a thing.

Many of the Jews who had succeeded in the difficult undertaking of escaping into Russia began to trickle back into Poland, and a few families even returned to Hrubieszow. Not all of them had come from Hrubieszow, however, and I of course did not ask why they came there, of all places. One of the families who returned to the city was the Katzhandel family, with their three daughters. Mania, the middle daughter, became a very close friend of mine. We were soon joined by another girl who was not originally from Hrubieszow, but who had returned from Russia with her father and her four year old brother, whom she cared for as if she were his mother. We were three eleven and twelve year old Jewish girls in a city that before the war had been largely Jewish in character and culture. We used to spend time together after school, particularly Mania and I. As I was not able to invite her to my house and as Manias house had everything a home should have, we spent a lot of time at her house with her family. Whenever I came to their house, Mania's mother always offered me something good to eat. Mania's younger sister Sarah also used to spend time with us, and, although we had no toys, we always managed to keep ourselves busy somehow. Our most enjoyable pastime was buying Napoleon cakes at a store that had opened up in the center of town.

As the days passed, a thin stream of Jews continued to flow into Hrubieszow. One day, three Jewish women arrived in the city: an older woman and two young women in their twenties. One of the young women was somewhat shy and had blonde curly hair. The other was a friendly, pretty woman with large brown eyes and blondish-brownish hair who came to Hrubieszow with the older woman, who was her aunt. I knew very little about them and nothing about their past. All I knew was that they arrived together. The handful of Jews that gathered in Hrubieszow immediately following the war created a new Jewish existence in the city.

Everyone knew that Hrubieszow was not their last stop, and because many people arrived on their own only to learn that their families had been killed and their homes had been occupied by Poles, they had no other choice but to live together. The most important thing was to find a place to live, and this is why couples and singles lived together in vacant apartments that had not yet been occupied by Poles. No one kept kosher any more, but rather ate whatever they were able to buy. They were simply happy to find food.

They also did not have a great deal of money. This situation, in which groups of individuals lived communally like families, often led to intimate relations and makeshift weddings. During such weddings, the apartments in which they took place had an air of festivity, despite the poor everyday conditions in which people were living at the time. Refreshments were minimal and the rabbi, who was simply someone from the community who volunteered to serve as a rabbi for the moment, was symbolic. All in all, such celebrations typically seemed somewhat unnatural. Gertel remarried in this manner, some time after I told him what had happened to his wife and son after the Germans discovered our hideaway and he knew for certain that he was a widower.

During the day, everyone was busy with their own affairs, but the evenings facilitated the emergence of a new Jewish life in which a handful of people would meet at someone's home and talk. During these gatherings, Gertel took special notice of the new woman with brownish-blondish hair, whose name was Sarah, and asked me to pass her a note saying that he would like to meet her alone. After Gertel read her response, I could see by the disappointed look on his face that she had declined his advance. But Gertel was not the only one who was disappointed. So was I. I liked the look of Sarah and I liked her openness. A few days later, Gertel asked me to deliver another note, this time to Matilda, the blonde woman, and the response was positive. For a few days, I delivered messages between the two until they decided to meet regularly. Just before the relationship between Gertel and Matilda began, Gertel's sister and brother-in-law arrived from Russia and of course came to live with us in our one room apartment.

All four of us now lived together in the same room, and within a day they improvised a bed for them. They had returned from Asiatic Russia, which to me sounded quite exotic. They brought pomegranate seeds wrapped in cloth inside a cardboard box, which they carried with them the entire trip. This was the first time I ever saw or tasted such a strange fruit. I was truly astounded by the seeds red color and slightly sour taste. I had not met Gertel's sister and brother-in-law before the war,   and for me it was like meeting strangers. However, it was not long before I became friendly with them. Gertel had told them about me.

On most days, we ate our meals in the home of the Drucker family, and this included all the occupants of the room downstairs. Much of the food, it appears, had been brought by villagers when they came to the apartment to purchase merchandise from Gertel and Drucker. Clearly, I had nothing to do with business matters in the house, aside from opening the door and greeting visitors when they knocked. I also sometimes sipped some of the vodka that was served to villagers upon their arrival, that is, until Mrs. Drucker noticed what I was doing and forbade me to drink. In the meantime, the meetings between Gertel and Matilda continued and increased in frequency. After some time had passed, they announced their intention to get married.

The wedding took place in the downstairs apartment. Mrs. Drucker cooked a large pot of meat and potatoes for the occasion, and there was no ceremonial canopy. The wedding was attended only by witnesses, who toasted the bride and groom and wished them mazal tov! Not only did the couple not have a honeymoon, but they were not even able to be alone on their wedding night, because neither I, nor Gertel's sister and brother-in-law, nor the other young man who arrived that night had another place to sleep. Neither did the young couple.

The day after the wedding, Matilda fell extremely ill, and nobody knew what to do. Eventually, Gertel asked me to go call the Jewish doctor who came to Hrubieszow from time to time and lived on the other side of town. I went to the doctor's house with a note from Gertel, but although he came to our apartment to examine her, he did not prescribe any medicine because there was none on hand. Matilda remained sick in bed for many days, and we were all worried about her, especially Gertel. Right after Gertel got married, they made me a new bed in a corner of the room, and when Matilda got back on her feet again, we were all relieved. I continued to go to school, but after school I usually went to

Mania's house. I told Mania everything that was on my mind, including my feelings about Gertel's marriage. Although for me he was still the same Gertel he had always been, I nonetheless felt somewhat like a third wheel. After all, what was I supposed to do with two people who just got married? In the meantime, they began to build a life together, and one day they told me that they had decided to leave Hrubieszow and to move to Lublin.

At that point, the movement of survivors from place to place was at its height. Everyone who returned to the city only to find that all their family members were dead and that their homes had been occupied stayed around for a bit and then moved on to other destinations. During the first few months after the liberation of Hrubieszow, most survivors flocked to Lublin, because it held the largest number of Jewish survivors. In the meantime, even before we moved, I had also learned that, while I was in Hrubieszow, a Jewish orphanage had opened in Lublin. The Jewish orphanage housed all the Jewish orphans from the area that had been liberated by the Red Army, including children who were partisans and children who had hidden with Poles.

13. THE ORPHANAGE OF THE RED CROSS AND THE JEWISH COMMUNIST COMMITTEE

As soon as Gertel told me that they were gong to Lublin, I asked their permission to join the orphanage. This would relieve them of the burden of taking care of me, and I felt that it would be best for them to live as a new couple, without me. After Gertel got married, I began to feel somewhat uncomfortable, as if I was in the way. After all, Matilda only met me after the war. Gertel, however, was not easily convinced to let me go to the orphanage. He did not want me to leave him, and he asked me over and over again if I was certain that that is what I wanted to do, which I apparently was.

In the end, Gertel and Matilda came with me and registered me for the Jewish orphanage. However, I was completely unprepared for the great surprise that awaited me there. When I arrived, I was astounded and overjoyed to find all the children with whom I had been at Majdanek. I simply could not believe my eyes: they had survived as well! Nonetheless, I was ecstatic for two reasons: first, because they had survived, and second, because I had suddenly discovered a group of friends who had suffered as I had.

When I first came to the orphanage it already held almost 200 children, and my arrival brought joy to the children of Majdanek in particular. After all, they also had not known that I had survived, and they too were also extremely happy to see

Shmuel Gertel, Cipora, and Matel Gertel, Lublin 1945

me. I also had to forge new relationships with the other children, which I did not find especially difficult. The beds in the orphanage were bunk beds, and I was immediately given a top bunk when I arrived. The bunk beds stood in a large hall, the walls of which were lined with single bunks. To a certain extent, they resembled the bunks in the camps. According to my own calculations today, it seems that I first came to the orphanage in February 1945. The children from Majdanek were among the first to arrive at the orphanage immediately following the liberation of Lublin, and I am still amazed by the fact that Sommerstein was unaware of this. Why else would he have sent me to a Christian orphanage? In no time, they were joined by children from many different places. In the meantime, the children managed to get acclimated and started attending school, and the older kids began studying different vocations. By the time I arrived at the orphanage, the children already knew one another and had started to form close friendships, boys with boys and girls with girls. I, however, had to find my own way and to enroll in a new school. Since I had been liberated, this was the third school I would attend in less than one year.

The Polish orphanage had enrolled me in the third grade, even though I had never attended the first or second grade. Nonetheless, the teacher had pointed me out as a very good student. When I arrived in Hrubieszow, I asked on my own initiative to be enrolled in the third grade. However, when I entered the Jewish orphanage after returning to Lublin, the teachers there, and perhaps the director of the orphanage herself, decided to enroll me in the fourth grade. The reason for this, it seems to me, was purely technical: as there was no space in the third grade in the middle of the year, I was placed in the fourth grade.

When I first entered the classroom, I realized that there were no children from the orphanage. Again, I was the only Jewish girl in the class, which made me feel very insecure. In contrast to my previous experience, my new class frightened me terribly. I was unable to concentrate, and I was especially intimidated by our math lessons, which were totally incomprehensible to me. There was no one in class I could turn to for help, and sometimes, when I told the educators at the orphanage that I was having difficulties at school, they added fuel to the fire by telling me that I simply needed to try harder. I was glad when the school year ended and the orphanage threw an end of the year party. The exceptional students were seated around a long, beautifully set table, and as a reward for their excellence, they were served plates of strawberries and cream, which was then considered a great delicacy!

The weak students, which included me, sat around a plain table. During her end of the year speech, the principal emphasized that the good students had been served strawberries and cream as a reward for their efforts, while the students who had not made an effort deserve nothing at all! For me, this was more than a stinging insult. I had not asked to be enrolled in the fourth grade, and I simply got lost there. Moreover, I started school in the middle of the year, only a month or two before the end of the year. Overall, I felt that her insulting attitude was unjustified.

Things were quite lively in the orphanage. New kids would join us from time to time, each with a terrifying story of their own. I remember two children who were brought to the orphanage in particular. The first was Dorotka, who had been found in the street by the Poles during the war with a note attached to her that said: Dorotka is seven months old. Although she was already four years old when she came to the orphanage, she could not yet walk or speak. All she could do was sit up. She was an unattractive girl with a face full of freckles and a shrill voice. Her strange appearance and behavior actually aroused in the girls a sense of motherliness and a desire to care for her. Indeed, we all took it upon ourselves to take care of her at different times. The fact that a four year old girl still could not talk made us extremely sympathetic and we wanted to help. After less than one year at the orphanage, she began to walk and her speech improved.

The second child I remember was well-dressed and approximately my age and did not look Jewish at all. She arrived with a Polish woman whom I remember quite clearly. The girl held on tight to the woman's hand and absolutely refused to enter the orphanage. A group of kids, mostly girls, including me, stood outside and tried to convince the girl to join us, but to no avail. When the Polish woman realized that there was no chance of convincing the girl to enter the orphanage, they said goodbye and left. We were a bit insulted that the girl did not want to join us. When we were already in Pietrolesie, the woman and the girl returned. This time, she went inside without any difficulty, and as time passed, she became involved in the social life of the orphanage and was quite popular. I admired her in particular.

After I entered the orphanage, I saw Gertel and Matilda once or twice. However, as time passed we lost touch for a long period of time, for in the meantime they had moved to Lodz.

After the city of Lodz was liberated from German occupation, Jewish survivors made their way there in droves. Now, Lodz became the major destination for survivors. After returning to Lublin and moving to the orphanage, I renewed my relationship with the family that had adopted me when I had been in the Polish orphanage, where I used to go to eat and to play with their daughters. I went to visit them once or twice, but they expected me to visit them more often, as I had done before. When I explained that I was unable to visit them as frequently as I had when I was in the Polish orphanage, they made it clear that they thought I was being ungrateful. I felt very bad about it all, but I truly was unable to leave the orphanage so frequently.

At the orphanage, there were periodic outbreaks of different strange illnesses. At one point, most of us had come down with the flu, including me. In order to prevent infecting all the children in the orphanage, they found a separate apartment for us on a different street. As far as I can remember, we were treated by nuns, who were also nurses. One day, while I was still sick in bed, I was stunned when my aunt Fayga and my cousin Tema walked into the room! There is no dictionary in the world that contains the words necessary to describe the emotion that gripped me during this reunion.

Crying appeared to be a good release for the burden of the tragedy that all the survivors carried with them deep in their heart. That is what we did during the sudden unexpected reunion. We cried. They did not know I had survived until they arrived in Lublin. They apparently learned about me from the Jewish Committee, which had registered me when I was still living in the Polish orphanage and I went to receive my allocation of sugar and soap. Until the moment they walked into the makeshift infirmary, I of course had no idea what had happened to them after I collapsed on the road during the march. After our initial emotions subsided somewhat and we were able to stop crying, I told them what had happened to me and they told me about themselves, how they had continued walking and were eventually put on a train to Auschwitz. From there, they were transferred to different camps in Germany. In one of the camps, they were separated from Uncle Yitzchak, who was sent to Mauthausen where he died from overeating two days after the camp was liberated by the Americans.

For them, Lublin was merely a stop on their way to Hrubieszow. They apologized that they could not take me with them at that point, because they had no money and no place to live. They first wanted to get to Hrubieszow and find an apartment, they told me, and then they would come and get me. I gladly accepted their apology, as I was sick and the orphanage was taking good care of me. I felt relatively settled with the children with whom I had managed to make friends by that point, and the fact that I at least had an aunt and a cousin made me very happy. They continued on to Hrubieszow, perhaps hoping to return to their home. When they got there, however, their home was nowhere to be found. It had been destroyed. In the meantime, I returned to the orphanage.

One day, we were informed that the entire orphanage was going to visit Majdanek. I was still weak, probably from the flu, and going back to Majdanek was the last thing I wanted to do at the time. Although I asked to be exempted from the trip as I truly felt that I did not need to visit there, my efforts were in vain. Almost a year had passed since I left Majdanek, and when I returned to tour the site as a free child, I noticed that many things had been changed. The pile of hair was no longer located where it had been when I had worked with some of the other children drying laundry in the gas chamber. Faded colored articles of clothing were scattered in disarray, and all in all the camp looked different than it had been when I was confined there as a prisoner.

Perhaps that was because I now saw things from a distance and was no longer in fear of the Germans. When I returned from the trip to the orphanage, I again fell ill. This time I was exhausted as well. It was the same exhaustion that struck me during the march from Majdanek, and I was barely able to climb up to my bunk. The educators thought I was faking the illness, and the children also looked at me suspiciously, as if I were just acting spoiled. I was alone. I felt abandoned and lonely, and I also thought that the staff was not giving me the sympathy I needed in my state. I needed some attention, and I was not receiving any at all.

Life in the orphanage flowed like a rough river, and there was no time for self pity. The problem of acquiring clothing for the children was extremely serious. All the children who came to the orphanage from the partisans, the hideaways, and Polish families arrived only with what they had on their backs, which was usually tattered and torn. In her memoirs, Mrs. Natanblut, the director of the orphanage, wrote the following:

Every day, new people would arrive at the Red Cross [the orphanage was run under the auspices of the Red Cross] dressed in tatters, some in Russian uniforms, fur hats, and ropes instead of belts. There were also women whose entire bodies were wrapped in blankets and whose legs were wrapped in rags, newspapers and ropes. The children from Majdanek came here.

The first money to support the most basic daily activities at the orphanage was provided by the Polish government, the Joint, and other public organizations. Private individuals also often made generous donations. Nonetheless, the money was not enough to pay for clothes for the children. However, even if there had been money, stores were not open and had no merchandise, as most of the clothing stores before the war had belonged to Jews. After their owners were murdered, the stores of course did not reopen, and the Polish authorities had not yet managed to gain control of the economic situation that resulted from the war's end. As the irony of fate had it, the creative solution for clothing the children of the orphanage was to send a few of the older kids to the laundry facilities at Majdanek concentration camp (where I had worked as a prisoner) on the outskirts of the city, to select clothes that would be suitable for children. They were garments that had been left behind by Jewish victims. In her memoirs, Mrs. Natanblut recounted how they found clothing for the children:

The Jewish Committee sent volunteers to the clothing warehouse at Majdanek to choose things that could be used in the orphanage. It was a huge warehouse with no windows, and it was filled up to the ceiling. The boys were astounded by the mountains of heavy shoes, boots, new children's shoes, elegant women's shoes, sandals, and more .

The number of children in the orphanage was always changing, with new children arriving every day. Some brought skin problems and lice, while others were simply ill as a result of malnutrition and medical neglect. For this reason, a strong, domineering woman who we referred to as Mrs. Doctorova was added to the orphanage staff. Although I am not at all certain that she was a doctor, we gave her the nickname because of her health and sanitation-related role in the orphanage. Mrs. Doctorova was extremely energetic and accustomed to being in command. But despite her domineering nature, the children knew that she was concerned about their health. This was especially true of the girls, from whom she demanded strict adherence to sanitary rules which often resulted in scandals. In one hall, she set up two quarantine rooms. Mrs. Doctorova fought scabies and eczema, and, despite the lack of proper medicine, she achieved results.

Some of the children in the orphanage were frightened and sensitive, but others were heroes who fought with the partisans, side by side with the adults. They were not scared of anything. The children went to the public school. In each class there were only a few Jewish children among the predominantly Polish student population, and fights broke out periodically between the Polish majority and the Jewish minority. Usually, the reason for these fights was pure anti-Semitism. However, the courage of our older boys typically enabled them to overcome their fear, and they often ended up fighting back against the Poles twice as hard. In some cases, the local police were forced to break up fights. Stones were sometimes thrown at the windows of the orphanage, and the staff always made sure to re-establish calm. In the meantime, new children continued arriving from all over Poland, and the orphanage became very crowded. The solution was a larger building located in Lower Silesia.

14. THE MOVE TO PIETROLESIE

In September 1945, the orphanage in Lublin was moved to a town in Lower Silesia that had belonged to Germany prior to the war. After the war, however, it was returned to Poland. In German, it was known as Peterswaldau, which means Peter's Forest, but the Poles translated the town's name as Pietrolesie.

It took more than five hours to travel from Lublin to Pietrolesie by train. The cars with seats were already full by the time we arrived at the train station, and the director asked for a few volunteers to ride in a freight car with one of our counselors, a young man whose name I cannot recall. I volunteered along with four or five other children, and that is why after all these years, I still remember the trip to Pietrolesie as a positive experience. I really liked to sing, and I had a good voice. Since I had been liberated, I had fallen in love with Russian songs, and I learned and sang them along with the Polish songs that were also very popular with the children at the time. The moment the train pulled out of Lublin, the instructor sat down in the doorway of the train car with his legs dangling down, and I sat down next to him along with another child. Together, we started to sing. We traveled a long distance in song, passing through beautiful landscapes of planted fields, thick forests, and train stations in different cities. For me, it was all so new and refreshing. I still remember the views from the trip. The experience I had on the trip was so wonderful that I would not have minded if it had gone on forever.

When we arrived in Breslau (Wroclaw), the engine was replaced and two German nuns boarded the train. At that point, many Germans were still living in the region. When the nuns saw the children in the car they did not dare enter, and instead sat outside the car in a little space near the car door. However, a few of our boys noticed them. Making their way toward them, they began to harass them and to shout derogatory names until one of the adults intervened and put an end to the episode.

We had different types of experiences during the trip. For example, when we arrived in Lower Silesia we saw long, crowded lines of Germans walking with their heads covered, carrying their belongings on their backs. The sight of entire German families being expelled brought us

200

enthusiastically to our feet. Hooray! we yelled, applauding loudly. Today, after so many years have passed, it may be difficult to understand the fact that we regarded the Germans as the devil incarnate and the degree to which the desire to take revenge against them ran deep in our badly wounded souls. The people walking were the mass of Germans that were being expelled from Silesia to West Germany. What a cleansing sense of revenge it was and how the scarred hearts of the children rejoiced to see the Germans in their misery.

In Pietrolesie, we were awaited by an enormous, multi-story building with beds that had already been arranged in anticipation of our arrival. On the ground floor near the entrance was a giant hall, which subsequently became our dining room. Although we were told that the building had previously served as Gestapo headquarters for the city or the region, there are a number of conflicting stories regarding the use of the building during the war. The building was almost new, and was surrounded by a large courtyard and a well tended, fenced off garden. As we began to settle-in and the staff determined who would live with whom and in which rooms, I found myself with Sonia, who was one of the older, more serious girls in the orphanage, and another girl about fourteen years old. I was almost twelve years old at time, which made me the youngest. It appears that we were intentionally divided up in this manner, so that the older kids could look after the younger kids. I liked my two roommates. They both kept secret diaries. During our first days in the new building, before our lives assumed a regular schedule, we had free time. Looking for something to do, we went through cabinets in the cellar in which we found photographs of Hitler. We decided to make the German children step on his picture, spit on it, and finally tear it up. This was also part of our campaign for venting our revenge.

A few German families still lived on the street across from the new building. At the same time, a few members of the orphanage staff were looking for places to live, as they could not sleep in the orphanage. They found an apartment that still housed a German family, which was about to be deported. As I was friendly with one of the women who were looking for a place to live, I went with her one day to the apartment when it was still furnished. Inside, there was a table covered with a tablecloth with the Hebrew word Shabbat embroidered on it. For us, this was proof that the Germans knew what was being done to the Jews of Europe. After all, their belongings were divided up inside Germany.

For many of us, Pietrolesie was a breath of fresh air and helped heal our wounded souls. We arrived around the time that the Germans were being expelled and the Poles were taking their place. But the rulers at the time were the Russians. Although it was a small town, Pietrolesie had a charming movie theatre. The movies we saw there were all Russian, and the subject was always the same: battles between the German army and the Red Army, during which the German cowards always lost to the victorious Russian heroes. After the victory, while still on the front line, the Red Army soldiers would celebrate, breaking into song accompanied by a harmonica and dancing the Kozachok. As I explained, we longed to exact revenge upon the Germans at every possible opportunity, and the Russian films served as an exceptional psychological outlet for this purpose. Every time a German soldier died at the hands of a Russian soldier, we broke into applause. We were overjoyed every time the Russians were victorious on the front. For us survivors, the Red Army was the savior that had delivered us from evil, and we worshipped them.

Pietrolesie also had a beautiful Olympic-size swimming pool that became a major attraction for us, which we visited frequently. One episode I witnessed there stands out in my memory. The children of the orphanage were not the only ones to go to the pool. So did dozens of Red Army officers. Simple Germans from the town no longer went to the pool. The pool was surrounded by a spacious, well-tended lawn that was meant for a variety of athletic activities. A diving board overlooked the pool, and the female German athletes who still remained in Pietrolesie were intent upon impressing the Russian soldiers. This was especially true of one woman in particular, who may have once been an Olympic high diver. She would perform acrobatics in the pool while diving from the board which was high above the water. In this way, she hoped to impress the Red Army officers. One day, her efforts to impress them and meet them came to annoy a senior officer, who jumped into the water after her and truly tried to drown her. The woman barely made it out of the water alive, and this impressed us to no end. As always, the Russian officer was the hero in our eyes.

By this time, we no longer lacked clothing. Every few days, the orphanage would receive packages of children's clothing in very good condition. We did not know exactly where the clothes came from, but we assumed that they had been removed from the homes of Germans who had been deported, apparently to West Germany.

I cannot remember if the woman who was responsible for preparing our food was already with us in Lublin. She may have been, but in Lublin I never went into the kitchen, and I therefore had no way of knowing who was actually cooking the modest meals we had been served. However, in Pietrolesie, we discovered that she was actually a young woman with light, straight hair who was always meticulously dressed, and who regularly had a horse and wagon at her disposal. Every day, we would see her ride off somewhere with an empty wagon only to return later with packages of food that were immediately brought into the kitchen.

Another woman, who was thin and sickly in appearance, also joined the staff of the orphanage. She looked young, maybe in her twenties, and was a pale, frail woman who taught us table manners. Some examples included: the rule that a person eating soup from an almost empty bowl should tilt the bowl away from himself, not toward himself; how to tie a napkin in order to stay clean while eating; and eating with ones mouth closed. She was responsible for all our cultural activities. She also knew how to play the piano, and she organized plays and dances with us. We liked her, and I personally liked appearing in the plays she organized, as well as the dances.

A French teacher was brought in to teach us once or twice a week. Why French, of all languages I have no idea. We, the children, ridiculed her and made fun of her to no end. She was an older woman with somewhat red, curly hair. At the time, learning French was not exactly at the top of our agenda. During the same period, kibbutz groups from all the different Zionist youth movements, especially Hashomer Hatzair, started to appear in Silesia, especially near Pietrolesie, not far from the orphanage. The movements tried with all their might to teach us about Israel, Zionism, and pioneering, but they did so secretly, without the knowledge of the orphanage staff. Perhaps this was because they knew that the orphanage was operating under the auspices of the Jewish Communist Committee, whose representatives were going to great lengths to persuade us to stay in communist Poland where they claimed that a rosy future awaited us. As I was one of the younger kids, I certainly did not understand the ideological aspects of the issue. All I knew was that I had an aunt in Palestine who lived in Tel Aviv, and that a blue JNF box had hung in my house before the war. My father had been in close contact with his sister and helped her, as far as I can remember. She had visited us in Hrubieszow the year before the war broke out.

15. Back to Hrubieszow with Aunt Fayga

Despite the intense efforts which the members of the Jewish Communist Committee made to persuade us that our future was in Poland, the older kids in the orphanage had a clear understanding of the orientation of the Jewish Committee and often told the younger children whom they should listen to more. One day, all the children of the orphanage had gathered for a discussion with one of the heads of the committee who came to speak to us. His message was that we should not believe things we were told about Jews in Palestine! As we sat listening to him, one of the teenagers in the orphanage, I believe it was actually the oldest boy in the orphanage, stood up and gave the speaker an exuberant Zionist speech. After he finished speaking, we looked upon the boy with total admiration!

In the meantime, life in the orphanage was relatively comfortable. We opened the Polish elementary school in Pietrolesie, and during the first few weeks of school we were the only (ostensibly Polish) children in the classrooms. German children no longer attended the school. However, it did not take long before Poles began to populate the town, which had been completely emptied of its German population, and new Polish children began to fill the classrooms. I do not know where the Polish teachers for the different subjects came from, but all the teachers were now Polish. Although my memory on this point is unclear, it seems to me that I was again enrolled in the fourth grade. However, I did not remain in that school for long, because one day my Aunt Fayga and cousin Tema showed up at the orphanage to take me back to Hrubieszow. I did not really want to leave the orphanage, because, I was finally relatively happy there. Not only was it comfortable and not only did I receive attention, but there was a pool and a movie theatre, and, most, importantly, the other children with whom I had already grown close. But my aunt's conscience would not allow her to leave me in the orphanage, and she was so intent on convincing me to return to Hrubieszow with them that I eventually gave in. Again, I packed my few belongings and made the two day trip on different trains, which at that time were virtually the only form of comfortable, rapid transportation. When we arrived in Hrubieszow, my cousin's boyfriend, who lived in a temporary apartment, was already waiting for us.

The Red Army had solidly established itself in Poland, although members of Stefan Banderas radical right wing organization in Poland attacked the Red Army wherever it could, killing large numbers of Soviet soldiers. After a week in the temporary apartment in Hrubieszow, my aunt told me that if I were to go to the local Russian authorities and inform on the Gotlewskis – the Polish family to whom my father had given the store and who had informed on us to the Gestapo, collaborated with the Germans, and eventually became Volksdeutsche – the Russians would evict them from the house and return it to me.

One morning, my aunt took me aside and said: Let's go say hello to the Gotlewskis so that they know you are alive and that the house belongs to you. When we went up to the house, the door was opened by Mrs. Gotlewski herself. She knew me well from the beginning of the war, as it was then that they received the store from my father and that I, as a little girl, had spent so much time in the kitchen of the restaurant they ran for German soldiers in the city. When she saw me upon opening the door, her face went pale and she started to tremble. She immediately started to kiss and caress me and invited us into the house.

Then, in the most demeaning display of obsequious flattery possible, she started asking me if I needed anything or if I wanted a new dress, food, or anything else. Remembering well what they did to my parents, I was capable of doing little more than answering no, in a weak voice, to everything she offered. I said almost nothing, as I too was overcome with emotion by being in our house again, the house my parents had built. In that instant, my entire life flashed before my eyes. In her uncomfortable nervousness, it is quite possible that Mrs. Gotlewski nonetheless noticed that I was not especially happy about the reunion and that I was not tempted by the many generous offers with which she hoped to bribe me. After a very short time, we left the house. We had achieved our goal. The Gotlewskis knew that a member of the family was still alive, and they were reminded of who they were and what they had done.

Of course, I do not know what went on in the Gotlewski house after I left, but a day or two later my aunt and I went to the city municipality that was now run by the Russians. I told them the entire story of the Gotlewski family and I asked for our house back. In less than a week, the house was vacated, and my aunt, Tema, Itsche and I moved in. I cannot remember all the details, but I know that we found beds and a table. Soon after we settled in, we were joined by a family with two children that had returned from Russia. As time passed, more Jews returned from Russia, and the house gradually filled up with many people. Two families lived in our large living room, and we lived in the bedroom. A different family with two children lived in the dining room, which was the largest room in the house. Each family took turns using the kitchen to cook. Everyone tried to come to terms with the conditions in good spirits and understanding, and I do not recall any arguments between families.

Actually, aside from helping my aunt sell clothes in what had once been a crowded market but which was now an empty lot in which we were the only merchants, I had a lot of free time on my hands. One morning on the way to the market, I noticed long lines of people walking with work animals, wagons, and horses. Their wagons were filled with adults and children, and even chickens. When I asked passersby where all the people were going, I was told that they were Ukrainians from the nearby villages who were being deported to Russia. The same spectacle repeated itself each day, with the human procession lasting for almost a week. As an adult, I have never heard of another evacuation on such a scale, and I have never read about one in the history books. I find it astounding that we know nothing about the people who were deported and where they were taken. Could it be that an entire population was transferred without anyone remembering it?! I cannot recall if I felt compassion for them at the time. After all, they were Ukrainian, and the Ukrainians were much crueler to the Jews than the Germans were. We used to call the Ukrainian policemen ravens, because of the black uniforms that their soldiers and policemen wore. We feared them no less than we feared the Germans.

During my free time, I tried relatively unsuccessfully to learn how to teach myself to read Russian, with the help of other occupants of the house who had returned from Russia. In the meantime, I found another girl my age in addition to Mania, who still lived in the city, and we became friends. She also had returned from Russia with her father and her younger brother, and she lived in the Zuberman house, which had been the location of our hideaway during the action. I took advantage of my visits to her house in order to explore the hideaway, which was still as it had been during the war, in search of the photographs my father had hidden between the rafters and the ceiling. My efforts, however, were in vain. As I could not remember exactly where he had hidden them, it is quite possible that the photographs are still there, somewhere between the rafters and the ceiling.

I have not yet mentioned the fact that the first time I returned to Hrubieszow, to Shmuel Gertel and Yechezkel Drucker, I told them that when we lived with the Zubermans, my father had hidden fifty pairs of shoes in a niche that was meant for firewood. He had sealed off the niche with bricks so that they would be indistinguishable from the rest of the kitchen wall. Every time I mentioned the cache of shoes, both Gertel and Drucker used to say, the kid's just talking. Neither of them took me seriously, as they thought I was too young to remember such details. One day, we happened to be passing by the Zuberman house and I begged them to go knock on the door of the house, which was now occupied by Poles, and to ask permission to take apart the wall in the kitchen. I swore to them that I was telling the truth.

I remember! I insisted with such certainty that it was impossible to doubt my words. In the end, they gave in to my request.

Let's give it a try, they said. What do we have to lose?

We knocked on the door and explained the situation to the current occupants. We also promised them that if we found the shoes, we would give them one pair for each of their children. From the look on their faces, it was clear that they were disappointed that they had not found the cache themselves. It did not take much effort to remove the four bricks and to find the fifty pairs of shoes that had been hidden there before the war. In addition to the shoes, which at the time were worth their weight in gold due to the severe shortage of consumer goods, I basked in the praise of Gertel and Drucker. The kid was not just talking, they said, she knows. I was quite proud of myself as well! From the shoes we found, I picked out a pair of pumps, which were very fashionable before the war. We sold the rest, and I do not recall exactly what I did with the money, although I think I used some of it to buy food.

Although I remembered the cache of shoes, I forgot about another cache of valuables, which I could have found when I moved back into my parent's house. Many years after the war, during an emotional meeting in our home in New York, a woman who used to work in our store asked me if I had found the cache of valuables my father had hidden, now referring to a different hiding place. It was only then that I suddenly remembered that I had been present when my father had hidden all the valuables in the house. She had been there too, but she remembered the event, while I had forgotten it. Who knows? Perhaps the valuables are still hidden there today.

During my second stint in Hrubieszow after being liberated from Majdanek, I have no memory of attending school. The city had only a handful of Jews who were always moving around. Everything was temporary, and each day brought with it new surprises, like the sudden arrival of my cousin Golda from Lodz.

Golda, the daughter of my mother's sister, was not in Hrubieszow when the war broke out. Her family had moved to Lodz shortly before the beginning of the war, and she had survived along with the last remaining Jews in Lodz. She somehow found out that we had survived, as well, and she decided to come see us. Most of us wore extremely basic clothes, but Golda dressed differently, and much more elegantly. She was an extremely attractive woman, and she made quite an impression. She arrived in Hrubieszow wearing only the latest fashions. After the emotions of the unexpected reunion had subsided and after we each told our stories of how we had survived, Golda stayed with us for a few more days and then returned to Lodz.

During this period the mail was also not functioning properly, and of course, no Jew had a permanent address. Under these conditions, if someone wanted to write to someone, they wrote to the local municipality where that person lived. This was especially true of Jews who were in Siberia during the war and who knew nothing of the fate of their loved ones. One day, I was summoned to the municipality and handed a postcard bearing the name of my brother Nathan. When I got home, I was so excited that I yelled to my aunt: I have a brother! I have a brother! My brother, who was then in Asiatic Russia, had written to the municipality and had asked if any of his family members were still alive. I immediately responded, in Polish of course, and told him that I was alive. Because the mail was not yet functioning properly, it took a very long time for postcards and letters to be delivered. I waited impatiently for a letter back from him. When I received no response, I decided to write another postcard, thinking that perhaps the first one had gotten lost due to disruptions in the mail service.

Then, however, I realized that I had lost the postcard with his address on it, and I felt terrible. It was as if I had lost my brother all over again. I had no address to write to, and I waited a long time for a reply, quite impatiently I might add. I eventually received another postcard from my brother, and it turned out that he had received my postcard in which I told him that I was the only member of the family who survived.

In his second postcard, he suggested that I come join him in Russia, and I was dumbfounded by the strange proposal. I wrote him back, telling him that I would not go to Russia, and instead suggested that he come home, although to which house, I could not say. I justified my response by explaining that I did not want to travel to yet another foreign location. After I sent my response to my brother, I was so worried about losing his address again that I sewed the second postcard I received from him into the lining of my jacket.

Our apartment had come to resemble a center for all the scattered remnants of the Jewish population of Hrubieszow including those that survived the camps and those that returned from Russia. The first stop of anyone new in town was our house. One day, we were visited by a Jewish native of Hrubieszow, who was a soldier in the Jewish Brigade. He told us that he lived in Tel Aviv, and I told him that I had an aunt in Tel Aviv. After I told him her full name, we quickly realized that he knew my aunt well and that they actually lived relatively close to one another. The soldier told us that he would soon get leave to visit home and that he would, of course, be in Tel Aviv. I jumped at the rare opportunity and wrote a short letter to my aunt, informing her that most of my family had been killed but that I had survived, that I was living with an aunt from my mother's side of the family, and that I hoped to come to Palestine. I gave the postcard to the soldier from the Jewish Brigade, who promised to give it to my aunt when he arrived in Tel Aviv.

The soldier traveled to Palestine and then returned to Hrubieszow. However, he did not bring a reply from my aunt, and I was very disappointed.

210

I was usually not involved in the discussions regarding plans for the immediate future of my Aunt Fayga and her family. It was therefore only after they had decided to leave Hrubieszow that they told me that we would soon be moving to Lodz, which then constituted the location of the largest concentration of Holocaust survivors. Any future plans would be decided upon there. My Aunt Fayga told me there was nothing left for us in Hrubieszow.

None of the few Jews who survived the Holocaust even considered the possibility of remaining in Hrubieszow, or in Poland for that matter. The vast majority of Poles did not express sorrow for the terrible tragedy that had befallen their Jewish neighbors. Clearly, some were even disappointed that a few Jews had survived. Whether from greed or genuine hatred of Jews, the Poles would not be sorry to see the Jews gone for good.

16. Selling the House

Because we were such a small number of Jews and because we knew almost everything about one another, Mr. Wyszynski also learned of our imminent departure from Hrubieszow. Mr. Wyszynski was a Polish butcher whose shop was located next to our shoe store and who had known my parents well. During the period leading up to our move, a Jewish man, whose identity I cannot recall, informed me that Mr. Wyszynski was interested in buying the house and suggested that I sell it to him so that I would have some money to support myself. After all, he told me, we would never be returning to Hrubieszow. The man also told me that one of the Orenstein brothers who was living in town was an attorney, and that he and Orenstein would serve as my guardians for signing the sales agreement. I too understood that if we left Hrubieszow this time we would never return, and that is why I had no hesitations about selling the house.

On the day I sold the house, I remember ascending the stairs to the municipality office accompanied by the two men who were acting as my guardians in that context. They put the money that Mr. Wyszynski paid for the house in a bag, and when we got home they gave me the bag with all the money in it. The next day, while looking for something else in which to put the money, I found a small raffia suitcase with a lock and key in one of the stores, and I was pleased with my new purchase. I do not remember how much money I received for the house, but I do remember suddenly feeling rich! After receiving the money, I went to one of the few meat stores open in the city, bought some salami, made a sandwich, and enjoyed it immensely. From that point on for the duration of my wanderings, the money remained in the same suitcase and I did not waste any more of it. I guarded the suitcase carefully wherever I went, until uncle Hershel, my father's brother, arrived from Russia and I gave it all to him. At that point, I was already eleven and-a-half-years old.

Our preparations to move to Lodz did not take long, and we had to vacate the house in any event after I sold it. We each packed the few clothes we had and I took the suitcase holding the money, and we went to the train station. As I said, the train was virtually the only mode of transportation at the time. Back then, riding on the train was somewhat like taking the bus in Cairo: in addition to the people crammed into the car itself, there were also people sitting on the roof and hanging on to the doors outside. The peasants in the area also used the train to sell their produce, and most Polish citizens at that time were moving around constantly. It was therefore no simple matter to get a seat on a train. Nonetheless, we somehow managed to squeeze onto one of the cars, and we even had seats for some of the trip. The train windows were open and the gusting wind that blew through the car propelled a small piece of coal into my eye, causing it to swell up immediately. When we arrived in Lodz, I was taken directly to see an eye doctor.

Cipora's family home

A look from a distance at our family house in Hurbieszow (center building).

17. Life in Lodz and Joining Hashomer Hatzair

I have no idea how we found the tiny apartment into which we moved in Lodz. The four of us lived together in one room and the apartment was in the center of the city, an area with a good-sized Jewish population. These Jews, like us, had come from all over Poland and Russia. As far as I can remember, the apartment was located on Kilingskego Street.

After the Red Army entered Lublin in 1944, the main Jewish center developed in Lublin. By the next year, Jews were concentrated in Lodz. They began to open Jewish schools and the different Zionist youth movements established 'kibbutzim' that successfully attracted many young people. An enormous amount of Zionist activity actually took place at the train station in Lodz. Each day, youth movement members were sent to the train station to entice young people who were returning home after spending the war years in Russia (some had been taken to Russia to work in labor camps; others had crossed the border in an attempt to save their lives after the German invasion of Poland). Now, with the war ended, Polish Jews were leaving Russia in droves.

The Zionist movement representatives worked hard to convince young Jews that their organization had the right approach, and the convincing often took place on the streets of Lodz. I experienced this phenomenon first-hand.

After we settled in Lodz, my aunt registered me for the Yiddish school that had been established there by the Left Poalei Zion. I think I was then in the fifth grade and could not write a word in Yiddish. I still remembered the entire Hebrew alphabet from when Chedva Russak had tutored me in my home after I could no longer attend regular school. This knowledge of Hebrew characters made it much easier for me to learn Yiddish, and it was not long before I had mastered reading and writing. All the other subjects were taught in Yiddish as well.

I remember that during this period I was a pretty good student and I liked going to that school, which was close to our apartment. Sometimes, on the way to school and on the way home from school, I ran into acquaintances, sometimes even people from Hrubieszow. Once, when I was walking along, two teenage boys approached me and asked me where I was from and whether I want to join Gordonia. "But I'm from Hashomer Hatzair!" I replied in no uncertain terms. It was not that I had ever been to a Hashomer Hatzair meeting or that I knew anything about the movement. I had said this because of my long-ago association with Chedva, my tutor, whose magical personality had had such a great influence on me. I still loved her deeply, despite the years that had passed since I had last seen her. Just the fact that she had been in Hashomer Hatzair, made me want to join the movement.

Every morning when I left the house for school, I saw a steady stream of people entering a wide gate into a courtyard just across the street. One day when I came home from school, I decided to cross the street and see what was going on there. To my great surprise, I discovered that the children going in and out of the gate were the children who had been with me in the Jewish orphanages in Lublin and Pietrolesie. When I got closer, they also recognized me immediately, and we enjoyed an emotional reunion.

I already mentioned that a kibbutz of the Hashomer Hatzair movement was located close to the orphanage in Pietrolesie. Teenagers from the orphanage used to go to the kibbutz in secret, concealing their activities from the Jewish communist directors of the orphanage. One night, after the older kids in the orphanage made up their minds that they wanted to join a kibbutz, a group of them ran away to the Hashomer Hatzair kibbutz.

Later, they came to the Lodz Hashomer Hatzair center, which was located in a large building at 49 Kilingskego Street, across from which my aunt just happened to find a vacant apartment. My reunion with the kids from the orphanage, who were now members of Hashomer Hatzair – Chedva's movement, made me want to join immediately. First, I ran home joyfully to tell my aunt whom I had met just across the street. Then, I went straight back to visit them.

In the kibbutz, I met more boys and girls from the orphanage as well as new children whom I was meeting for the first time. One of the older ones took me to meet their counselor, who was circulating around and talking to different kids. She's one of us, he told her, referring to the fact that I had been with them in the orphanage. Within a few days I had convinced my aunt that I wanted to join my friends in the kibbutz, and that is what I did. Leaving my aunt's house was not only an important emotional step for me. Although I was unaware of it at the moment I made my decision, it was also an ideological step: the school I had been attending when I lived with my aunt was a Yiddish school run by Left Poalei Zion. Their ideology was inconsistent with that of Hashomer Hatzair. That being the case, my counselors in the movement insisted that I transfer from the Left Poalei Zion school to the Hebrew school, which was attended by youngsters from all the different youth movements, as well as by children whose parents planned to move to Palestine.

The teacher who tested me when I moved to the new school realized that I knew how to read and write in Hebrew, which remained with me from my time with Chedva. On this basis, he decided to enroll me in the fourth grade. During the years following the war, children who had survived the Holocaust were not placed in grades according to their year of birth. Rather, classes contained students of different ages. A fourth-grade class could contain children between the ages of nine and fifteen or sixteen, depending on how old they were when the war broke out and the number of grades they had completed before that. In the fourth grade in the Hebrew school, all subjects were taught in Hebrew, including language. I do not know if the man who taught fourth grade in the school was a teacher by profession, or if he was just someone who happened to know Hebrew. This fourth-grade class, which I joined in the middle of the year, had young kids like me, as well as kids as old as age seventeen.

In contrast to the Left Poalei Zion school, which I had liked very much, going to the Hebrew school became a daily ordeal. The teacher, who was supposedly a trained educator, was a tall man with a combed-back forelock, which drew attention to his menacing eyes and his buck teeth. I found him extremely intimidating. I had usually gone willingly to every school I had attended, regardless of the difficulties. I was always interested in my studies, and at times I even excelled. The Hebrew school, however, became a nightmare for me, even though all the students were Jewish and I walked the short distance to the school with other kids from the kibbutz.

216

One day around Shavuot, the festival of first fruits, the teacher was explaining the meaning of the holiday to the class in Hebrew. Suddenly, toward the end of the lesson, the father of one of the weakest and most disruptive students in the class walked into the classroom carrying a basket full of all the best produce, which in those days were true luxuries. The father presented the basket to the teacher in front of the whole class as a holiday gift. The same evening, there was a Shavuot party to which the parents of the few non-orphan children were also invited. The party was held in one of the large classrooms, and after the official holiday speeches, the same teacher stood up and began commending the students on their academic achievements.

As he stood before us, he gave a report on the class during which he pointed out the top student in the class. This turned out to be none other than the worst student in the class – the son of the father who had given him the Shavuot basket. The other kids in the class were dumbfounded by the choice. He then identified me, in front of everyone, as the worst student in the class. In reality, I was a mediocre student with a Hebrew level that was too low to enable me to fulfill the teacher's expectations. I'm sure he didn't consider this at all in his calculations. More importantly, I lacked a father who could present gifts to the teacher and thus influence his feelings about me.

After the party, many children approached me and offered their encouragement. While I was clearly embarrassed and deeply hurt by being designated as the worst student in the class, I also learned an important and unforgettable lesson on the subject of bribery. I knew that the basket of produce had served its purpose. All the other students, who now began speaking disparagingly about the teacher, also realized what had taken place and why. This was the first time I did not like school and actively looked for reasons not to attend, such as rotational duties in the kibbutz. Fortunately, what had happened in school did not affect my social status in the kibbutz. I was an active member of the community and well- educated on the values of kibbutz life. We conducted ideological discussions and learned songs that expressed a yearning for the Land of Israel. The living conditions were not the best, the food was not especially good, and we had very little clothing. However, morale was high, as reflected in the wild hora dancing of the kids in the kibbutz. Life in the kibbutz was extremely well organized. We were divided into age-groups, and the adults who lived with us, in a different part of the building, took care of our financial and physical needs. Our counselors were adults who had been movement members before the war.

18. THE REUNION WITH MY UNCLE
AND LATER WITH MY BROTHER

One day in the middle of the week, my friend Mania from Hrubieszow, arrived in Lodz. She and her family had also moved to the city, and I was quite stunned by her unexpected arrival. When she saw me from a distance, she yelled, Your uncle! Your uncle has come from Russia. He's waiting for you now at our house. Come quick! When I heard the news, I was filled with joy. After informing my counselors, I left.

Mania did not live far from the kibbutz, but I was so impatient to see my uncle – my father's brother – that the short distance seemed never-ending. He was an uncle that I had really liked, and he was actually the only uncle on my father's side that I had met before the war. He used to visit us often for reasons related to his joint shoe business with my father. Whenever he came to our house, he would bring us special salami from Radom. I was somewhat spoiled when it came to food; the salami was delicious and I loved it. He was my father's younger brother and a bachelor, and he enjoyed taking walks and playing with me. So, I loved his visits and developed a close relationship with him.

I was out of breath when I finally reached Mania's apartment, where I found my uncle sitting in the living room. He looked a bit different than I remembered him, but his face had not changed. The moment he saw me, he stood up, gave me a bear hug and began to sob uncontrollably. Actually, we were both crying, but I managed to stop quickly. He continued crying and could not stop. For over an hour, he stood there hugging me and crying. When finally calmed down, he told me that my brother, Nathan, was on his way and would arrive soon.

As far as I can remember, my uncle stayed with the Katzhandels (Mania's family) for only a few days; he found an apartment within a very short time. I went back to the kibbutz, but from that day forward, we met every day.

My uncle took it upon himself to be responsible for me. As a result of his efforts, the Hebrew school finally agreed to move me into the third grade, where I began to thrive. The teacher was not only a real teacher but a good person, and I understood the Hebrew he taught in class. Now that I had my uncle, I entrusted to him for safekeeping, all the money from the sale of the house. I have no idea how much money it actually was, but I do know I had managed to save most of the money. Shortly after my uncle arrived, my Aunt Fayga left for Germany with Tema and Itsche, and we parted for good.

Life in the kibbutz and the education we received, which was geared towards preparing us for emigration to Israel, were quite unrelated to events going on in Poland at the time. I certainly never followed current political affairs. Perhaps the only exception was the one time I went to a kiosk to buy something and learned that the Russians were changing their currency, meaning that I could only pay with old money until a certain date. We had also heard about the pogrom that occurred in Kielce just before we were about to leave for summer camp at Helenowek, a village close to Lodz where the kibbutz organizers had rented a farm.

HaShomer HaTzair Youth Group "Ken" (nest); Bad Reichenhall, 1946. The drummer in front is Cipora.

220

As a consequence of that horrific event, we were accompanied that summer by adult members of the kibbutz who served as armed guards.

Summer camp filled us with new vitality. We hiked through the woods collecting berries, played scouting games such as "capture the flag", and spent time outdoors, breathing in the fresh air. One young counselor named Moshe was particularly active in organizing our activities, and all the girls were in love with him. During the summer, we felt as if we were children once more. On Lag B'Omer, our counselors assembled us in a clearing in the woods for a discussion and a meeting with an emissary from Palestine. She told us that the kibbutz children were looking forward to our arrival with great excitement. We were left with hopeful expectations regarding what we would find when we'd first set foot in Palestine. After darkness fell, a campfire was lit. We had an inspiring ceremony. Each of us was given a piece of paper with our name written on it in Polish. Then, after casting the notes into the fire, we each chose a Hebrew name for ourselves. Until that moment, I had been Fela, or Faygeleh. From then on, I was Cipora, which is still my name today.

After we returned to the routine of the city and school, my uncle informed me that someone had told him my brother was on his way and would be arriving any day. My ears pricked up any time footsteps could be heard outside my classroom door, in the hopes that they were the sound of someone coming to find me to announce my brother's arrival. I was in a constant state of anxiety. The Hebrew school building had several stories, and if I remember correctly my classroom was located on the second floor. One day, a girl burst into the classroom happily shouting that my brother was in Lodz and was waiting for me at the home of friends who lived near the school. Without asking my teacher's permission to leave in the middle of the lesson, I dashed out of the classroom. I was so excited, and I was running so frantically, that I fell down the steps and hurt my leg on the way. When I finally reached my brother, I recognized him immediately. His facial features had remained just as I remembered them, except he had aged and looked more serious. For my brother, however, it was a different story. He claimed that he would not have recognized me even if we would have passed each other in the street. It took us both some time to recover from the shock of seeing each other again. He continued to stare at me, and I at him. Our excitement was infectious and everyone around us was overjoyed about the reunion. I have a brother! I said to myself. I have a brother!

When we finally relaxed and sat down, he told me that, throughout his long difficult journey to Siberia, to the coal mines, and through Asiatic Russia, he had managed to keep the pictures of the family that our parents had packed for him the night after the death march, when they had smuggled him into Russia. When I heard that he had those pictures of our loved ones whose images I carried with me only in my memory, my excitement knew no bounds. I burst into tears at the sight of the first picture my brother took out of his wallet, which was of my other brother Shalom who was killed when he was sixteen. I saw the pictures of my parents through my tears and continued to weep. I cried uncontrollably for four hours, without a break. I simply could not stop crying. All the people around me, including my brother, begged me to stop, and I wanted to. But I could not stop. There was only one good thing: the storm of emotions and all the crying made me completely forget about my leg, which I had hurt falling down the stairs at school. But seeing the photographs rekindled in me all the pain of my past.

Once again, I was reminded of my lost mother and my father and the good home I once had. I was reminded of how much I regretted not having had the chance to say goodbye to them before they died. My uncontrollable weeping served as a catharsis, releasing all the tensions, fears, and loneliness that I had experienced. During my reunion with uncle Hershel, it was he who was unable to control his tears. Now, I was the one who was falling apart. It was the first time since the end of the war that I had cried so hard. The reunion with my brother remains deeply engraved in my memory and on my heart. Despite the more than six decades that have passed since then, it is a memory I will keep with me until the day I die.

For the time being, my brother stayed with his friends, a family he had become friends with in Russia, and I returned to the kibbutz with a bandaged leg. When I went back to school the next day, I explained to my teacher why I had run out of class so suddenly. My teacher of course understood the situation, and forgave me immediately.

My brother was unable to find work or an apartment in Lodz. He was lonely, and after some time, he joined the adult members of the kibbutz. Unfortunately, he had very few options in the new situation in which he found himself; and joining the kibbutz seemed like the most promising path to take. Like many others during this period, he did not join for ideological reasons.

19. Our Flight From Poland

The month my brother joined the kibbutz, the counselors gathered together all the kids and told us that we would be leaving Poland and going to Palestine in only a few days. We would not be traveling legally, we were informed. Rather, we were fleeing the country, fleeing Poland. During the meeting, we were told that trucks would come to the kibbutz building to take us to the Czech border, where we would be met by people who would help us cross the Tatra Mountains into Czechoslovakia. We were also told that because we were crossing the border somewhat illegally, we would not be crossing as Jews but rather as Turks. For this reason, we were instructed to leave behind anything that could identify us. People with pictures bearing dedications in Yiddish, Hebrew, or Polish were requested to erase them in order to prevent being identified. At that point, pictures were virtually our only possessions.

After the meeting, I went to my bed, found my pictures among my personal belongings, and erased anything that was written on them, which usually included dedications from other children. All the other children did the same thing. To this day, I have pictures from this period of people whom I am unable to identify. For us children, it was very common to give pictures to one another as a token of friendship. The announcement that we were going to Palestine was meant only for the young members of the kibbutz, and the adults had been instructed to remain in Poland for the meantime. Only parents and a few relatives were permitted to come along, and my Uncle Hershel joined the group. However, my brother, with whom I had been reunited only one month earlier, remained with the adult kibbutz in Lodz. Again, we were separated.

One afternoon, a tarp-covered truck pulled up to the gates of the kibbutz at 49 Kilingskego Street. Carrying our meager belongings, we approached the truck silently, so as not to raise suspicions. We boarded and began the trip. Because the truck was covered, we were unable to see where we were going. The counselors who accompanied us told us that we would first travel to Silesia, to a location from which we would cross the border. From there, they explained, we would begin climbing the Tatra Mountains. We tried to remain silent the entire trip, and we were all lost in our own thoughts. That was my last day in Poland.

We reached the border after nightfall and quietly alit from the truck. A few of the adults who had been awaiting us explained that we would be led to our destination by someone who knew the trails. We would not be able to talk, because someone in the mountains might hear us and inform the authorities. We would need to remain close to one another, and in some places we would need to lie down and hide behind thick trees, in order make sure that we were neither seen nor heard. My uncle and I had almost no belongings, aside from a small suitcase and a bag. Before leaving Lodz, my uncle decided to buy a gift for his sister who lived in Palestine, and he also had some Polish money, which he wanted to use. (But, unfamiliar with the climate of the country, he used some of the money to purchase a second-hand three-quarter length mink coat to bring to his sister!)

From there, we started ascending into the wooded foothills of the Tatra Mountains. All in all, the climb was no easy undertaking, one filled with tension, as we so feared getting caught. This fear prevented us from making any noise during the steep ascent. Every once in a while, we were allowed to rest and have something to eat. And so we walked, under the clear nighttime sky, in total secrecy and with complete obedience to those responsible for us. We accepted the tension as a necessity of reality. At the same time, our hearts beat with the lofty hope of the Land of Israel, which, we thought to ourselves, made the effort and the fear well worth it. When dawn broke, we were already descending the mountains on the other side of the border, next to a Slovakian village. When the dogs of the village heard us, despite our efforts to walk quietly and not be heard, they began to bark. When we first heard the barks we held our breath, and were immediately ordered to lie down on the dew-covered ground. Only after some time had passed were we permitted to get up and continue to the pick-up point, which was located on a broad plain. From there, we were taken to some sort of camp containing long barracks with many beds, which reminded me a great deal of the camps in which I had been imprisoned. Years later, I read that we had been on the outskirts of the city of Nachod. In this camp, we were checked for cleanliness, and if I am not mistaken, our heads were sprayed with D.D.T. or a similar chemical. After a short time in the camp, we boarded another truck which took us to Bratislava.

In Bratislava, we were taken to a giant field where we found hundreds of other Jews already waiting. From the looks of it, they also had stolen across the border. I was quite surprised by the large ramp holding crates of fruit that stood at the edge of the field. It had been years since I had seen so many different types of fruit in one place. The image of the fruit on the ramp still appears to me from time to time in my imagination as a colorful, vivid photograph. We stayed at that field for quite some time, and people started walking around and looking for people they knew. At one point, we heard spontaneous cries of joy, and learned that a boy who had been with us in the kibbutz actually found his mother in the densely packed crowd. Neither one had known that the other had survived, and the reunion was like a rebirth of the dead.

We sat on the field without knowing who would provide us with new information or where we were headed. On the one hand, we sat in an atmosphere of great tension awaiting some sort of announcement. On the other hand, we were obedient and quite glad that we were being well taken care of. After a few hours, our counselors told us that we would be traveling by train to Bavaria, Germany.

20. In the Displaced Persons Camps

The train ride to Prague took hours, and from Prague we continued by train to Bad Reichenhall, Bavaria. In Bad Reichenhall, the few parents and relatives who had accompanied us were told to say goodbye to the children. They would be staying in displaced persons camps in the city, they were told, and only the kibbutz children would be travelling into the French Zone, where, in a monastery called Jordenbad, a Hashomer Hatzair kibbutz had already been set up.

The train rides went on for days and became almost routine. Eventually, we arrived at the Jordenbad convent. There were still a few German nuns there who had been expelled from the large houses in which they had previously lived; we were now housed in their stead. The Jordenbad convent was situated on a large piece of land and was a beautiful place, with well-tended gardens kept by the German nuns. It had a small pond with goldfish, which for us seemed magical. As the site was originally a convent, it had everything the kibbutz needed for communal life: a spacious dining room, extensive laundry facilities, a large well-equipped kitchen, and sick rooms. The nuns maintained cleanliness in all of the public areas.

The kibbutz in Jordenbad was divided into three age-groups, in accordance with movement tradition: The adult kibbutz (hakibbutz haboger), to which our counselors belonged; older scouts (tzofim bogrim); and younger scouts (tzofim tzeirim). Each age-group lived in a different building. I, of course, belonged to the younger scouts. Most of our activities focused on the fact that we would build a kibbutz when we arrived in Palestine, and our counselors gave us the feeling that we were old enough to do so. I do not remember them talking to us at all about going to school or studying. We spent a great deal of time engaged in sports competitions, cleaning our rooms, and other such non-academic activities.

When I got to Jordenbad, I was wearing boots that had been sewed for me by a shoemaker in Hrubieszow according to my shoe size right before I left the city. I wore them as I climbed up and down the Tatra Mountains, and at the time they were my prettiest, most precious possessions. They were known by the fashionable name of Officerki (officer boots).

Because I loved them so much, I ignored the fact that one of the boots was pressing hard on my heel, in the hope that the discomfort would pass. When I got to Jordenbad, however, the pain in my heel became unbearable and the doctor discovered that my heel was full of pus and that an operation would be necessary to drain it. I already mentioned that, in Jordenbad, there were sick rooms that had previously been used by the nuns but now served the kibbutzim and the Poles who had survived forced labor in Germany.

Another girl lay in the sick room with me. She was Polish, and she was completely paralyzed. She had been kidnapped by the Germans to serve as a forced laborer in Germany, and while in Germany she was tortured and was now unable to move. Her parents in Poland were still unaware that she was alive, and for that reason she lay in the sick room at Jordenbad. I told her my story in brief, and there, in the sick room in Jordenbad, we became partners in the suffering we had both experienced during that terrible war.

After some time had passed, my brother also joined Uncle Hershel in Bad Reichenhall. On the way to Germany, the kibbutz members with whom he left Poland had passed through Vienna, and there he left the kibbutz and joined our uncle. They had both endured the war together in Russia, and they had lived together for a long time as father and son. When my brother arrived in Bad Reichenhall, he found Uncle Hershel sick in bed and wrote me a postcard that I should also come there to help take care of him. At the time, I was still in bed after having undergone surgery. I was in great pain. I wept when I read the postcard. I was all alone and my leg hurt me a great deal, and my brother's postcard made me even lonelier. I wrote him back and told him about my heel, and explained that in my condition, I would not be able to care for Uncle Hershel. Nonetheless, I wrote, I would try to make it back to them.

I was still limping when I left the hospital. When I got back to the kibbutz, I learned that our counselor Junia had been replaced. The subject of the evening activities had changed with the new counselor. Now, they focused on the idea that, in Palestine, we would be able to go back to school and re-experience our youth, and on how we would be absorbed into the country and the kibbutz. Because most of our previous discussions had revolved around establishing a new kibbutz and building the country, the subject of returning to school was a sudden and surprising change. We did not like the change and we voiced our opposition to the ideas of the new counselor; the atmosphere in these discussions was negative. As a result we rebelled, and I was one of the rebels. I decided to leave the kibbutz and join my brother and uncle in Bad Reichenhall. The counselors did not let me travel on my own, and found an adult movement member to accompany me on the journey. When I reached my uncle and my brother, they could not find me a bed, so they set up a military stretcher next to my uncle's bed, which became my bed. Until that point I had slept on the wooden bunks in the camps and on chairs, floors, and other unusual surfaces. For me, sleeping on the stretcher was no problem whatsoever.

The displaced persons camp in Bad Reichenhall was enclosed by a fence, and inside stood rows of grey, multiple-story buildings, one across from the other. A wide street separated the buildings from one another and became the center of the camp. The camp, it seemed, had previously served as a military base. We lived in one of the buildings, which had extremely large rooms, each housing a number of families. In my uncle's apartment, we lived with another family which consisted of a couple with two sons, more or less my age, and the father's brother. In order to facilitate a degree of privacy for each family, the room was divided by blankets hung on ropes. The husband and his brother were both tailors, and thanks to them I now had clothes to wear. They even used old clothing to sew me a dress and a sporty suit and a hat. I became friends with the two boys who were my age and they provided me with good company.

Bad Reichenhall was a very large displaced persons camp. Almost all of the Zionist youth movements, including the partisan organization known as Pachach (Hebrew acronym for Partisans, Soldiers, and Pioneers), coexisted in the camp. At Bad Reichenhall there was also a Hashomer Hatzair kibbutz and movement chapter. I joined the chapter at almost the moment I arrived, and my counselor was none other than Yehoshua Ravitz, father of the well-known Israeli singer and songwriter, Yehudit Ravitz. I went to the Hashomer Hatzair chapter every evening and became the drummer in the movement parades that were conducted in the camp from time to time. The camp also had a Hebrew school in which my uncle enrolled me as soon as I arrived. After my unpleasant experience in the Hebrew school in Lodz, I decided that this time I would begin in the third grade. I was not embarrassed by moving down a grade, because by that point it seems that I was already aware of my own limitations, particularly in Hebrew. My teacher in the school in the camp was a wise man: he knew Hebrew well and was a teacher by nature. With this teacher, I became the best student in the entire school. In contrast to the suffering and embarrassment I had experienced in the Hebrew school in Lodz, I truly enjoyed going to school in Bad Reichenhall. I was happy and I flourished.

The cultural atmosphere in the school also had a positive impact on me. It had a children's choir in which we learned Hebrew songs and performed for the general camp population, as well as for special guests from Palestine such as Zrubavel, the then-leader of the Left Poalei Zion. There was also a drama group in which I participated and a local theatre with actors who had been Yiddish theatre actors in Warsaw and Lodz before the war. One production of the local theatre needed a child actor to play a Jewish partisan during the war. When the director asked the school for a suggestion of someone to play the role, my teacher suggested me. I became the child theatre actor of Bad Reichenhall. The production was extremely successful and one day the theatre director told me that the troupe wanted to do a tour of all the displaced persons camps in Germany. He wanted me to participate and told me that this tour would require me to take a break from school. I liked school so much at that point that I decided not to join the troupe for its performances outside of Bad Reichenhall. The other actors tried hard to convince me, but I resolved on my own to stay in school. Unfortunately, my refusal caused the entire troupe to stop the production. I was very sorry about this, and I felt rather uncomfortable about the fact that I was the reason they would not perform the play again. Still, I did not want to miss school.

During the time I was acting, I – like the other actors – received special packages from the American Jewish Joint Distribution Committee (known as the Joint). The packages included chocolate and chewing gum and other things that were very expensive at the time. My brother and my uncle who together constituted the entirety of my small family, enjoyed the luxurious supplement as well. Although I could not at all understand how someone could chew gum when I was first introduced to it, people with more experience eventually persuaded me that I should give it a try, and I found that the gum really tasted very good indeed.

I have fond memories of my time in Bad Reichenhall, particularly of the movement activities during which we hiked through the surrounding area, the breathtaking natural setting, and the two-kilometer high mountains, which towered above the city. During movement activities, we took the cable-car up the mountain, visited the salt mines, and traveled to Berchtesgaden (which had been Hitler's summer residence) and was a town with a breathtaking view. I was attending a school that I liked and I had a teacher that I appreciated. I also took piano lessons from a German woman in exchange for bread and a token fee. At the time, the citizens of Germany were hungry, but we did not feel sorry for them. I do not know how long I remained in Bad Reichenhall. When my teacher at school learned that my uncle and I were going to the displaced persons camp at Bergen-Belsen in order to travel from there to Palestine, he wrote a letter bearing the school stamp recommending my acceptance into an acting school in Palestine.

Because the Bergen-Belsen D.P. camp was located in the British zone of occupation and because the residents of the camp were eligible to receive certificates to move to Palestine as British citizens, the camp became a springboard to Palestine. Not all the Jews in the camp wanted to move to Palestine, however, and many chose to immigrate to the United States, Australia, and Canada instead. Some people's decisions also depended on where they had relatives. The Jews in the camp who were not planning to move to Palestine sold the certificates to which they were eligible on the black market.

Uncle Hershel was still safeguarding the money from the sale of our house. A good friend of his in the Bergen-Belsen D.P. camp had written him a letter telling him that certificates could be purchased on the black market in the camp, but that one first had to live there for a period of time before receiving them. I have no idea how much a black market certificate cost at the time, but my uncle said that the money we had was only enough for two certificates and I was again separated from my brother. I said goodbye to my teacher from school and my friends from the movement chapter whom I had to leave behind. My uncle and

I packed the few bags we had and went to the Bad Reichenhall train station. From there we made our way by train to Bergen-Belsen.

When the train that left Bad Reichenhall reached the border between the American-occupied zone and the British-occupied zone, we stopped for a border inspection. The train was boarded by German policemen, who checked our travel papers. The citizens of Germany, which was then occupied by four countries, were hungry. Acquiring food was very difficult, and the black market for foodstuff blossomed. The German policewoman who boarded the train was tall and had a wide body, blue eyes, straight blond hair, and a threatening gaze. She immediately brought back memories of the female guards in the concentration camps, not just because of her physical appearance but because of her angry look and her way of speaking. The mere sight of her frightened me. The benches in our train car lined the walls and were not arranged in rows as in typical train cars.

Sitting right next to us was an elderly German couple, and under their bench they were hiding a basket of eggs, which were then sold primarily on the black market. The moment the policewoman began searching the car, the German couple moved the basket so that it was underneath our bench. We did not notice, and when the policewoman found the basket, she fixed her menacing eyes upon us. The elderly couple, immediately pointed at us, falsely and shamelessly insisting that we were the owners of the basket. Overflowing with anger, I opened my mouth and, like a steam engine, roared in defiance in either Yiddish or German that the basket belonged to the elderly couple, not us. Although it was hard for me to accept at the time, there were also a few humane Germans on the train who confirmed my version of the story and that the basket was not ours, but rather belonged to the German couple.

The policewoman summarily confiscated the basket but left the couple on the train without punishing them. Instead, it was my uncle she ordered to leave the train and enter the police station located adjacent to the tracks. I was left alone on the train, and I was very frightened. Now, the policewoman focused her harassing attention on me alone, and started to search me from head to toe. I felt as if I was back in the concentration camp. I was now absolutely incapable of keeping quiet, and I gave her a piece of my mind, saying, You Germans have searched me enough, I screamed, in what I think was Germanized Yiddish. Now we are free, I continued, unlike you Germans. I was upset and my face was red. But I was also trembling with fear at the possibility of her finding the dollars I had hidden in my socks in order to buy the certificates. Perhaps because of how upset I was and perhaps because she knew the train was about to start moving again, she suddenly stopped bothering me, leaving me amazed that she did not discover the money in my socks. Regardless, I was relieved when she finally left.

My uncle had not yet re-boarded the train when the train workers sounded their whistle. I stood by the door trembling with fear. I was alone among all those Germans, and I was scared that they would delay my uncle in the police station and that I would remain on the train all alone. He arrived just as the train wheels began to move, and the tension and my fear of remaining on the train all alone evaporated the moment I saw him. As the train resumed its journey, we understood that Germany was still deeply dedicated to its hatred of the Jews and that its citizens were still as cruel as they had been when Hitler ruled. The Germans did not seem to regret what they had done to Europe and the Jews. Their only regret was that they had lost the war!

After a long exhausting journey, we finally reached the Bergen-Belsen Displaced Persons camp. My uncle's friend and his wife and their small baby received us warmly and invited us to stay with them in their apartment. I know nothing about the arrangements my uncle made in the camp or whether we paid any expenses while we were living with the family. The DP camp was less organized than had been the camp in Bad Reichenhall. The buildings were different sizes, and the camp had a rather dilapidated appearance. Although after a short time in the camp I learned that it too had a Hashomer Hatzair kibbutz, I made no effort to make contact or to join it, or any other group framework for that matter. In the Bergen-Belsen DP camp, I established no social connections because we were going to be there for only a short time.

About two weeks after our arrival, I began menstruating for the first time. For an entire day, I had terrible cramps in my stomach. When my uncle asked me what was causing the pain and if I had perhaps eaten something that might have been spoiled, I could not think of what to say. As the pains continued, he simply had no idea what to do with me. I was also unaware of the cause, and there was no doctor to be found. It was only in the evening when I went to the bathroom which was located outside the apartment that I realized why my stomach hurt. As no one had ever talked to me about these intimate things, I was rather frightened by the development.

Instead of approaching my uncle, I asked my uncle's friend's wife what it was. Congratulations, she said, you are now a woman. She did not offer her help in handling the situation, as she lacked the material means to do so herself. I had only two pairs of underwear, and there was no place to find another pair. For ten days, I suffered through my first menstruation with no hygienic supplies whatsoever, not even a rag. I did the best I could by using regular paper I happened to find here and there, and when at one point a young woman told me where a rag was, I ran there to look for it. I was embarrassed to tell my uncle what was bothering me. Perhaps he guessed himself, but even if he did know, he had no way to help me. I was almost thirteen, and I was miserable.

Another emotional experience of a completely different kind was the commemoration of the second anniversary of the liberation of the Bergen-Belsen concentration camp. The displaced persons camp was located relatively close to where the concentration camp had stood. On the anniversary of the liberation, a large crowd from the D.P. camp made their way to the site and, as far as I can remember, stood next to the gallows. After the ceremony, people gave speeches in memory of the victims. Suddenly, as we stood there and listened as one of the speakers expressed the wounds that had not yet healed, I noticed people running to a point some distance away from where the ceremony was taking place. I also left the ceremony to find out the reason for the commotion and ran to where people were now gathering. When I got there, I found a crowd of people surrounding an extremely embarrassed woman, whose head was turned downward. The people were beating her and screaming, Murderer! Murderer! Now we'll murder you! It seemed that she was a German who had served as a guard in the concentration camp, and that, on the very spot where she stood during the ceremony, she had once beat a young Jewish woman to death.

Someone in the crowd had been in the concentration camp at the time. He identified her and, with great emotion, explained to the people who had gathered that he could not understand why she came to the camp on the second anniversary of its liberation. Why had she returned to the site where she killed a Jewish woman? Was it regret? Who would ever know? In any event, the crowd surrounding her was trying to lynch her then and there, when the camp's Jewish police force showed up, loaded her onto the back of a pick-up truck along with a few survivors of the camp, and disappeared. As a result of the commotion, I have no memory of the official ceremony. However, I will never forget the spectacle surrounding the former camp guard.

The Jews in the displaced persons camps in Germany often tried to identify German criminals who had guarded them in the concentration camps, and this was not the first such case I had witnessed. Once, I was riding on a train with some other girls when one of them identified a former female concentration camp guard. The woman claimed that it was not her, but her denial was in vain. The girls called the police and she was taken away.

During most of my time in the displaced persons camp, I was bored as I had very little to do. Sometimes, I just played with the baby that lived in the apartment where we were staying. In addition, the food there was not very good. Most of my time was spent waiting impatiently for the day we would leave the camp and continue on our journey. Finally, the big day arrived. One afternoon, my uncle told me excitedly that he had been instructed to report to a certain location, and from there we would travel by train to Marseilles. In the camp, my uncle had managed to purchase a few used shirts and trousers so as not to arrive in Palestine with nothing. He bought me a shirt, which I really liked, and a few dresses. All in all, we had one small suitcase and a large bag. We thanked our hosts and said goodbye, and set out on our journey, this time to Palestine.

21. Immigrating to Palestine

Again, I found myself on the train. This time, we were traveling through Germany until we reached France. I had already gotten used to train rides, and I always loved to sit by the window and enjoy the new views. When we reached Marseilles, we were met at the train station by a group of Jews. We were given a place to sleep not far from the port in a structure that was actually a giant warehouse. I do not know who organized our accommodations and our food, or who arranged our passage by boat and informed us of our date of departure. We were part of a group of approximately 300 people of all ages, including one baby. I did not know most of the people, but I did spot a few acquaintances who also came from Bad Reichenhall and who also apparently purchased certificates the same way we had.

In Marseilles, we waited two weeks for our boat. In order to stave off boredom while we waited, we took trips in the area from time to time. We did not do any shopping, because we did not have any francs. We also did not know French, and we therefore did not venture too far from our temporary place of residence. One day, we arrived at the shore. It was the first time in my life that I had seen the sea. The moment I reached the water, my head started to spin and I began to panic that the water would engulf me. The horizon over the sea frightened me as well. I began to ask my uncle geography questions that were perhaps more typical of a six-year-old. I was simply dumbfounded by the fact that I was standing on the beach by water which seemed to go on forever. My uncle smiled and reassured me that I would not drown while standing on the beach.

During our two weeks in Marseilles, my uncle told me that we had close relatives in Paris and suggested that we go visit them first instead of going directly to Palestine. This was the first time I knew about having any relatives in France. But because we had come to Marseilles solely for the purpose of using it as a stepping-stone to Palestine, we immediately ruled out the possibility of staying in France. Just then, a voice over a loudspeaker announced that our ship had arrived! When we reported to the port where the boat was supposedly anchored, we did not see a ship. Instead, we saw a rather small tourist yacht flying a Panamanian flag with the name 'Valena' painted on the side. It appeared to be meant to carry approximately fifty rich people, while we totaled more than 300 people, including the additional families who had joined us in Marseilles. When we were then told to board the boat, we were shocked and began to complain in vain. The crowding on the boat was unbearable, as was the heat in the cabins. Although almost all of us received cabins, each one holding a few families, most of us remained above deck in order to breathe fresh air. The rough waves rocked the small boat from side to side almost incessantly from the moment we set sail.

At the beginning of the trip, the passengers walked around on deck nervously, because of the high waves, which knocked against the small boat causing it to rock from side to side. It was only when we got out to sea that the waves calmed. The boat stopped rocking and the people relaxed somewhat. Sailing on the open sea, an activity to which I had just been introduced, was a traumatic experience for me. The entire time, I feared that the tiny ship would capsize. After all, it was carrying such a large number of passengers, who were packed so densely. It was the calm faces of the sailors that gave me the most comfort, for if they were not scared, I thought to myself, then the boat was surely not about to turn over.

Although the fear of drowning was disconcerting, the food was actually good and quite filling. The cooks were from Greece and they prepared wonderful Greek dishes. Breakfast was first served on a long, beautifully-set table around which the passengers sat. The menu included large black olives of the highest quality. The first person to dare to taste the olives decided that it was a rotten plum and spit it out. In the meantime, reports of his reaction had spread among the diners at lightening speed, and no one touched those rotten plums. The Greek waiters could not understand why we were boycotting the olives and tried with all their might to convince us that the olives were, in fact, expensive and of excellent quality. It took a few days until several intrepid passengers tried them again; I was one of the brave ones. After that, I learned to love olives, which was a fruit that I had neither seen nor tasted until that voyage. Later, my familiarity with the taste of olives helped me adapt to the food in Israel. Ever since then, I have had a taste for olives.

The trip lasted for many long days, and it felt as if we would be at sea forever. After at least ten days of sailing, my uncle told me that he had sent a telegram from the boat to his sister, my aunt, informing her of our date of arrival in Haifa. He was hoping that the family would be waiting for us when we arrived in the country. One afternoon, after approximately two weeks at sea, when the waves were calm, someone standing on deck at the bow of the boat began yelling hysterically that he could see land, and that the land he could see was the mountains of Haifa, Mt. Carmel. This encouraging news spread like wildfire among the passengers, all of whom now came on deck and stood on the side of the boat from which land could be seen. As the boat continued sailing we were able to see the land more clearly.

All of the passengers were now on their feet and filled with emotion, with tears in their eyes. And when the voice of Yaffa Yarkoni suddenly emerged from the loudspeaker, singing Artzeinu Haktantonet (Our Tiny Country), the members of the teary-eyed emotional group, who were all standing on the left side of the boat from which they could see Haifa, began weeping hysterically. At that point, the crew members began yelling that we must stand on both sides of the boat. But by now, everyone was talking and yelling. In the midst of the excitement and commotion that engulfed both the immigrants and the crew, two gigantic ships suddenly appeared in close proximity to our boat and were heading directly toward us. We could hear the skipper of our boat explaining to the captains of the British vessels that his passengers had certificates and that the boat was therefore legal. We were treated to a British escort into the port of Haifa.

22. Absorption in Palestine

With great emotion and little baggage, we began to disembark from the boat. A small wooden desk with a stack of papers on it stood at the bottom of the stairs. Next to the desk sat a representative of the Jewish Agency charged with the task of recording our names and other personal information. When our turn came, he asked me about my parents, and when he realized that I was an orphan, he immediately declared that I must go straight to a kibbutz. I, however, still did not want to part with my uncle, and I had also been waiting to see my aunt who lived in Tel Aviv. After all, my uncle had sent her a telegram from the boat indicating our date of arrival, and we both assumed she would be waiting for us outside the port. The official was not very pleased by the fact that I didn't want to go straight to a kibbutz, and he tried as hard as he could to persuade me in a variety of different ways. At one point, he told me that if I did not go to a kibbutz directly from the port they may very well not accept me later. In addition, if they did accept me, someone would have to pay for me.

As soon as we left the port, we began scanning the passersby in search of my aunt. We waited there for a long time in the hope that she would come and that perhaps she was just late. But when it started to get dark and we saw that nobody was waiting for us, my uncle walked over to one of the taxis waiting nearby and we took it to Tel Aviv, HaAliya Street, where the Jewish Agency absorption camp was located. At the time, a number of long barracks stood on a hill overlooking HaAliya Street. To me, the surroundings seemed quite dismal. That was my first encounter with the country. After we were again registered, a Jewish Agency representative escorted us to one of the long barracks containing iron beds, and the clerk pointed to two beds on which we could sleep. By then, we were very tired and quite agitated, and that is how we spent our first night in the country, on Jewish Agency-provided beds.

The next morning, we each received five pounds from the Jewish Agency, and we used this money for cab-fare to get to my aunt's house. Like the cab driver who had driven us from Haifa to Tel Aviv, this cab driver was also excited to meet new immigrants, and he greeted us warmly. After the initial excitement of our first visit with my uncle's sister, my

238

uncle began to look for work in his profession, the shoe business. At the same time, I began to practice my Hebrew on the kids who lived in my aunt's building. Not much time passed before I went to the Jewish Agency in order to sign up for a kibbutz. The first time I went to their offices, I was told that my relatives would have to pay for me. I explained to the clerk that I had no one to pay for me, but the clerk nevertheless insisted on payment. I went back to my aunt's house, disappointed and in tears. In front of the building I was met by a neighbor who asked me why I was crying. Naively and greatly disillusioned by the Jewish Agency clerk, I told her what he had said and I waited for an expression of sympathy. Instead, however, she gave me a stern lecture, You new immigrants think you deserve everything, she told me. We suffered here and drained the swamps and received nothing in return. And here you are, only a week in the country, thinking that you deserve everything!

I explained to her that she had misunderstood the situation. My parents had been murdered and I had no one to pay for me. Don't you understand what we have been through and the conditions in which we lived? I asked her. I also told her about my desire to go to kibbutz. As I walked away, the response of the woman who had been in the country for much longer than I had made me cry even harder. The clerk at the Jewish Agency and the lecture delivered by my aunt's neighbor, hurt me deeply.

After a short time had passed, I went back to the Jewish Agency, which was located on the second floor of a building on HaYarkon Street. As I was walking up the stairs to the offices in which children were registered for kibbutz, a clerk wearing a skullcap who was also walking up the steps stopped me and asked me what I needed. I came to sign up for a youth group on kibbutz, I told him.

Were your parents in Poland religious? he asked me. When I told him that they were, he said, Well, if that's the case you need to join a youth group on a religious kibbutz. As we talked, we continued ascending the stairs to the Jewish Agency offices. When we got to the correct floor, we entered a corridor. To the left of the door through which we had entered, stood another man. The man who had walked up the stairs with me pointed me out to the other man, and said, This is a girl from a religious home. She needs to be registered for a religious kibbutz.

239

Although I was only thirteen years old at the time, I immediately, assertively, and unhesitatingly told them that I was a member of Hashomer Hatzair and that I would not go to a religious kibbutz. After a bitter argument, the man standing by the door eventually persuaded the other man to leave me alone, and he did. I then went over to the door across the hall and knocked on it. After I heard a voice say yes, please come in, I opened the door to find another clerk sitting behind a desk, who received me warmly. I explained my situation and that I had no one to pay for me, and I told him how much I wanted to go to a kibbutz of Hashomer Hatzair. This time, I succeeded.

I arrived at Kibbutz Beit-Zera accompanied by my uncle, and I joined a youth group of children from Romania who had already been there for six months. Because my Hebrew at the time was on a par with the children's Hebrew, the teacher in charge of the group allowed me to join their class at school. At Beit-Zera, I again unexpectedly met Rafael Feldman, who had found me standing by the Jewish Committee building in Lublin. Our unexpected reunion filled us with overwhelming emotion. We were so happy to be on the same kibbutz at the same time. On the day I arrived on the kibbutz, the only person sitting on the bench in front of the kibbutz dining room in the sweltering afternoon heat of the Jordan Valley was Yehoshua Ravitz, my counselor from Bad Reichenhall. I was also very happy to see him, and it was a good beginning for me. I felt at home at Beit-Zera. The kibbutz gave me a sense of belonging and a new childhood. During my adolescence, I managed to shed the torments of my childhood, and I actually felt lucky to be what appeared to be the only surviving Jewish child from Hrubieszow.

When I got older, I served in the Israeli Defense Forces and for a number of years was a youth leader in the Hashomer Hatzair movement in Israel. In 1955, an Israeli Army unit was stationed in Kibbutz Bet Zera, which included a group of Hashomer Hatzair members from the United States. They were true pioneers who swam against the stream of American Jewish life; among them, I met my future husband, Ariel Hurwitz. After a while, the unit was moved from Bet Zera to Kibbutz Nirim on the Gaza border. On May 30th, 1955, Nirim was shelled from Gaza and in that shelling one kibbutz member was killed and four others seriously wounded, including Ariel. His recovery took some time. After their Army service was completed, the American group joined Kibbutz

Galon in the Northern Negev, then a young kibbutz existing in difficult, pioneering conditions.

In 1956, Ariel and I were married, and I joined Ariel on Kibbutz Galon. We had three children – two girls and a boy. As a mother, I fought unsuccessfully for the life of my daughter Galia for many years. This is a wound that will never heal.

Ariel and I were eventually sent by the Jewish Agency as emissaries to South Africa and to the United States to work with Jewish youth. I attended a teachers's college and after graduation, taught Hebrew in High School and in an Ulpan for new immigrants until I retired.

I only returned to the subject of the Holocaust when Poland opened its gates to group visits. Because I was the youngest child to survive from Hrubieszow, and because I survived, I feel it is my duty to give testimony in schools and I.D.F. units throughout Israel and to accompany high school students on trips to Poland as a witness. I do this primarily so that the young generation will know about the German extermination of the Jews. While telling my story to the groups it also allows me to commemorate my friends and family who did not survive – and who have no grave, no name, and no one else to remember them.

This book concludes the part of my life story that I shared with the teenagers who came to Poland to tour the death camps and the extermination facilities. My story is a testimony in the name of the dead.

In 1998, I was asked by Moreshet to speak at the Holocaust Remembrance Day memorial ceremony at Kibbutz Yad Mordechai (named after Mordechai Anielewicz, the commander of the Warsaw Ghetto Revolt). I include the text of my speech from that event below because it reflects my experiences and my aspirations as a young survivor when I came to Israel. In these memoirs, I have not shared everything, as some details, moments, and situations are better left unsaid. In Israel, I lived like any other person.

23. At the Yad Mordechai
Holocaust Remembrance Day Ceremony
April 23, 1998

European Jewry was destroyed when I was a five-and-a-half years old. Then, the land was covered with darkness. During the war, my childhood, which until that point, had been a happy childhood in a warm and loving home, was trampled by iron soldiers of destruction. My parents, like the millions of other Jews living in Europe, neither clashed with another nation nor threatened another people. They were simply Jews living their everyday lives. They never imagined that such an evil force, unprecedented in human history, would emerge and make the determination that being a Jew is a crime punishable by death. This was what they called "the final solution."

I cannot explain why I, a spoiled little girl, was able to withstand the hellish suffering of the final solution. I managed to hide in a niche of an oven, and I survived. I stood at inspections in the freezing cold, and I did not catch a cold. I engaged in forced labor and I was able to complete it. I hungered for a piece of bread, and I persevered. I witnessed executions, and my spirit was not broken. I stood next to the crematorium in the Majdanek death camp and smelled the stench of burning human flesh, and I continued breathing. When I was liberated at the age of ten and a half, I was exhausted and ill.

My parents were murdered, and no one knows where they were buried. My brother was forced to dig his own grave, in which he was subsequently shot to death.

I survived with only a thin dress clinging to my skin. Good people and institutions helped me get back on my feet again. As a girl who grew up before her time, I not only stood on my own two feet, but demonstrated the courage of my convictions. Because I came from a Zionist home, I was attracted to anything related to the Land of Israel. I made the decision to join the Zionist youth movement of Hashomer Hatzair, and there I found other children and teenagers who, like me, had experienced the worst of all human atrocities. Together, we tried to repress and erase our unexplainable past and to heal the wounds of our completely trampled childhood in order to return to the joys of youth and to dream of a better future. We dedicated all our youth and all our desires to the dream of building up the Land of Israel. In contrast to our exile, the Land of Israel seemed like the actualization of everything: Israel, where the sun rises, where everything is green, and whose population of pioneers was waiting only for us.

Although we had no idea what a kibbutz was, we were called 'kibbutz' and we felt that we were a kibbutz. Our lives revolved around the dream of immigrating to the Land of Israel. However, this dream was not realized without dangers, threats, and dangerous turns in the road. We stole across borders and entered Czechoslovakia as Turks. We did not come to Israel on an El Al flight and no one played Shalom Aleichem for us upon landing. We came to Israel on rickety, overcrowded boats and were received by British destroyers. Most of us did not make it to the safe shores of Haifa immediately, but rather experienced again the familiar barbed wire fences of camps in Cyprus. When the long-awaited day finally arrived and we saw the Carmel Mountains on the horizon, we also heard the thunder of cannons of the War of Independence. When we stepped foot on the soil of this country, we fulfilled a dream based on personal desire.

Today, new historians are trying to distort that reality.

Our understanding that we were meant to use the rest of our lives fulfilling a greater mission led most of us to volunteer in the war effort and to take part in building the country. By contributing to the revival of the country and by making sacrifices for the sake of its security, we felt that we, too, were being rebuilt. This feeling enabled us to withstand every danger we faced and all the sufferings we experienced.

When we dreamed of the Land of Israel over there, we had no idea that our meeting with the veteran residents of the country would not live up to the dream. Although we were integrated into the country in all realms of life, we were not always treated as equals. Moreover, our suffering over there was not always heard by sympathetic ears here. We did not demand rights and we did not receive rights. We came here to contribute and to establish roots.

Far from the raging flames over there, we lit a torch of freedom here in Israel, transforming the memory of our destroyed home into the cornerstone of the foundation for a new life. The wounds of the past have not yet healed and never will, but our desire to lay down roots has enabled us to reach the present as people whose dignity had been restored and whose spirit is still undaunted.

The statue of Mordechai Anielewicz,
at Kibbutz Yad Mordechai

244